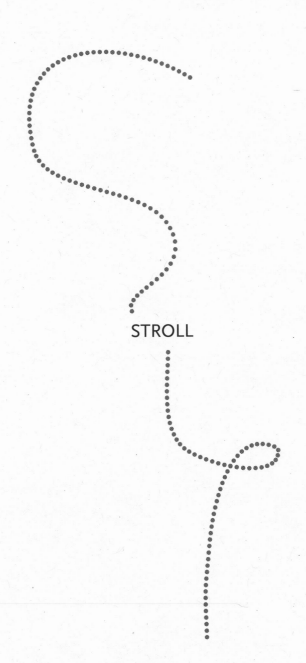

STROLL

STROLL

Psychogeographic
Walking Tours of Toronto

Shawn Micallef
Illustrations by Marlena Zuber

Coach House Books
EYE WEEKLY
Toronto

First edition, second printing, July 2010

Co-published with   **EYE WEEKLY**

 Canada Council   Conseil des Arts   ONTARIO ARTS COUNCIL   Canada
for the Arts   du Canada   CONSEIL DES ARTS DE L'ONTARIO

Published with the generous assistance of the Canada Council for
the Arts and the Ontario Arts Council. Coach House Books also
acknowledges the support of the Government of Ontario through
the Ontario Book Publishing Tax Credit and the Government of
Canada through the Book Publishing Industry Development
Program.

LIBRARY AND ARCHIVES CANADA CATALOGUING IN PUBLICATION

Micallef, Shawn, 1974-

   Stroll : Psychogeographic Walking Tours of Toronto / by Shawn
Micallef ; with illustrations by Marlena Zuber.

Includes index. Collection of author's expanded *EYE WEEKLY*
columns.

ISBN 978-1-55245-226-4

   1. Toronto (Ont.). I. Title.

FC3097.3.S87 2010   971.3'541   C2010-901999-7

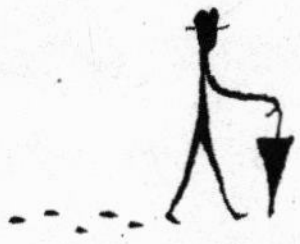

Table of Contents

Foreword

A new, cool style of engaging and enjoying metropolitan realities
has recently emerged in Toronto among certain young writers,
artists, architects and persons without portfolio. These people can
be recognized by their careful gaze at things most others ignore
places off the tourist map of Toronto's notable sights, the clutter
of sidewalk signage and graffiti, the grain inscribed on the urban
surface by the drift of populations and the cuts of fashion.

Their typical tactic is the stroll. The typical product of strolling
is knowledge that cannot be acquired merely by studying maps,
guidebooks and statistics. Rather, it is a matter of the body, knowing the city by pacing off its streets and neighbourhoods, recover-
ing the deep, enduring traces of our inhabitation by encountering
directly the fabric of buildings and the legends we have built here
during the last two centuries. Some of these strollers, including
Shawn Micallef, have joined forces to make *Spacing* magazine.
But Shawn has done more than that. He has recorded his strolls
in *EYE WEEKLY*, and these meditations, in turn, have provided
the raw material for the present book. The result you have in your
hands is a new introduction to Toronto as it reveals itself to the
patient walker, and an invitation to walk abroad on our own
errands of discovery, uncovering the memories, codes and
messages hidden in the text that is the city.

– John Bentley Mays

Flâneur Manifesto

With each step, the walk takes on greater momentum; ever weaker grow the temptations of shops, of bistros, of smiling women, ever more irresistible the magnetism of the next streetcorner, of a distant mass of foliage, of a street name.

— Walter Benjamin, *The Arcades Project*

When I was growing up in Windsor, Toronto seemed to be a spaceport city made up of the Eaton Centre, Ontario Place and the CN Tower. It had subways that ran like an electric bloodstream underneath the city, promising total freedom and complete mobility. The city I saw on occasional visits was all *A Clockwork Orange*–style modernism, yet through the gaps I'd catch glimpses of row houses, ravines and streets like Dundas or Davenport that weren't space-age at all. These places seemed like a kind of remixed British colonial landscape, and I didn't know how they fit with the Toronto I thought I knew. The city was asking to be explored.

When I moved here in 2000, I realized that my internal Toronto map had big blank spots. Not knowing where the streets ended made me nervous, so I started walking. I walked out to the Beach and the Kingsway, negotiated the PATH system, tried to make it across Rosedale without ending up where I started, and forgot about food and water as the city distracted me. In short, I turned into a *flâneur*, someone who wanders the city with the sole purpose of paying attention to it. I've been taking notes for this book ever since.

In the beginning, I wrote down what I saw on my walks and emailed these thoughts in dispatches to friends. Some asked to be taken off my list, but I kept walking, and trying to figure out how this city works, who's here, how it's all put together, what's a street or two over, where the curve in the road leads and, ultimately, what Toronto means. I'll likely never completely figure out that last point, so I'll keep walking.

Over and over, we're told that Toronto is not Paris, New York, London or Tokyo. We've been trained to be underwhelmed.

There are references all over the city that remind us that this place started out as a provincial city in a distant part of the British Empire, with streets named after places and people in the mother country, reminders of how Brit-focused we were back then. Today, Toronto gets to play all kinds of places in film and TV productions, but it rarely stars as itself. We see cameras taking pictures of NYC cabs on our streets, but not of the Royal, Beck or Co-op companies that Torontonians know.

Since Toronto seems to exist without design or reason, we don't expect to turn the corner and see beauty or be amazed. Canadians from coast to coast are taught to hate Toronto, even if they can't always articulate why. But when you ask Torontonians about their city, why are so many people genuinely amazed about being Torontonian? (Only after they've run through the perfunctory down-on-Toronto spiel to assuage their guilty feelings about the matter, of course.) Any Toronto *flâneur* knows that exploring this city makes the burden of civic self-deprecation disappear. And anybody can be a Toronto *flâneur*. More people should take the opportunity because this city is more than the sum of its parts, and those parts can be found only on foot. As American essayist Rebecca Solnit wrote in her book *Wanderlust: A History of Walking*, 'Cities move at the speed of walking.'

A *flâneur* is anyone who wanders, and watches, the city. The nineteenth-century French poet Charles Baudelaire called the *flâneur* a 'perfect idler' and a 'passionate observer.' Baudelaire was a *flâneur* himself and, when he wasn't writing poems and spending his trust fund on dandy outfits and opium, he drifted through the streets of Paris. Later, philosopher Walter Benjamin collected a chunk of thoughts on the idea of the *flâneur* in his epic volume of notes on Paris, *The Arcades Project*. The *flâneur* wanders the city, slightly invisible, just on the outside of everything – he or she observes from an anonymous perspective. That invisibility can disappear, however, if your gender is a little more female or your skin colour a shade or two away from white. What I've done in this book – walk largely unnoticed – may not be possible for everybody. I'm been lucky – I fit the mould of *flâneur* more easily than many others. The old notion of the *flâneur* will be different for whoever engages in this activity, even in a diverse metropolis such as Toronto. But that doesn't mean that other *flâneurs* can't carve out ways to navigate the city comfortably, recording their own insights and noticing the ways their own particular bodies and histories interact with the cityscape.

Around the same time I began walking, I started to find other people who were deeply excited about Toronto. (Back then, people tended to keep that kind of feeling in the closet.) One night, in the Suspect Video store buried into the side of Honest Ed's on Markham Street, I picked up a zine called *Infiltration* off the magazine rack and paged through it. Published by the late Jeff Chapman, who went by the name Ninjalicious, *Infiltration* was legendary in urban exploration circles – Chapman even coined the movement's name – for taking readers to the behind-the-scenes places where Toronto's pipes, boilers and exhaust fans do their business. I realized then that other people thought about the city the same way I did, that others saw it as a seemingly infinite and mysterious place waiting to be explored and discovered.

Chapman's first issue of *Infiltration* chronicled his adventures in the Royal York Hotel, a place he loved, and where he later spent his honeymoon, shortly before he died of cancer in 2005. Subsequent issues detailed places like Union Station, City Hall, a drain under St. Clair Avenue and St. Mike's Hospital, where he wandered the halls with his IV pole during his illness. Chapman's dedication inspired us all to uncover and listen to our own fascination with the layers of Toronto you see when you're on foot.

At a party sometime during my first year in Toronto, the hostess took me aside and introduced me to Todd Irvine, who, she said, liked to walk too. After some initial awkwardness, we were soon comparing the worn-out soles of our shoes. We figured a walking date was appropriate, so we met the following Thursday at his house on De Grassi Street. We walked west. We were nervous. And sometimes we would bump into each other because our eyes were on the buildings. We were on something like a date. We crossed the empty West Don Lands – now a completely changed landscape – and eventually ended up at a bar.

We walked again the next week with Marlena Zuber, who has filled the book you're holding with psychogeographic illustrations and maps. On subsequent Thursdays, more people joined us. Walks became our weekly thing – our mobile salon. Our practice

was simple: we picked a meeting spot and started walking. Sometimes there were two people, sometimes twenty-five, and we
drifted through the city, each corner or fork in the road presenting
a choice.

Toronto is big – the fifth biggest municipality in North America –
and that can be a daunting thing when you start exploring. The
best way to start is just to walk. As Glinda the Good Witch of the
South says in the *Wizard of Oz*, 'It's always best to start at the
beginning – and all you do is follow the Yellow Brick Road.'
Though there is no beginning to Toronto (and no Yellow Brick
Road, for that matter) you can follow any of the thirty-two walks
in this book, veering off whenever you want in whatever direction
you like, or you can put this book down now and start out on your
own, in any direction, to find Toronto. You can start your own
society whenever and with whomever you want. While there is a
general route described in each chapter, my notes are really just
starting points for your own walks through the city. If things go
right, you'll even get lost sometimes. That's good. You'll eventually find your way back to someplace that looks familiar, or you'll
find a bus to take you to a subway station.

This kind of walking is also called *psychogeography*, a term
invented by Guy Debord and the Situationists in 1950s Paris.
They were concerned with the effects of geography on human
emotions and behaviour, so they did absurd things like walk
around Paris using a map of London. They got lost, and we try
to do the same by breaking out of our usual routes, by following
our fancy rather than our logic, by going to places we wouldn't
normally choose to go because they aren't on our mental map
of the city. We named ourselves the Toronto Psychogeography
Society, and where the Situationists were trying to strike a blow
against capitalism and society, we take a lighter view of psychogeography best expressed by Christina Ray, the founder of New
York's Glowlab gallery, when she described it as 'simply getting
excited about a place.'

Walking this way makes Toronto new. The edges of the
416 are different from the centre; the alleys are different from
the streets. When you walk through places that don't fit your
mental picture of the city, you create what Bertolt Brecht called

a *Verfremdungseffekt*, a 'distancing effect,' taking what's familiar
and making it strange. By removing yourself from your habits
and context and letting some unpredictability seep into your
routine, you're better able to see what all the excitement is about.

We all took what we wanted from these walks. We've found
parts of the city we didn't know existed, and its public spaces have
become personal. Some of us enjoy going into dark ravines with
the comfort of a group. (That's one way of mitigating the limita-
tions for would-be *flâneurs* who don't fit the traditional model of
who's allow to walk wherever and whenever they want.) Others
used it in their own work. Marlena started interpreting our walks
in paintings, illustrations and, later, maps. I collected details and
they fed my writing on the city. Walking also helped inspire
[murmur], a mobile-phone oral history documentary project I
co-founded in 2003. We record short stories and anecdotes people
have about specific locations and put a sign in that spot with a
phone number that passersby can call to hear that story in the
place where it happened. Working on *[murmur]* gave me an excuse
to ask people about their memories and experiences of Toronto
and to get underneath the surface of this city a little bit more.

A former poet laureate of Toronto, Pier Giorgio Di Cicco, said in a
2004 speech that the city is falling in love with itself 'as a haven
against, and a cultural blueprint against, globalization, and as a
great experiment in the rehumanization of contemporary life.
There is an excitement that carries its own momentum.' Toronto
is always changing, always reinventing its parts, working from a
Victorian base that serves as a kind of scaffolding for all the new
people, with their new ways of doing things, who have changed
and continue to change the city into something bigger and more
interesting.

I undertook many of the walks in this book either alone or
with one or two partners for company. Either way is fine – you'll
see different details with different people, and when in a group
your conversation will start to bounce off the geography and take
both your body and your mind to places you didn't expect. Sometimes I covered similar ground again with the larger Psychogeography Society and saw different things and took other detours.
Though I've been walking since I moved here, the walks in this

book took place between 2004 and late 2009, and though the early walks were revisited and updated, the city is always changing and my words are snapshots in time. These essays are just starting points and initial sketches – it's up to you to fill in the spaces between with whatever you find on your own walks.

– Shawn Micallef
Toronto, April 2010

The Middle

Yonge Street

 day trip

 dress to impress

 scenic views

Connecting walks: Harbourfront, Nathan Phillips Square/PATH, YMCA, Dundas, St. Clair, Eglinton, Finch Hydro Corridor, Sheppard, Downtown East Side.

Towards the end of high school – circa 1992 – four of us from Windsor got into a Dodge Shadow and drove up the 401 to Toronto for our first real road trip. We didn't know much about Toronto other than the tourist places like the CN Tower or Casa Loma – neighbourhood names like the Annex, Rosedale or even Kensington Market had only a faint ring of familiarity – but we knew the first place we had to go was the Yonge Street strip. We parked, we walked back and forth and eventually we were served drinks at a second-floor bar, staring in awe into the giant rotating neon discs of Sam the Record Man. We were in the promised land.

If you're from a small town or a car-dominated city like Windsor, your initial moments along Yonge are made up of all the big-city clichés: crowds of people, amusements, stores open late into the evening and Swiss Chalet restaurants next to sex-toy shops. And though you can still see wide-eyed tourists taking it all in the way we did that first time – the most euphoric of them ready to throw their hats in the air like Mary Tyler Moore did when she moved to Minneapolis – Yonge Street isn't what it used to be. In fact, it's a little boring, and poking around the history of this stretch might leave you wishing for a return to the days when Toronto presented a big-city show, long before it ever worried about being world class.

Despite being this city's main street, and though it holds a mythic place in the Canadian psyche, Yonge occupies a strange place in our imagination. We all know it's important, but we often ignore it. It's not the main shopping street anymore. The seedy bars are seedy in the wrong way. And nobody really calls Yonge home. Yet when the city needs to come together, it comes here. This is where a million people gather for the annual Pride parade, and it's the only place to go when a sports team wins – if the Leafs ever do win the cup, the street will likely burn to the ground from the heat of all that pent-up fan adrenalin. But perhaps most telling of its importance to Toronto are events that, nearly thirty years apart, came to symbolize our collective anxiety about being a big city.

Yonge starts right at Lake Ontario. It's an inauspicious beginning for such a mythical street – at least it is right now, as this part of the waterfront is in flux, and has been for a while. To the west are the condos – some new, some old – that Torontonians often complain about. To the east lies the post-industrial Port Lands landscape, which we also complain about, a place where decades of unfulfilled plans have bred a waterfront cynicism into the city that we're slow to shake, even as development appears imminent.

Still, there are spectacular attractions, like Captain John's floating seafood restaurant, which is docked in the harbour at the very foot of Yonge Street. Should you venture onto the ship, you'll find a surf-and-turf cocktail-lounge time warp of tuxedoed waiters and deep-fried foods. The ship itself is a relic from the former Yugoslavia. The restaurant's owner, Captain John Letnik, sailed the ship to Toronto in 1975 after purchasing it from the Yugoslav government for $1 million. He put it up for sale in 2009, so it may yet see the high seas (or lake) again.

If you look along the sidewalk here, in front of the ship, you'll see a short metal balcony that extends over the water and lists the distances to various Ontario towns on the 'world's longest street' – it reminds me of the directional sign that pointed to other cities in the movie version of *M*A*S*H*. Though Yonge's longest-street claim is challenged by some, as you stand here, looking north, it's a

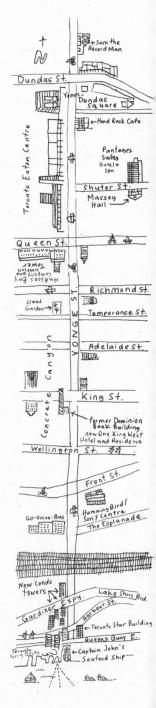

good way to feel connected to the rest of the province on a street that everybody knows about.

Yonge's first hundred metres are wide and, though the parking lots that languished for years here are being filled in with new buildings, it is still a frumpy start – or end – to a main street. The Gardiner, just to the north, always blamed for cutting off Torontonians from our waterfront, is being consumed by condo towers on both sides. The raised expressway isn't exactly disappearing, but it is becoming just another part of this landscape rather than the dominant view. Once underneath the much longer railway underpass, Yonge rises up to the original shoreline of Lake Ontario and crosses what is now Front Street. Here, at the southeast corner, is the Sony (née Hummingbird, then O'Keefe) Centre, a perfectly modern performance venue designed by the late Toronto architect Peter Dickinson.

Between Front and Richmond streets, Yonge is a concrete canyon. Day trippers returning from the Toronto Islands on the Ward's Island ferry can get a wonderful glimpse of it from the water. While no longer a particularly interesting pedestrian experience – much of the on-street retail and human energy has, as with much of the financial district, disappeared into the underground PATH tunnels – One King West catches the eye as it rises out of the former Dominion Bank Building. The original 1914 structure serves as a plinth for an impossibly razor-thin, fifty-one-storey condo tower that slices through the downtown sky like a schooner. As impressive as it is, though, it's a subtle part of the skyline. From many angles, it's just a nondescript part of the familiar clump of downtown buildings, so its narrow form can surprise when viewed from the north or south.

'The Yonge Street Strip' – the part that matters to Newfoundlanders and Windsorites alike – runs roughly from Richmond Street up to Wellesley Street. In its glory years, it was what the internet is to us today: a place where sex, drugs and rock 'n' roll are just a step away from all things moral and upright. What made it magnificent is that it all played out in real time, in real space.

This *Midnight Cowboy* Toronto included places like Mr. Arnold's, 'Canada's adult entertainment centre,' which boasted uncensored stag movies for $2, or $1 for seniors. In 1971, the

Toronto Star reported on the Catholic Church's concern that 'sex shops and pornographic bookstores are destroying Toronto the Good.' In fact, it was first- and second-hand knowledge of Yonge Street's tawdry spectacle, the one you can see if you watch the Canadian cinema classic *Goin' Down the Road*, that made the notion of 'Toronto the Good' a bit of a mystery to me for years.

Toronto's tolerance for this activity ended in July 1977, when twelve-year-old Emanuel Jaques, a Yonge-and-Dundas shoeshine boy, was raped, drowned in a sink full of water and ultimately dumped onto the roof of 245 Yonge, just south of where the Hard Rock Café is today. The clean-up of the street that followed grew bigger than originally intended, eventually leading to a moral panic and a gay witch-hunt that reached its peak with the infamous bathhouse raids of 1981.

Those raids had a galvanizing, Stonewall-like effect on Toronto's gay population, which had long been concentrated along Yonge north of College Street. Many of Toronto's early gay bars were located here, including the St. Charles Tavern at 488 Yonge (a former fire hall that today sports a refurbished Victorian clock tower) and the Parkside Tavern at 530 Yonge (now a twenty-four-hour Sobeys). It had long been a Toronto tradition for mobs of people to gather by what is now the Courtyard Marriott hotel to,

The Yonge Street strip in 1973 in all its smutty, exciting glory.

heckle the drag queens as they moved from the Parkside to the
St. Charles each Halloween night. Many came just to watch and
enjoy, as people do on Church Street now, but violence was never
far away. In 1968, police found several gasoline bombs behind the
St. Charles and, by 1977, a 100-officer-strong police square was
needed to control spectators who tossed insults, bricks and eggs.

Yonge was decidedly queerer than the rest of the city, and it
was also wetter. This is where Toronto the Good's lapsed Presbyte-
rians came to drink, at places like the Silver Rail at Yonge and
Shuter Street, which opened in 1947 as one of Toronto's first
licenced cocktail lounges. Half a block south, a three-lot strip on
Yonge facing the Eaton Centre is strangely derelict, at odds with its
ornate and storied past. At 197 Yonge stands the dirty and fenced-
in former Canadian Bank of Commerce building, built in 1905.
Just north, at 205, you'll find the former Bank of Toronto, built in
1905 by E. J. Lennox (of Old City Hall and Casa Loma fame).
Between them, there's a park disguised as a forbidding vacant lot.
If you're feeling particularly romantic, the small raised 'stage' area
can be viewed as an homage to the Colonial Tavern that once stood
here. On the Colonial's stage, jazz greats from Gillespie to Holiday
to Brubeck played in surroundings so intimate people could chat
with the performers by the stage after the show. Years later, in a
basement space dubbed the Meet Market, notorious Toronto punk
pioneers the Viletones further eroded Toronto's morals just as
their contemporaries in New York did at CBGB.

So where have you gone, Yonge Street? Walking along, it's hard to
find a drink in reasonable surroundings, and the good bands and
DJs don't play here anymore. The centre of the strip now would
appear to be Yonge-Dundas Square, probably the most controversial bit of real estate in the city. Everybody, it seems, has something
bad to say about it, but I'm not sure why. At most hours, and when
the square isn't being rented out for a private function (a valid criticism of the management of the space), it's full of people enjoying
themselves and watching the fountains or whatever performance
is going on. Surrounding it is our very own vulgar display of electric power, which takes the form of walls of advertising. On humid
nights, the air glows hundreds of metres into the sky around the
square, as if filled with electrified neon. While it may not be to

everyone's particular taste, it's helpful to view Yonge-Dundas Square as a shock-and-awe commercial pressure release, where anything can and will go. Just as long as it doesn't spread to the rest of the city, we can enjoy it for what it is. Many of us already appear to be doing so.

Though Yonge-Dundas Square's beloved/unbeloved status is in flux, almost everybody can agree that 10 Dundas East – the building on the northeast corner of the intersection, formerly known as 'Metropolis,' and as 'Toronto Life Square' after that – isn't inspiring in its architecture or interior design. At one of Toronto's most visible locations, an entirely appropriate place for movie theatres and stores, the view from Yonge-Dundas Square looks straight into the heart of a dowdy Future Shop utility corridor on the second floor. Watch as employees make their way from a pair of washrooms to their break room, which is littered with cheap folding chairs and tables.

Another long-time anomaly sits at the northwest corner of Yonge and Gerrard. Though home to one of Toronto's most unfortunately prominent parking lots, plans are underway to build 'Aura,' a 'supertall' condo, here. Development has been a long time coming to this parcel of land. The Great Depression has been over for nearly three-quarters of a century, yet this lot has languished since then, when economic collapse thwarted the Eaton family's empire-sized dreams for the location. The Eatons opened their flagship store at the north end of this block in 1930, and while still a magnificent example of art moderne architecture, it was just one part of a bigger plan to build the largest office and retail complex in North America. The downturn nixed plans for a thirty-six-storey Empire State Building–style tower, and the surrounding land was filled with unsympathetic structures and, eventually, parking. If you happen to find yourself in the seventh-floor Carlu – the streamlined reception and concert hall where Lady Eaton lunched and Glenn Gould liked to play – check out the huge architectural model on display and see what could have been. And though some may lament the Winners discount store that has moved into the main shopping hall downstairs, it's closer to the Eatons' mass-retailing, something-for-everybody ethos than anything that has been in this space since Eaton's vacated the site when the Eaton Centre was opened in 1977.

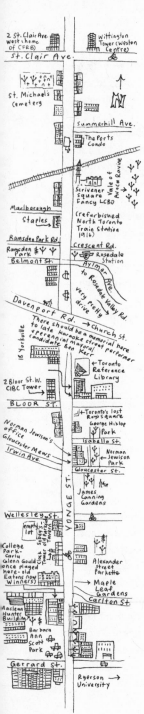

Though Toronto derives its name from an Iroquois word, *Tkaronto*, which means 'place where trees stand in the water,' examples of First Nations public art around the city are rare. One giant exception is found in the atrium of the former Maclean-Hunter building at College and Bay streets, one of Toronto's more 'unsympathetic' structures, depending on your sensibility. The plain glass tower's basement houses the *Three Watchmen*, three totem poles (one fifty feet tall, the other two thirty feet) by artist Robert Davidson of the west-coast Haida Nation. Maclean-Hunter may not exist anymore (it was subsumed into the Rogers empire), but Davidson's contemporary totems mark the day in 1984 when a Canadian print media company was mighty enough that it could afford its own skyscraper.

North to Bloor, Yonge is a jumble of shops and restaurants without a particular identity. Perhaps that's the fate of a main street: it must represent the whole city so it becomes a kind of pastiche of other neighbourhoods. For a change, take the Yonge passage, which runs parallel to the street just a few steps east between Bloor and Wellesley stations. A series of pedestrian passageways that include three linear parks sit where structures were cleared away for the Yonge subway line. (Subway nerds will notice that north of College station, the Yonge subway line shifts to the east and runs just adjacent to the street rather than directly under it.) To walk the alternative passage, start at James Canning Gardens, which is at the south end, a block north of Wellesley, and continue north through Norman Jewison Park, named after the Canadian film director whose dedication to Toronto has kept his 'Yorktown Productions' office in a neighbouring yellow building. The northern park is named after the late George Hislop, the longtime gay activist who ran as an MPP in 1981 after the Toronto bathhouse raids, and was later involved in the class-action lawsuit that saw same-sex pension benefits applied retroactively to 1985, the year the Charter of Rights and Freedoms was amended to include gay and lesbian equality rights. The passage then leads through a parking garage to what was once a collection of low-rise buildings on the Yonge and Bloor corner. In 2007, eviction notices were sent to the businesses in these buildings in preparation for the construction of an eighty-storey condo-and-hotel tower. Though some critics were perhaps a tad harsh when they called the old corner an eyesore, it certainly wasn't one of our most beautiful intersections (especially for such a prominent one), and this is an appropriate place for a tower of this size. But as of this writing, the company behind the planned condo had gone out of business, so Toronto has a rubble-strewn parcel of land on its hands. The real shame is that in the process of clearing this space, Toronto lost Roy's Square, a pedestrian laneway that ran behind the former buildings. It was a rare, almost European-style arcade passageway of small shops that made coming from and going to the Yonge and Bloor subway a pleasure.

Across Bloor on the northeast corner of Yonge stands the kind of building that gives concrete a bad name. Perched on what is arguably Toronto's most important corner, the Hudson's Bay building presents an impassable, wraparound wall of concrete. The adjacent Royal Bank branch, which is raised above street level, even had a 'No sitting' sign on the steps until recently. The money may be safe, but what about the people? Who thought this was a good way to attract customers? The dowdy buildings on the southeast corner are now gone, and renovations to the CIBC building on the northwest side have fixed some 1970s mistakes. Why doesn't this building follow suit? A memorial to late street performer and perennial mayoral candidate Ben Kerr, who stood here playing his guitar and singing for years (it was his audience that prompted those 'no sitting' signs), would be welcome too.

The micro-cultures that made their homes along this part of Yonge have either moved to other parts of the city or on to the internet. A walk along Yonge is not without excitement and charm, but as the old-timers will say, it isn't like it used to be.

Yet, even as many other streets can make a claim to being the heart of Toronto, Yonge can still grab us by the throat, as it did on Boxing Day in 2005 when fifteen-year-old Jane Creba was killed during a gun battle right near the spot we had those high-school drinks back in 1992. There are many reasons this event so deeply affected Torontonians during the so-called 'Year of the Gun,' just as Emanuel Jaques' murder did in '77; one of them, surely, is that both traumatic events played out on the street that is our collective living room, even if it's one we don't use all that often.

Yonge tends not to elicit such high emotional and cultural impact as it passes quietly through some of Toronto's more genteel neighbourhoods north of Bloor. The first stop along this stretch may just be the smartest place in the city. If this town had a physical brain, the Toronto Reference Library would be it. It's big, it's public and it's one of the few places where all types can bump into each other. Men in suits read statistics near the guy who waves his arms and reads to himself aloud, consumed by madness and Heidegger. I often sit on the fourth floor by the north windows, surrounded by students calculating things on folding computers while they share tables with retirees reading journal articles.

Pierre Berton researched many of his novels here, the inventors of *Trivial Pursuit* dug up some of their answers in the stacks, back when the questions were actually hard. The TRL's resources

The Toronto Reference Library's very quiet and very big atrium.

are so deep that most of us can find a bit of ourselves somewhere in it – like an old City of Windsor directory from 1966 that listed my grandfather, then a recent émigré to Canada: 'Micallef, Paul C. Labourer, Chryslers. 816 Dougall Avenue.' Line by line, Toronto's and Canada's stories are told as a matter of fact, with no embellishment needed.

I've found out more about what it means to be a Torontonian (and a Canadian) inside the TRL than anywhere else apart from walking around. When I show people Toronto, I take them here and make them ride the glass elevator to the top of the enormous five-storey atrium. It's like the opening shot of *Metropolis*, all the layers and movements visible at once. An echo of this can be found in another of Raymond Moriyama's buildings, the former Scarborough City Hall (now home to City of Toronto offices and open to the public), which has an equally impressive atrium.

Inside the TRL's front doors lies a cement pond and waterfall, above which a fabric sculpture by Japanese-Canadian artist Aiko Suzuki used to hang like a jungle. The sculpture was made of a million feet of fibre, separating the chaos outside from the order inside. I hope it's not gone forever; it belongs here just like the orange-carpeted walls and the hanging plants that used to dangle over the edge of each level. Built in 1977, all are vestiges of the (Prime Minister) Pierre Trudeau and (Mayor) David Crombie years, Toronto's last great era of city-building. That the library survived the lean years intact, and that it is used and loved by all kinds of Torontonians – manufacturing a steady stream of public intellectuals – could be why a civic renaissance is even possible today.

Though still a vision of utopian, modern architecture, the thirty-plus-year-old building is currently being updated by Moriyama's son, Ajon. The changes preserve the space-age-ness of the original design, and include a new glass entry, an interior expansion and the addition of the Bluma Appel Salon on the east side of the building. The Toronto Public Library system is the busiest in the world, and this is its mothership.

Across the street sits 18 Yorkville, a narrow 'point tower' that serves as a glassy distraction from the heavier CIBC and Bay towers to the south. Designed by Toronto architect Peter Clewes and his firm, architectsAlliance, it's a fine example of the kind

of neo-modernism style that so many new Toronto buildings have
followed. On the ground, things are just as nice. Toronto has many
parks but very few of them are formal. With the construction of
18 Yorkville, Toronto also got Town Hall Square, opened between
the Yorkville library branch and the condo building. Named after
the former Yorkville town hall that used to be nearby, the park is
modelled after a French parterre (a formal garden of paths, plant-
ings and trimmed hedges) and designed by Toronto landscape
architecture firm Janet Rosenberg + Associates. It turns the top
of an underground parking garage into a geometric green maze
that invites exploration.

Yonge continues north along the open-air trench of the
subway line, flanked by a jumble of low- and high-rise buildings.
Rosedale station is built into the side of the ravine and feels leafy
and bucolic, like so many of the Tube stations in the suburban
parts of London that follow the English Garden style of development. A dip in the road at Ramsden Park marks where Castle
Frank Brook once crossed Yonge, flowing eastwards towards the
Don River. Here, Yonge becomes Rosedale's 'main street,' with,
appropriately enough, a building that houses one of Toronto's
more expensive home-decorating shops.

At first glance, the Staples at Marlborough, a few blocks north
of Ramsden Park, is a big-box blight on Yonge and out of step with
the other high-end businesses, but take note of the gargoyles on
each archway, which survived an unsympathetic renovation. Built
in 1930, this was originally the ornate showroom for the Pierce-
Arrow Motor Car Company, a Buffalo-based luxury automobile
manufacturer that went out of business in 1937. The showroom
was eventually bought by the CBC in 1954 and turned into a television studio that housed iconic Canadian shows like *Wayne and
Shuster*, *Front Page Challenge*, the *Tommy Hunter Show* and even a
production of *Macbeth* starring a pre–*James Bond* Sean Connery.

Across the street, midtown's refurbished North Toronto Train
Station, built in 1916 at Summerhill by the firm Darling and Pearson (they also did the Dominion Bank building at One King West),
houses the world's fanciest liquor store. Restored and retrofitted in
2004, its interior was hidden behind acoustic drop ceilings. Out
front is Scrivener Square, the kind of small urban square Toronto
needs more of. Designed by Toronto architect Stephen Teeple and

named after the late MPP Margaret Scrivener, it includes a 'tipping fountain' by artist Robert Fones and a series of small, angular streams and ponds that are refreshingly free of the unnecessary safety barriers that too often ruin good urban design. Those who want green can walk east between the two condo buildings and eventually find a passageway to the Vale of Avoca Ravine and the wonderful *Swiss Family Robinson*–style trails high on the ravine wall.

As Yonge dips under the set of railway tracks that once served the North Toronto station (and may again one day), it starts moving uphill. On the east side, a condo tower called the Ports vaguely resembles the decks of a cruise ship. The name is even more appropriate considering that this was, until 1983, the site of the Ports o' Call, 'a drinkers' Disneyland' of Polynesian-, Western- and Roman-themed restaurants and lounges. Long-time Toronto jazzman Ian Bargh played the Polynesian room and once told me Ports o' Call was a hotbed of the Toronto jazz scene in the '60s. How such a weirdo place existed in famously uptight Toronto is a mystery on the surface, but Toronto the Good could be a wonderfully bad place when that Orange and WASP-y surface was scratched. That the condo developers saw fit to memorialize this place in the new name should inspire other developers to give their buildings names that actually mean something to Toronto.

Further up the hill sits the long-time home of the historic CHUM DIAL 1050 sign, though, due to various media buyouts and reorganizations, it has recently been reinstalled at Duncan and Richmond streets. On May 27, 1957, 1050 CHUM became the first Canadian station to play rock music

The CHUM radio sign before it was moved to Richmond and Duncan streets.

exclusively. Later, as an oldies station, it reminded baby boomers of their golden youth. CHUM sat on top of 'Gallows Hill,' so named because a fallen tree here once resembled the beam of wood that hangmen found so useful, though it's not so much a hill as just part of the escarpment that runs along midtown Toronto and marks the shoreline of ancient Lake Iroquois. When CHUM's tight rotation allowed them to play Bowie's 'Rebel, Rebel,' it would've been easy to pretend it was an homage to William Lyon Mackenzie's rebel forces, whose advance was stopped here in 1837.

Unless you peek down an alley running west off Yonge, just south of St. Clair Avenue, it's easy to miss St. Michael's cemetery. Opened in 1855 when the area was countryside, it's now tucked in behind buildings. When I lived nineteen floors up, across Yonge Street on Pleasant Boulevard, I used to watch kids igniting fireworks there at night, briefly lighting up the vast darkness, as would the ultra-bright beams of police spotlights that would pan back and forth between the tombstones soon afterwards.

Some thirty thousand Catholic Torontonians lie buried behind St. Michael's gates, many of them Irish immigrants who fled the potato famine – their county of origin is often listed on the markers – including John Pickford Hennessey, grandfather of 'America's Sweetheart,' actress Mary Pickford.

In the middle of the cemetery sits the octagonal 'dead house,' the mortuary vault where caskets were stored during the winter months. It was designed in 1856 by Joseph Sheard, the only architect ever to become mayor of Toronto (and, incidentally, the guy who thought a civic holiday in August might be nice – another reason Ontario should be kind to Toronto).

When I stand at Yonge and St. Clair, I find it striking that the intersection is so unsung. Most mid-sized towns around Canada dream of a downtown filled with this much activity. After a year of living there when I first moved to Toronto, it did sometimes feel like I was living at the mall – there was an It Store across the street at the time – but it has a certain urban elegance to it.

The night we moved in – my first sleep in my own Toronto home – after hauling our stuff up nineteen floors, I went for an exhausted and overwhelmed walk through the warm May night. To the east, I discovered the huge St. Clair Viaduct that crosses

the Vale of Avoca Ravine and Yellow Creek.
Far below in the darkness, the treetops swayed
gently in the wind, alternately sinister and
magical. I had heard of Toronto ravines and
seen them from Highway 401, but this was
my first real encounter with one. Margaret
Atwood's novel *The Blind Assassin* opens on
this bridge where, in 1945, a car gets stuck in
the streetcar track, flies off course and plunges
off the side. There are no rails on the bridge
now, but Atwood was right about the streetcar
presence: the buried corpses of those old rails
push up through the asphalt just east at Mount
Pleasant.

On later walks, I discovered a network of
trails that extend below the viaduct, good for
long runs with no traffic and thick, oxygenated
air. (Entrances go north up the vale and you
can find a secret back entrance to Mount
Pleasant Cemetery, but be careful not to get
locked in at closing time.)

The area up top is called Deer Park. In
1837, Agnes Heath and her son Charles Heath
bought forty acres of land here and raised deer.
Local historian Joan C. Kinsella writes in the
Toronto Public Library–produced *Historical
Walking Tour of Deer Park*, that the deer
'roamed through the area as far east as Parliament Street and were quite tame. The deer
always knew when it was dinner time at the
hotel at St. Clair and Yonge and would gather
at the corner to be fed by the guests.'

The deer are gone now, but there are lots
of places to feed here. When I first moved to
the area in 2000, there was no Tim Hortons
yet, so the only late-night coffee available was
at the original Fran's diner (home to a Fionn
MacCool's pub now). The takeout coffee was
dispensed from those irritating pump jugs,

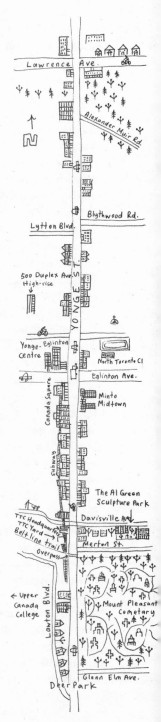

but it gave me time to look at the regulars who hung out there, like the woman who painted on one-inch-thick eyebrows. Glenn Gould used to have his own booth there too. In its own understated way, Yonge and St. Clair is a perfect urban corner.

A little to the north, Mount Pleasant Cemetery pleasantly disrupts Yonge's urbanity. The cemetery property runs from Yonge's east side over to Bayview, a massive green rectangle that sprawls across midtown Toronto. Apart from the buried dead, it can be considered one of Toronto's largest and nicest parks. Mount Pleasant makes a point of being open for the living – whether walking, jogging or biking along the gently curving roads – and also functions as an arboretum, playing host to a wide variety of trees. Here, Canada's not-so-famous are buried next to the famous. Some, like the Eatons and Masseys, lie in massive crypts, while others, like the Blacks, rest in large family plots – and yes, there is enough room to accommodate Conrad one day. Explore Mount Pleasant without a map; after many such trips, I finally found, by chance, former Prime Minister William Lyon Mackenzie King's grave, complete with fresh flowers and a Canadian flag.

Back on Yonge, the street dips where Yellow Creek once flowed before it was filled in. Opposite the cemetery lies the Davisville TTC yard, so this bit of Yonge feels quite open. The old railway trestle that crosses Yonge above the cemetery is part of the Kay Gardiner Beltline Park. Cutting a northwest line through central Toronto, it's the city's thinnest park, named after the local councillor who was instrumental in converting the former railway into a cycling and walking trail. Originally a commuter railway, the Belt Line opened in 1892 and ran forty kilometres out from Union Station, up the Don Valley and through new suburban neighbourhoods in Rosedale, Moore Park and Forest Hill. It operated only for two years before going bankrupt, but left a right of way that today allows for a continuous backyard glimpse into Forest Hill.

Near the corner of Davisville sits the W. C. McBrien Building, the TTC's headquarters. Built after the Yonge subway line opened in 1954, it's now the start of a modern highrise community that houses a near-secret sculpture garden. As one of the three founders of Greenwin Property Management, Abraham 'Al' Green was able to see his passion for art has result in exceptional bits of

modern sculpture placed around his Toronto developments, beginning long before the practice was *de rigueur*. Many sculptures can
be found on the lawns surrounding the tall white Greenwin buildings, which spread east from Davisville station between Davisville
Avenue and Merton Street. On Balliol Street, the Al Green Sculpture Park is home to twenty-five sculptures by Canadian public-art
giants of the '60s and '70s such as Kosso Eloul and Sorel Etrog,
as well as some by Green himself. A walk here is a journey from
utopian modern buildings to our avant-garde past.

Yonge reverts, as it often does, to a low-rise landscape of two-
and three-storey retail and restaurants (this is the default typology
of Yonge, interrupted only when new developments have gone up)
until a few blocks south of Eglinton. If Woody Allen set movies
in Toronto they would be shot at Yonge and Eglinton. It's vertical,
the sidewalks are full of people wearing lululemon – Toronto's
equivalent of Allen's tennis racquet conversation prop – and it's
upwardly mobile. It both functions and is known as the city's
uptown, even though North York denizens might disagree, since
the megacity amalgamation rendered Yonge and Eglinton
Toronto's geographical midtown.

This area is the kind of place where the cool kids don't hang
out but the 'Young and Eligible' folks do. This civic dynamic of
uptown-downtown is universal, and there has always been an
awkward relationship between the two. In *How Insensitive*, his
1994 novel about Toronto's cultural scene, Russell Smith wrote
of a late-night arrival in the neighbourhood: 'Ted got off the
subway at Eglinton. John had told him to just walk north until
he saw the cars. He had never been to this part of town before;
it was where John had grown up. John never talked about it. Go-
Go had sneeringly said it was white, just white and nothing else.
In the dark, Yonge Street seemed deserted and sterile. There
seemed to be a disproportionate number of specialty food shops
with baguettes and jam jars and italic lettering in the windows, all
closed. In between them were dry cleaners, a dark Second Cup, an
imitation British pub at the base of a mirrored office building.'

The shops and bars in and around Yonge and Eglinton tend
not to be destinations for people from other neighbourhoods
(restaurants are an exception), and this area has always suffered
from a sense of being off the trendy beaten path, a foggy 'place up

there.' In an article in the *Toronto World* newspaper from 1907 on
the area, then the frontier of Toronto's manifest-destiny surge into
rural Ontario, it's clear the neighbourhood has always been off
everyone else's civic radar: 'A good deal is being heard of this most
beautiful of Toronto's suburbs, North Toronto, but few people
indeed know where it is situated and when the question is asked
"Where is North Toronto?" the answer generally is ... altogether
wrong.' The article goes on to describe the area in topographic
terms that current residents might not object to: 'This high altitude secures the town's inhabitants' pure air, as the atmosphere
is not contaminated with coal smoke and other foul-smelling,
disease-producing and death-dealing odours; and consequently
makes it a very desirable spot to live in.'

Yonge and Eglinton still is a desirable place to live and, when
the subway opened in 1954, a new pressure was added: developers.
Eglinton was the end – or beginning – of Toronto's nascent
subway system, and it transformed what was a sleepy streetcar
suburb into a hub. When you stand on one of the western corners
of the intersection, you can still see the transformation happening:
in places, Yonge looks like it could still be in the Diefenbaker era,
with low-rise and some single-storey retail buildings lining the
street. Look the other way, though, and all you see are skyscrapers.
From a distance, Yonge and Eglinton is an impressively silhouet-
ted skyline knuckle on Toronto's Yonge Street spine.

The black glass towers of Canada Square – previously called
Foundation House – were the first to lead Yonge and Eglinton into
the postwar modern age. As it did in the early 1960s, Canada
Square embodies an unapologetic big-cityness, with movie theatres
and corporate head offices attached to underground trains. TVO
even broadcasts from the basement – guests on Steve Paikin's
current-events program *The Agenda* can feel the subway rumbling
a few feet below. Nothing was more modern than TV in the postwar
era. Toronto's 1964 'Plan for Eglinton' summed up the spirit of the
time: 'To the Torontonian boarding a subway train to the City in
the morning, or motoring up Yonge Street in the evening rush
hour, the Eglinton District presents the picture of dynamic growth
and change. Impressive glass office towers, bustling stores, high-
rise apartments and the busy intersection of Yonge Street and
Eglinton Avenue all contribute to this new image.'

This intersection is still a contentious place, growing always taller and denser. The giant memorials to the recent growth spurt are the Minto twin towers – nobody seems to call them by their *James Bond*–ish official names, Quantum North and Quantum South, perhaps because even the as-advertised lifestyles of their occupants can't live up to that much fiction. The anti-tower crowd points to them as the neighbourhood-killer. In a February 2009 *National Post* article, Councillor Michael Walker called them 'monsters' and added that 'you have to feel for the residents of Yonge-Eglinton' – a strange sentiment given that he represents a lot of folks that seem quite happy living tall and, perhaps more importantly, that the area went vertical over forty years ago.

During the growth of the 1960s, many residents were all for this vertical expansion. An archival collection of letters to City of Toronto planners in response to the 1964 plan that called for the blocks surrounding the main intersection to be covered in high-density apartments were largely positive. It's strange to read them now, conditioned as we are by decades of consultation where the predominant word is 'No.' True, some of the homeowners were likely in favour of the plan because they could sell their property to developers at top price. Today, though, there are only four or five blocks of apartment buildings, which easily give way to a neighbourhood of solid, single-family homes.

To wander the surrounding blocks today is to travel through a kind of modern wonderland. Low-rise and (very) high-rise buildings with names like the Lord Elgin, the Imperial Manor, the Rosemount, Place de Soleil and Americana capture the optimistic modern thinking of the era while still being connected to our colonial past. The Berkeshire House and the Canterbury House, two magnificent 1970s concrete buildings found behind the rather ugly and austere RioCan buildings on the northwest side of Yonge and Eglinton have much in common with brutalist buildings in Britain that have similar traditional 'house' names.

Lingering by the fountains in the Anne Johnston Courtyard, which is sandwiched between the two Minto towers and named after the local city councillor who gave up her political life to defend Toronto's right to skyscrapers, you can easily forget that there are many storeys above. Done right, tall buildings aren't wastelands at the bottom, and aren't an eyesore on the horizon.

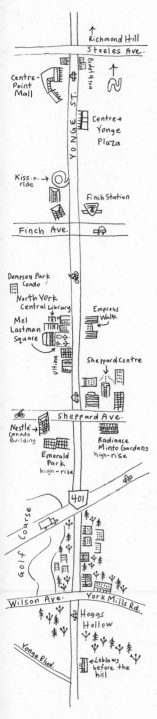

We often waste the opportunity to put tall buildings where they belong: in the middle of a major hub. The fact that the thirty-seven- and fifty-four-floor Minto towers are shorter than planned is one of Toronto's latest failures to recognize that it is a vertical city. The long, drawn-out 'fight' over height in this neighbourhood was over when Trudeaumania began, yet the abandoned TTC yards adjacent to Canada Square, where a proposed tower development tweaked the perpetual kink in Councillor Walker's neck back in February 2009, still face opposition. Tall buildings are coming. Why not let them be as tall as they can be, and let Yonge and Eglinton be the metropolitan centre it's been turning itself into for decades?

Towards Lawrence, Yonge defaults low again, another pleasant strip of pleasant stores. The area is perhaps a little more diverse than Russell Smith gave it credit for, though in the mid-2000s, *Globe and Mail* columnist John Barber referred to North Toronto, the area around Yonge and Lawrence, as our city's only real ghetto (a rich white one). I worked up here for a while and met some of the nice ghetto denizens. They shop at the upscale supermarket Pusateri's, send their kids to Upper Canada College and, when giving me a ride to the subway, they would point out fancy homes where important wives had left important husbands. As with so many Toronto neighbourhoods, it functions like a small town, where everyone knows everyone and gossip flows through the streets.

Just south of Lawrence and east of Yonge lies the former farm of gentleman farmer John Lawrence. Just before the First World War, this land was subdivided by the Dovercourt Land Building and Savings Company into the

Lawrence Park Estates, designed as 'a high-class suburban site.' However, the war and recession resulted in an auction, in 1919, of the many unsold properties at 'any price the public will pay.' Today, people pay upwards of $1 million to live on these leafy streets. Unfortunately, some of the Craftsman houses in this neighbourhood have been torn down to make way for atrocious monster homes that must make the old money shudder.

South of Lawrence Park stretch the ravines that follow Burke Creek, starting with the Alexander Muir Memorial Gardens. These gardens were originally located north of St. Clair but, in 1952, the TTC spent $100,000 to move them to make way for the subway. Muir's massive 1867 top-forty hit 'The Maple Leaf Forever' isn't sung much anymore, but his park has lovely red crushed-stone paths, a nice change from boring pavement.

Wander deeper into ravine and you'll find old-growth forests with a 'super canopy' of white pines that is the natural equivalent of the city's high-rise buildings (those buildings seem far away down here). A pitched battle between dog owners and dogless residents took place here during the 1990s, similar to the ones brewing around the city today; the dog-owners won in this case, and dogs now have ample off-leash areas to roam, including a network of fenced-in pathways that keep the sensitive ravine slopes safe from doggy disturbances. There is even a dog drinking fountain dedicated to 'mankind's best friend.' From the plaque: 'We wish them Fun Walks. Happy times. Cool drinks. Willy, thanks for getting us walking in this beautiful park. This clean water is for you and the little fur people … drink, my loves.'

North of Lawrence, Yonge continues in its default low-rise retail incarnation until it arrives at the end of the old City of Toronto, where it dips deep into Hoggs Hollow, the scourge of north-south cyclists, a place that divides the city deeper and wider than the Don Valley. At the southern crest, across from the Loblaws – where the Yonge streetcar line used to terminate – there is a giant surveyor's compass called 'Toronto's Northern Gateway.' It's a vestige of old Metropolitan Toronto and used to sit on the border between Toronto and North York. Like all borders that don't exist anymore, we cross it without thinking, only occasionally noticing something that reminds us it was there. A little further north, there's an apartment building called 'Top of the Hollow,' which marks an entrance into the community of Hoggs Hollow, a wealthy enclave of big homes and twisting country-like roads. Hoggs Hollow sits at the bottom of a valley, and walking down into it, you can feel the temperature drop and the humidity go up, a sign that water is near. Some homes even have lawns of ferns, which makes the area feel almost like a North Vancouver neighbourhood.

Unlike so many of Toronto's lost streams and rivers, the West Don remains open in places, weaving its way through the big lots in this area. The small bridge that crossed it here was destroyed by Hurricane Hazel's storm surge in 1954. There is a small plaque on the new bridge that doesn't mention what perhaps many are left wondering: what will happen to all these houses, built on a flood plain, when the next Hazel hits? Nearby, in the park at the entrance to Hoggs Hollow, there is a monument for artist C. W. Jefferys, whose home and studio still stand on Yonge just north of York Mills. The studio site is surrounded by a cluster of mid-rise glass office buildings that occupy the bottom of the valley. They're tucked into the trees and the Don Valley Golf Course. They're big – one building houses a football-field-sized customer service centre – but most Torontonians likely miss both as Yonge is fast here and the slow pedestrian view is easy to neglect.

If you're on foot during the frozen winter, wander onto the golf-course grounds. The entrance is just before the Highway 401 overpasses, and access to the grounds is easy when the clubs are in storage. All paths lead to a vast, cathedral-like area underneath the quadruple bridges of the 401 high above. One frozen night we ventured down here, with the constant hum of traffic above and light dripping over the sides from the jumbo-sized light towers. On the west side of the grounds, we scrambled up the banks of the ravine and popped our heads up in the space between the east-bound express and collector lanes. The sound and fury are airport-runway worthy. The 401 is usually seen from a distance or from within a fast-moving vehicle. Being so close to the flow is like waking up in the middle of a rushing river of steel. We were safe behind the barriers, but close enough to feel the air move as each vehicle passed by.

Yonge itself doesn't pass under the 401 pleasantly, especially when you're on foot. This is the least pedestrian-friendly stretch of the street, and though there are sidewalks, it feels at times like you might be walking on the 401 itself. Beyond the on- and off-ramps, North York civilizes somewhat as Yonge approaches Sheppard and the in-transition mix of high-rises and 1950s and '60s low-rise plaza developments clash. North York City Centre, our uptown 'billion dollar downtown,' is new and will always be compared to the streetscape south of Hoggs Hollow, which was established before the automobile changed the way we do streets. In the middle of all this is one of Toronto's most important public spaces, Mel Lastman Square, named after the long-time mayor of North York who went on to become the first mayor of the amalgamated City of Toronto. This is the uptown-downtown that Lastman built, but this legacy didn't turn out exactly as he planned. In an unguarded moment in the 1990s, Lastman told former mayor John Sewell, who was then writing a column about city politics for *NOW* magazine, that 'the streetscape turned out like hell. It's awful. It's not what I wanted.'

Places that need to use the word 'city' in their name usually betray a civic insecurity, but long-time residents have no such anxiety here; some of them still list their address as Willowdale, Ontario, avoiding any reference to Toronto. Right now, it's one of the most interesting places in the city because new and old collide block by block, like two glaciers, complete with archetypal progress scenes where little bungalows cower next to shiny glass towers.

The growth of Yonge was a key issue in the 1985 North York municipal election. Lastman offered a gung-ho approach and his opponent, Barbara Greene, pushed for slower 'good development.' Proof of Lastman's overwhelming victory is on record, but also in the air. North York has a real big-city skyline, just like Houston, Calgary or Dayton, Ohio – kind of impressive but ultimately forgettable and generic, and peppered with a few exceptions, such as the former North York City Hall (now simply city government offices), with its dramatic slanted roof and, next to it, the building that houses the North York Central Library.

Inside City Hall, a building that had its political power sucked out of it when the megacity was created, there are happy photo montages of North York declaring 'Dave Winfield Day' in 1993 and 'Wendel Clark Day' in 1994. (Only Winfield cared enough about the honour to wear a suit for the occasion.) If the library reminds you of the Toronto Reference Library or Scarborough Civic Centre, it's because it, too, was designed by Raymond Moriyama, the architect behind Toronto's most impressive public atria and zigzagging staircases.

Adding to the movie-set strangeness of North York City Centre are the overwrought, nearly baroque condo names: Cosmo, the Monet, the Majestic Phase II, Platinum Towers, Spectrum and the Ultima at Broadway. How do you invite people over for dinner with a straight face when you live at the Grande Triomphe at Northtown? Even the Vatican has less hubris.

The Residences of Dempsey Park is one of the few buildings with a historical reference in its name. The Dempsey hardware store stood at Yonge and Sheppard, a local landmark since 1860, but moved a few blocks away, to Beecroft Avenue, before construction of the Sheppard subway line began in '90s. You can now find the store hiding, like the rest of Willowdale, between and behind the new city centre.

The condo towers begin to thin out at Finch Avenue, and the remainder of Yonge and North York is low-rise and bungalow heavy. Though there are many buses running up Yonge at this point, the fact that the subway ends at Finch gives this bit a cutoff and farther-away feeling. All this is – or was – Newtonbrook, an early-nineteenth-century village. Most traces of this historic village disappeared when the area was subdivided into a huge residential development in the 1950s. Lost, too, was the Methodist manse at the corner of Yonge and Hendon Avenue where Prime Minister Lester B. Pearson was born. His term as prime minister is partly responsible for Newtonbrook's contemporary multiculturalism as his government started opening Canada's doors to newcomers in a big way. Today, his intersection is home to the Finch subway station's kiss 'n' ride depot, certainly a fitting memorial to the Nobel Prize–winning peacemaker.

At the end – or beginning – of Toronto, there's a store called Bidet4U. It welcomes travellers coming south along Yonge from Richmond Hill to the big city, where anything is possible and all manner of foreign toilet experiences are easily within reach. Standing at the Steeles Avenue curb, where Yonge Street continues into the clutches of the rest of Ontario, we might be tempted to call this place the crossroads of nowhere, but it's as busy as

Yonge and Bloor. Buses from York's Rapid Transit service, Viva and standing-room-only TTC caravans pass by constantly. Even Brampton and Bramalea transit make their way through here.

At mid-afternoon, pedestrians are everywhere, crossing all seven lanes of Yonge or Steeles. Some of the pedestrians cross north to Richmond Hill – big-sky country. You can't really see Richmond Hill from here, but the signs assure you that it is indeed there, sprawling, like many other GTA municipalities, up to Lake Simcoe and beyond.

Any lingering doubts as to this place's importance are cleared up by Centerpoint Mall's self-assured modish logo of four arrows pointing inwards. Inside, it's the standard Toronto second-tier mall mix of rug emporiums, fly-by-night electronics and leather goods stores and women pushing small dogs in Zellers carts.

Centrepoint was originally going to be called Sayvette City when it was planned in 1961, but changed names before opening in 1964. It, like its popular cousin, Yorkdale Mall, is a bit of a modernist gem, with horizontal windows along the tops of corridors and a huge round room with a sweeping ceiling that feels like a 1960s airport – though it was ruined at some point to make way for an oversized Buck or Two shop.

Back outside at Yonge at Steeles, the quieter Richmond Hill streetscape is a contrast to the remarkable chaos of Toronto strip malls, like at the Centre & Yonge Plaza – across from Centerpoint – an old cedar-shingled building that houses Iranian butchers, Chinese florists and the Love Shop adult novelty and video store, a landscape of suburban pleasures and multiculturalism, together at last. Yonge Street, from top to bottom, can accommodate such variety, both human and architectural.

The Toronto Islands

 pack a lunch bathing suit recommended

 admission

Connecting walk: Harbourfront.

During the summer, at about noon on Fridays, Toronto starts to empty out. You can almost hear the slow drain to the north as tens of thousands of Torontonians make for the highways on their way to odd-sounding places like Wasaga, Bala, Bobcaygeon and Killbear. Those of us on the wrong side of the cottage gap are left with a quieter city – some Sunday afternoons feel downright apocalyptic in their emptiness. We're left no choice but to find our adventures in the urban wilderness and, often, on the Toronto Islands.

The Islands are to Toronto what the seaside resorts of Brighton and Blackpool were to Britain: a place where working- and middle-class folks could take cheap holidays of their own. Blackpool would heave with factory workers from the north of England, while Brighton, just a short train ride from London, was an escape from the tumult and pollution of the city. The resorts were full of amusements from giant Victorian piers to streets called the 'Golden Mile.' (Our own Golden Mile is in Scarborough, but that's another story.) Until the 1970s, their beaches and promenades were packed with people; there was nowhere else to go.

With the advent of cheap holiday packages, lobster-red Britons now choose to sun themselves on the Mediterranean shores of Ibiza, Majorca and Malta. The old resorts are seen as melancholy places where the skies are perpetually cloudy and the beaches cold and windswept. Morrissey summed up the sensibility best in 'Everyday is Like Sunday,' perhaps the most apocalyptic pop song ever written: 'Hide on the promenade / Etch a postcard / "How I Dearly Wish I Was Not Here" / In the seaside town / That they forgot to bomb / Come, Come, Come – nuclear bomb / Every day is like Sunday / Every day is silent and grey.'

Though I'd love an excuse to take maudlin trips to the Toronto Islands and sing sad songs to myself, I can't, because there isn't much that's depressing about the place, even if it functions in much the same way as the British resorts did. Today, the Islands are as busy as they were in 1813, when an early European settler, D.W. Smith, observing the First Nations people who boated to the Islands, recorded in the *Gazetteer* that 'the long beach or peninsula, which affords a most delightful ride, is considered so healthy by the Indians that they resort to it whenever indisposed.'

floating dinks and boobs
mostly dinks though

Certainly Smith paints too rosy a portrait of aboriginal life under British rule, but I too like to sneak over when 'indisposed,' or even when I'm disposed; on at least one occasion I've participated in a conference call while lying on the beach there.

The ferry trip to the Islands makes the separation between here and there official. Visitors to Centre Island are met with some of the softest, greenest grass I've ever seen in a public park and one of the famous Toronto Parks and Recreation signs that invite people to 'Please Walk on the Grass.' On weekends, these greens are packed with large groups of new Canadians cooking food and playing games or just going for walks. Many, especially the South Asian men, wear dress pants and shirts to the park, even on 'heat alert' days, just as most men did here sixty years ago.

Near the docks lies Centreville, a cute little amusement park not unlike those found on the British piers. It's more small-town fair than Canada's Wonderland: the theme is quaint and slightly cheesy and the rides' modest speeds are unlikely to shatter any world records. Yet even without the fake mountain, the kids (and their adult handlers) seem to love it. At the snack bars, nearly everything is deep-fried, just like in Britain.

To the south, beyond Centreville, a series of formal gardens with Pearson-era fountains lead to the Islands' only pier, which juts out over Lake Ontario. I wasn't around for it, but this is what I imagine wandering the modern public spaces at Expo 67 felt like. Little modernist pavilions from the same time also dot the island. The only amusement on the pier is the view, but on shore whole families rent strange looking quad-cycles to explore the Islands, often going wildly off course.

TORONTO

Clothing optional
Beach

To the west lie the natural and less-populated parts of the Islands. The main road leads along a narrow peninsula between Lake Ontario and the interior waterways (rent a kayak on the mainland and paddle over for a completely different view of island life). As the trail curves north towards the Island Airport, small signs direct the curious to Hanlan's Point, Toronto's clothing-optional beach.

People wear as much or as little as they want at Hanlan's. The naked coexist happily with people less willing to burn their sensitive parts. On one occasion, I saw someone lounging in what looked like a woolen Victorian bathing costume, while another time, a man in a three-piece suit walked the hot sands. It's Toronto's most liminal of spaces, an in-between place in our civic backyard that somehow feels far from home. Like our ravines, Hanlan's is one of the places where nature and metropolis collide and, unlike the largely private cottage country to the north, it's home to a very public beach culture that allows Toronto's urban mix to express itself even more than it does on Queen Street or in Kensington Market. It's easy to forget the city, but then the occasional glimpse of someone's painful-looking genital piercing reminds me that we're still safely surrounded by Toronto's urbanity. It's sometimes an uneasy mix – you'll sometimes hear grumblings from the committed nudists, who complain about the people who don't get completely naked – but this beach is the ultimate manifestation of the kind of freedom Toronto represents: everybody can simply be how they like without segregation or categorization.

Wander south, away from the crowds, and you'll find secret coves and water so clear it seems downright Bahamian, while the long walk north, into the 'clothed' area, passes through a wonderful dune-and-grass scrubland that continues until a hundred or so metres from the airport runway. During the airshow, this is the best seat in Toronto: the planes fly so low overhead that the pilots' heads are visible and the water vibrates from the sound.

Torontonians have been taught to think that we're surrounded by a toxic soup fit only for three-headed fish (as people have in many Great Lakes cities), but Lake Ontario is just fine to swim in – in some places, it's even cleaner than some of the world's more celebrated beaches. In fact, six Toronto beaches regularly fly a Blue Flag, the internationally recognized eco-label awarded to beaches that meet a list of twenty-seven criteria related to water quality, environmental education, management, safety and services. Other unflagged beaches are often fine to swim in as well.

East of the centre pier lies the residential side of the Islands, where two communities were saved from demolition in 1980, when then Ontario Premier Bill Davis prevented the razing of dozens of cottages. During the 1970s, the Metro Toronto government was intent on making the island 100 per cent parkland, and removing the small resortish main street and adjacent houses was part of that progress. While much of it was removed, two clusters of cute streets with even cuter cottage-style homes on Algonquin Island (which can be reached by a short bridge) and at the end of Ward's Island (near where the island was once attached to the mainland) were preserved. Many people resent the Islanders' presence, and still wish the bulldozers had completed their work and cleared the Islands completely of homes. This is always curious to me, as I like that people live here. I don't feel jealous because I can't think of a worse place to live. It isn't easy, bringing everything you need over by ferry in bike trailers, competing with the crowds in the summer and enduring no ferry service at times, especially in the frozen winter. Yet, looking over from the mainland, it's comforting to know there are people there, watching over it and populating the place. During summer days it's a crowded place, but at night and when the colder winds blow, the Islands empty out. The city has more than enough empty green space, and the Islands' residents are something unique to Toronto (though at times they can be cranky, and their in-fighting is legendary). Perhaps even a return to that resort 'main street' with a few bars and hotels might be all right too.

Like anybody, I happily take a weekend at the cottage when one is offered. But the Islands and their Disney-like perfection are a good substitute – and the ferry ride back at the end of the day beats the Highway 400 crawl back into town.

Harbourfront

neighbourhood jaunt

bathing suit optional

offspring friendly

Connecting walks: Yonge, Toronto Islands, Bathurst, Spadina, CNE/Western Waterfront.

When the *Toronto Star* decided to move into the poo-brown monster of a building at the foot of Yonge in 1971, Queens Quay was lined with dying industry and railroad tracks. They were redevelopment pioneers and, as early as 1963, they wrote poetically about the future of the waterfront: 'On stage is a panorama of rails, rust and rot ... waiting in the wings are magnificent plans to transform it into office, motor hotels, a marine park, a heliport and ferry terminal extraordinaire.'

Heliports were hot in the '60s and all the best buildings had them, but the jet age didn't make it to the waterfront as quickly as the *Star* predicted, and the rot continued to rot. Fast-forward forty years and the *Star* was still on the eastern frontier of Toronto's waterfront development. Queens Quay became unfit of its royal name; its semi-industrial scrubland remained relatively contiguous all the way to Ashbridge's Bay, near the Beach neighbourhood.

Only in the latter part of the 2000s has progress been made, first with a design competition for Sugar Beach, a park along the Jarvis Slip, opposite the giant Redpath Sugar factory. Further east, the new Corus building, a square, low-rise box with angled top designed by Toronto's Diamond and Schmitt Architects, is bringing people and life to an area that, until recently, was where nightclub- and concertgoers would park their cars before heading to the Koolhaus (née Warehouse) and Guvernment (née RPM) mega-clubs.

As the neighbourhood changes, operations that were once remote are no longer. The clubs will now have to contend with more uptight neighbours, for one. Redpath Sugar shows no sign of leaving the area, which is a good thing. Freighters are often docked next to the building, unloading unrefined sugar from the Caribbean; if the wind is blowing right, sparkly smoke or steam blows into the skyscraper cluster. The plant employs a lot of people who make a physical product (a novel thing in the 'creative city'), but it's also a reminder of Toronto's industrial heritage and of our once-working waterfront. The area beyond, for years a refuge of odd industries, including a golf dome, will see change come more quickly now that the Corus beachhead has been made – though one risks falling into the *Star*'s 1963 trap when making predictions like this.

Excitement about Toronto's waterfront is nothing new, but neither is disappointment – the *Star* itself inadvertently started the now infamous waterfront wall of 1970s concrete so reviled in our city. In 1964, Bauhaus school founder Walter Gropius, then a professor at Harvard, saw the plans for new developments as very exciting, saying 'Toronto is fortunate that its cross-town expressway was built north of the reclaimed land' – observing that, though Torontonians hate it so, the Gardiner could have been much worse, as waterfront freeways are in many other cities.

The main culprits behind the post-Gardiner barrier to the water are the Westin Harbour Castle Hotel and the neighbouring residential towers of Harbour Square, built in the early 1970s by

Robert Campeau, the now-deposed king of Canadian development, an eventual victim of 1980s excess. If you walk by at street level, the buildings have all the charm and romance of the fan entrance to a football stadium where only losing teams play. The hotel's gaping mouth contains the most elaborate and well-lit parking ramp in the city. Figuring out how to walk into the hotel is a challenge, and guests dodge tourists and suvs with every step. The Toronto Islands ferry docks behind the hotel block public thoroughfare (in fact, the docks are one of the few places this happens, as pedestrians can walk directly at the water's edge along much of the downtown waterfront).

Harbour Square is redeemed by its lakeside public spaces. There are wooden docks with stairs that lead down to the water and lots of green mixed in with the concrete, and these spaces are populated and well-used. From the ferry, the building looks beautiful and utopic, like a futuristic *Star Trek* city rising out of blue and green nature. Up close, a giant concrete public-art 'ball' seems to float with the lily pads in a fountain. The ball is hollow, with a suspended walkway and an observatory-like view of the Islands from inside. This is concrete used for good rather than evil, and though the south side of the complex is awful, the lake side of Harbour Square is a fine and unsung pedestrian promenade.

People don't move down here for the sidewalks, though – these towers would be empty if they did. It's the view from the top that counts. In the early 2000s, on one of those summer nights when the city takes over and seems to make plans for you as you walk along through random encounters (this is in the days before I had a mobile phone), I ended up at a party thrown by someone I didn't know on the thirtieth floor of Number One York Quay, one of the blue-and-beige towers next to Harbour Square. There was a tub full of beer, a grand piano, torch songs and a stunning view from the balcony. The Gardiner and the city sparkled into the humidity and smog, magically disappearing, an anonymous view high above a street that's undergoing constant improvements and may one day match that view.

At York Street, our lakeside concrete canyon starts to lighten up with the Queen's Quay Terminal, a giant old warehouse with a glass condo sprouting out of the top. In 1982, Zeidler Partnership Architects turned the 1927 Terminal Warehouse – the first poured-concrete building in Canada, and known as a 'fisherman's dream' for all the products it housed – into offices and luxury condos that eventually became the home of former Ontario Premier Mike Harris, Mr. Anti-Toronto himself.

It couldn't have been his pad that caused his hostility to our city; it's a brilliant building. Take the southeast corner, hollowed out four floors high, as if Lake Ontario storms had worn it down to its skeleton over time. The main floor was supposed to be high-end retail, a sort of Hazelton Lanes on the lake, but the rich, like a lot of Torontonians, thought the Gardiner was more of a barrier than it really is, and didn't come. Tourist-trade retail moved in, like the iconic Tilly Endurables and their 'guaranteed for life' slogan. (Unfortunate, really: clothing that's designed to make people look frumpy should at the very least disintegrate as quickly as possible.)

The most promising development in the area has been the addition of a Sobeys in the Queen's Quay Terminal. People who don't live near a major grocery store often say it's their neighbourhood's missing ingredient, and Sobeys has been very good at inserting small, urban-sized stores into neighbourhoods around Toronto. The terminal building is part of the twelve acres overseen by Harbourfront, a federal crown corporation – and now a charitable organization – established in 1972 to revitalize Toronto's waterfront. Though it runs the risk of becoming a tourist trap – it's one of those places where Freedom-55ers, sometimes with grandkids in tow, come in from elsewhere to see 'the city' – it's a good place and it works. On warm nights, it's teeming with people from downtown, uptown and beyond, and there's opportunity for nice cultural collisions when an indie band is playing on the open-air stage and folks who might not normally listen to this music, let alone attend a show, get to participate. This is how cities should work.

On one summer trip here, I came across a group of Bible-camp teens in the little pocket of grassy knolls by the Power Plant gallery. They were sitting in a circle, asking each other, 'What would Jesus do?' while, a few trees over, a guy in acid-washed jeans dry humped his date behind a shrub. For a more subtle display, look at the tiny cubes of light scattered in the pathways that change colour over time. It's little details and moments like this, the things you don't see at first but might discover on your seventh visit, that make this place special – like the gardens that were planted in 1996 along the western wall of the Power Plant by Gene Threndyle, a demolition worker and, apparently, an artsy gardener too. Included among the flora are chunks of a Shaw Street sidewalk, which make the connection between the waterfront and the city it's attached to. It all mixes just fine in the shadow of the Power Plant, our miniature version of London's Tate Modern, which is housed in another (much larger) former power plant on the banks of the Thames.

The metal-and-wood pedestrian footbridge that crosses the marina to the west of the Harbourfront stage area was my preferred route around the area until Waterfront Toronto opened the third of their innovative wave decks at Simcoe Quay in 2009. The undulating wooden sidewalks are dream-like, as if what we know about urbanity has suddenly become an absurd cartoon. In officious Toronto, the wave decks are an audacious addition to the streetscape and, perhaps predictably, within months of opening were already the subject of one lawsuit from a man who hurt himself while trying to walk them and wanted to blame somebody for his fall.

The bustle of Harbourfront quiets down beyond the Radisson Hotel, a rather regrettable mirror of a building on an otherwise decent stretch of waterfront made even better with the recent addition of $H_T O$ Park just to the west. Designed in part by Toronto landscape-architecture firm Janet Rosenberg + Associates, the $7.5-million park stretches over four hectares and includes rolling, grassy mounds of earth, trees, Muskoka chairs, sand and a terraced cement beach, all reminiscent of the Paris Plage, where the banks of the grey Seine are turned into a sandy beach each summer. It's the kind of natural-but-not landscape that we expect from great cities, where humans invent environments that put them in touch with the natural world – Lake Ontario in this case – but without the terror of actual wilderness. Though many beaches in Toronto are perfectly fine for swimming, signs here prohibit such activity, and this is the only ingredient missing in a place that attempts, more so than any other place along this part of the waterfront, to get us as close to the lake as possible.

Just as good as $H_T O$ Park is the naturalized area at the foot of Spadina, beyond the Spadina Wave Deck, where plaques describe the flora and fauna as well as how the shoreline has shifted and expanded over the decades. Even more fun are the secret paths

Muskoka chairs and sand at HTO park. (No swimming, please.)

through reeds where your feet squish in the muck, and where you can stand in the place where the lake and land mix together in soft and dirty ways. An acquaintance of mine said he and his partner came down here the night of Sept. 11, 2001, sat on the rocks and smoked pot, thinking it was a good way to hide from that bad day, to let nature somehow make up for the things people do to each other. Nearby, during summer months, tall(ish) ships rock in the swell.

These wetlands lead to the high and dry Toronto Music Garden, inspired by Bach's *Suites for Unaccompanied Cello*. In the mid-'90s, landscape designer Julie Moir Messervy worked with omnipresent cellist Yo-Yo Ma to interpret the piece in flora based on its six dance movements – Bach's 'Prelude' became 'an undulating river-scape with curves and bends' while his 'Sarabande' became 'a conifer grove in the shape of an arc.' However, on an overcast day, I found Prince's 'Purple Rain' worked well with the space, too, which means they did a good job on the park. The garden's trails weave in and out like a song, and there are secret spots and spiral paths between bushes that lead up to an iron maypole. There is even an underutilized amphitheatre on a grassy slope, waiting for some-

Bach interpreted: bring your iPod to the Music Garden.

body to stage a Fringe Festival play or perhaps some other kind of gentle guerrilla theatre. Across the way, Arthur Erickson's King's Landing condo looks, with its terraced floors, like a white cruise ship ready to set sail into Lake Ontario. It, like many of the condo buildings past Spadina, are not the buildings people talk about when they scrunch up their noses at waterfront residences.

The stretch ends with a nice mix of condos and co-ops, complete with a community school where you'll find the most urban-looking basketball courts – in the *Sesame Street* sense – in the city. It's a real waterfront neighbourhood that's socially and economically diverse. The Toronto Island airport proponents who often claim this is just the wealthy elite complaining about the airport's existence have probably only ever seen the neighbourhood from the air. It's not exclusive, and though that rhetoric flares up from time to time, just crank the Bach and Prince and go for a waterfront walk and you won't hear anything about that.

The CN Tower

  neighbourhood jaunt

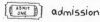 dress to impress

admission

Connecting walks: Nathan Phillips Square/PATH, Spadina.

Every time I walk south on Ossington Avenue, a block north of Bloor, I register the CN Tower in my peripheral vision, but when I turn to look at it, I'm surprised each time because what I'm seeing isn't the tower, but rather the dome of the Ukrainian Catholic Church of the Holy Protection on Leeds Street. Houses along this part of Ossington block the view of the actual tower, but it's the landmark that calibrates my mental map of Toronto, so my brain replaces what's actually there with the CN Tower. Wherever we are in Toronto, we can either see or sort of feel the tower's position and proximity to us. It's the compass that lets us know where we are.

The CN Tower has so penetrated our civic consciousness that it hardly matters that after over three decades as the world's tallest freestanding structure, it was surpassed in 2009 by the Burj Khalifa (Dubai Tower) in the United Arab Emirates. When our tower was built, its world's-best status was a matter of civic and national pride, transcending regionalism the way Expo 67 and Wayne Gretzky and the rest of the 1980s Edmonton Oilers did. The CN Tower gave all Canadians bragging rights.

Planning for the tower began in 1971 when CN and FM radio signals that originated downtown began to be blocked by Toronto's growing skyline. The Sky Pod and Space Deck were added during the planning process, as builders realized they had a tourist attraction on their hands, 'a goldmine in the sky selling rides to the top at $2 to $3 each,' according to a 1975 *Toronto Star* article. A few extra feet were added when builders realized it could beat Moscow's Ostankino Tower. When it finally opened in 1976, the *Toronto Star* reported that people in cottage country had discovered new programs on radio and TV, prompting the mayor of Bracebridge to ask, 'You can't get us some American channels, can you?'

Airborne concrete: the CN Tower's space-age pod under construction in 1974.

Strangely, though it stayed on top of the world for all those years, that record alone was never enough. The CN Tower always tried to outdo itself, as if our confidence as a world city (municipally) or as a middle power (nationally) was so deeply insecure it required constant maintenance.

In the late 1970s, Jimmy Conklin, the 'Carny King' who ran games and rides at the CNE, set up Undercurrent, installing $750,000 worth of arcade amusements in the basement of the tower, hosted by costumed attendants Glitch and Short Circuit, creating an 'unsleazy' arcade that newspaper reports said 'appealed to the whole family.' In the 1980s, Citytv's Moses Znaimer produced the Tour of the Universe space simulation ride that he hoped to turn into a North American franchise. In recent years, a glass floor was added to the pod, its strength measured by the weight of hippos (fourteen of them), followed by a long overdue LED lighting scheme in 2007. It's as if the comparative height never really mattered at all, so why would it matter now that we were no longer on top?

Though it's a local icon that we share with the rest of the country, the CN Tower is unmistakably Toronto, and it will continue to mean a great deal to this city. Returning to Toronto, even by plane, I experience that special moment as it finally comes into a view, when the relieved feeling of being home sets in: I'm safe again

The CN Tower takes another hit for Toronto.

and that which lies beyond our city's walls has not managed to destroy me.

We've all got our favourite view of our tower. It's said that tower architect John Andrews' favourite place to view it is from the northeast corner of Bay and King, where it's framed perfectly by the austere black towers of the TD Centre. From there, the Space Pod seems as oversized as the moon does in the posters for the movie *E.T.*, but the tower itself seems almost short and stubby. From the west, around Liberty Village or Fort York, it's suddenly standing alone, far from the downtown cluster, its spectacular size even bigger than you might remember.

Though it looks different depending on the perspective, the tower dominates the skyline from anywhere in the city. When it opened in 1976, the late alderman, journalist and architect Colin Vaughan wrote that 'some people [complain] that you can't go anywhere in Toronto without having the CN Tower come along too. Turn a corner on a street, look out a window and the tower seems to be there, always present whether you like it or not.' But after nearly two generations of it hanging around every day, losing it would feel like having a civic limb removed.

Imagine a Toronto without the CN Tower. Darren O'Donnell did in his 2004 novel *Your Secrets Sleep with Me*, in which he wrote of a tornado toppling it into Lake Ontario, forever placing his book into the local dystopia section at the Toronto Public Library. We would be as lost and just as freaked out without our concrete compass as New Yorkers were when the World Trade Center catastrophically disappeared from their lives, leaving that city's citizens guessing at where the tip of Manhattan was and, consequently, where they were, both physically and existentially.

Amy Lavender Harris, a York University professor whose 'Imagining Toronto' project comprises the most complete collection of Toronto-based literature in the city, outlined literary representations of the tower in Coach House Books' second uTOpia anthology, *The State of the Arts: Living with Culture in Toronto*. In it, she finds the tower irreplaceable: 'Without the CN Tower we would lose our bearings,' she wrote. 'And its coordinates are useful for far more than guiding us when we stumble out of an unfamiliar subway station. It also reminds us of our identity: a city striving for recognition on the world stage. Its architectural clumsiness mirrors our own.'

Opinions on the tower have always varied wildly. There are those, like Harris, who love it but find it kind of awkward, and those who take cheap shots at it by dragging out the tired old 'phallus in the sky' criticism,which says more about what's on their minds than about what the tower does for us. I've always thought it was the sleekest thing around, like the skinny architectural version of an Airstream trailer: that long, perfect curve to the ground, the Space Pod looking like a glass-and-steel pill I wish I could ingest. The CN Tower is weird-looking, which is why we haven't been able to stop looking at it all these years. It's like those supermodels who are so beautiful they're kind of ugly. We can't take our eyes off any of them.

Being on top didn't cure our insecurity, and though it gave us the chance to boast a little when visitors from abroad were around, it hardly matters that the CN Tower is no longer the tallest freestanding structure in the world. Its usefulness to us has gone well beyond a world record, so Dubai can have that record. From the looks of it, they're even more insecure than Toronto is.

Nathan Phillips Square and the PATH System

neighbourhood jaunt

dress to impress

scenic views

Connecting walks: Yonge, Harbourfront, CN Tower, University, Dundas, Downtown East Side.

One night in the mid-2000s, a small group of people active in City circles – architects, writers, councillors, urban planners and even an activist or two – gathered in a room at Grano restaurant on Yonge Street, a few blocks north of Davisville. Roberto Martella, Grano's owner, has turned his restaurant into a kind of civic salon, hosting talks and dinners about what it means to be a city. On this deep January night, Projects for Public Spaces (PPS), a non-profit organization from New York 'dedicated to creating and sustaining public places that build communities' talked about their efforts to make Mississauga's public places walkable, people-friendly and inviting. They also said something that caused an audible gasp in the room: 'Nathan Phillips Square, on a scale of one to a hundred, ranks zero.'

They might have been playing the role of American dilettantes, trying to shock us out of our provincial complacency, but that gasp turned into a collective hiss because, as everybody in Toronto knows, the square works. The folks from PPS were suffering from a condition we can call modern-hate, an orthodoxy that says that any big concrete space is automatically a wasteland. That's not the case in Toronto. Nathan Phillips Square is a sacred civic space, perhaps the finest concrete manifestation of peace, order and good government in Canada. During the day, it's enjoyed by seemingly everybody: scores of office people, wayward hippie girls with backpacks twice as big as they are, lobbyists on cellphones, some homeless folks on the periphery and a constant stream of people crossing the square on their way to City Hall. Crossing the square is a ceremonial march: you're forced to regard City Hall from afar and approach it on foot – it's huge, but you can walk right in. When Old City Hall opened in 1899, then mayor John Shaw said, 'Great buildings symbolize a people's deeds and aspirations.' He could have easily been speaking at the opening sixty-six years later of New City Hall , a place that has become Toronto's agora.

Maximum Canadiana on the Nathan Phillips Square rink.

In ancient Greek city-states, the agora, or 'place of assembly,' was the centre of civic and democratic life, the place where citizens would gather to discuss politics or listen to public speeches, and to run into other citizens. Sometimes the square would also host a market, but generally, it was just a large outdoor space surrounded by public buildings. The agora in Athens included fountains, trees and temples for various gods like Hephaestus, Zeus and Apollo. The agora provided space for citizens to meet and and a home for institutions that represented the Athenian state – all the elements of a formal public space that became a civic living room.

There are earnest expressions of what it means to be a Torontonian all over Nathan Phillips Square, like at the Speakers' Corner podium – so wonderfully, frustratingly, officiously Torontonian that it includes a warning that, while dedicated to the concept of free speech, 'speakers are reminded that the Criminal Code prohibits slanderous statements or statements promoting genocide or hatred against an identifiable group or race.' The middle 'freedom arch' that stretches over the pond at the south side of the square houses a chunk of the Berlin Wall, which I dare anybody to resist touching.

Nathan Phillips Square is located in what was once a dense slum known as the Ward. This was where Toronto's original downtown Chinatown began, before it was aimed north towards Dundas.

In the late 1950s, when the area was cleared for the new City Hall project, there was no large open downtown space in Toronto. As a result of the project, the city got a clean and modernist expanse of concrete, the preface to the two crescent-shaped buildings that surround the spaceship-like Council Chamber.

The small collection of Chinese shops and restaurants on Dundas Street between Bay and University is all that remains of Toronto's first Chinatown. It migrated west along Dundas when the Ward was cleared out, eventually establishing a new community at Spadina Avenue. Two plaques in the northwest corner of Nathan Phillips Square – part of Heritage Toronto's 'Plaques and Markers' program – commemorate one of this city's earliest ethnic areas, lost to the march of progress.

In the Peace Garden on the east side of the Square, a very Torontonian plaque reads 'CAUTION: ETERNAL AME.' It should read 'CAUTION: PEACE GARDEN' – the well-intentioned gesture is a design mistake that was added to the square in 1984, and that messes up Finnish architect Viljo Revell's original clean design. Among the lesser consequences of the escalation of the Cold War in the 1980s was the desperate need for peace gardens. But good

sod   flame   christen

intentions can run amok, even when you get Pierre Trudeau to turn the sod, the Pope to light the flame with an ember from Hiroshima and the Queen to christen the whole thing. This story was certainly a cautionary tale for those involved in the 2007 design competition to 'revitalize' the square.

Broaching the plan to revitalize the square with green roofs and improved facilities was a delicate endeavour: how do you fix up a sacred space? The Projects for Public Space people encourage programmed human activity in public spaces, and see a modernist expanse like Nathan Phillips Square as empty and maybe even totalitarian. But we don't always need designed distractions when in public. What's most noticeable about Nathan Phillips Square is the lack of physical 'stuff.' Apart from the Peace Garden, the skating rink with its three Freedom Arches, the statue of Sir Winston Churchill and the Henry Moore sculpture in front of the City Hall doors, the square is respectful of the robust democracy it represents (that 'peace, order and good government' thing). It allows for large groups of people to gather without barrier, even if they're angry with the government of the day. It respects the right and need of citizens to gather. Where else would you want to welcome a Canadian hero like Terry Fox as he triumphantly runs into the city, as he did during his Marathon of Hope in 1980? Thousands cheered as he was given the key to the city in the place that best represents the city.

The flyer distributed to invited guests to the opening-day celebrations in 1965 included the statement of guidance that accompanied the launch of the worldwide design competition for New City Hall initiated in 1957. The statement asked architects to 'find a building that will proudly express its function as the centre of civic government.' Revell, whose design ultimately won the competition over the 520 other designs submitted, called the square and City Hall 'the eye of government' (the 'spaceship' has been called the eyeball and the two towers the eyelids). In that respect, the square is the place where Torontonians can either step back and observe the centre of civic power, or walk right up to the front door unencumbered and continue inside. Critics of the square, and of modernism in general, say the square is sterile. But the fact that there's nothing physically in the way of people looking at or accessing City Hall says a remarkable amount about the faith the design has in the intelligence of the average citizen and government's non-cynical relationship with the people it represents.

The square and City Hall instantly came to represent Toronto's bright future, and signalled the beginning of its shift from Canada's second city to its cultural and business capital. Though the CN Tower provides some stiff competition, Nathan Phillips Square is the iconic image of Toronto, a symbol it was meant to become from the beginning. (A stylized outline of the two buildings, which meet to form a 'T', can be seen on Toronto's flag.)

That opening-day flyer also included a quote from architecture critic Sigfried Giedion: 'It is the first civic centre of this century worthy of the name.' It's a sentiment that survives today: even the language from the design competition to fix and update the square described a revitalization of 'the city's greatest public space' rather than a complete redesign. The winning design by Plant Architect and Shore Tilbe Irwin and Partners added a forested perimeter, a cleaned-up and reorganized peace garden and, in the architect's words, made an 'explict attempt to bring out the square's role as an agora but also as a civic theatre of focused gathering.'

Take a moment to compare the mid-century era of civic-square building to one a few decades later. The Peace Garden in Nathan Phillips Square has much in common with Mel Lastman Square, located in front of what was North York City Hall prior to amalgamation. Completed in 1987, nearly ten years after North York's City Hall opened (unlike Nathan Phillips Square, it wasn't one cohesive design, but rather two separate initiatives), it was named after the very much alive and in-office mayor of North York, Mel Lastman. Stand on Yonge Street and look west into the square and your path to the front doors of North York's former City Hall (now the North York Civic Centre) is blocked by a number of obstacles. There's a 700-seat amphitheatre, a stream that flows over a waterfall, a wedding chapel and, like Nathan Phillips Square, a reflecting pool that doubles as a skating rink in the winter months. The

Mel Lastman Square and the former North York City Hall.

square is also multi-level, with staircases leading up and down to areas of different height, a jagged foothill-like topography laid out before the sharp and severe slant of the mountain range that is the civic building. The actual entrance to the building is obscured in a sunken area well below street level. Wherever your eye lands, there's something new to look at. It's the architectural equivalent of MTV-style television editing: no long takes, designed for short attention spans.

Back downtown, the Sheraton Centre Hotel, located across from City Hall, is for many people everything that's both right and wrong with modernism. The reason it draws so much civic ire is its unforgivable treatment of Queen Street: solid, impenetrable cliffs of concrete and parking lot entrances render the sidewalk in front of it unpleasant and desolate. This trend is continued around the new Four Seasons Centre for the Performing Arts a block west, a sharp contrast to the open spaces found on the north side of Queen. Yet, from the east and west, the Sheraton's forty-three floors look impossibly razor-thin, and from Nathan Phillips Square at night, the building is a shimmering wall of light. At any given time during the day, you can see somebody peering out of its wide facade, giving Nathan Phillips Square a gazed-at sense that makes every movement made there seem more important. The Sheraton Centre's finest details are the interior terraced gardens and water-falls that run nearly the length of the hotel. If you hate this build-ing, take a peek inside and let it give you something to love.

Like City Hall, the bowels of the Sheraton are connected to Toronto's PATH system, the twenty-seven-kilometre-long network of underground passages and tunnels that connects over fifty downtown buildings. You can start exploring the PATH here in the heart of the city or from any of the connected buildings in the financial district. The PATH has no beginning or end, but for a good suggested starting point, walk north on Bay Street from City Hall to the Greyhound bus terminal just north of Dundas. Along the way, you'll find Larry Sefton Park tucked directly behind City Hall. It's a cute and brutalist pocket park that was commissioned by the United Steel Workers of America in 1977 in memory of Sefton, a long-time union leader. Some of the benches and the built-in fountain are broken, and the indestructible steel I-beams bursting dramatically out of the concrete make this quiet place seem like Superman's Fortress of Solitude.

In the fine old bus terminal building, an underwhelming (compared with the older parts of the building) staircase leads down to the entrance to the car-free boulevards of the PATH. A short passage underneath Bay Street leads into the mall-like space of the Atrium on Bay building; the entire system generally alternates between these two typologies. Over 100,000 commuters pass through here each day. Those with a good sense of direction can meander from the bus depot down to the Convention Centre at Front and John and back up to the Sheraton and City Hall without ever stepping outside, though it's a challenge to navigate as familiar landmarks disappear and one's sense of direction, even if excellent, becomes easily flipped around.

The PATH is Toronto's version of Paris's arcades, 'a world in miniature' where philosopher Walter Benjamin wandered in the 1920s when trying to understand that city. At first glance, the PATH is a fairly generic shopping mall, but the impressive sum of its parts and the people who populate it make it remarkable. As you walk through it, the stores start to repeat like the background in a cartoon chase scene. It's architectural déjà vu, a dream world where the parts are the same, just arranged differently.

In the 1990s, the City of Toronto installed a wayfinding system to aid movement between sections, but it's intentionally subtle: each section of the PATH is privately owned, and like window-and-clock-free casinos, they don't want to provide you and your money with an easy escape. The Toronto-Dominion Centre was long an exception to the generic look of much of the PATH. Architect Mies van der Rohe laid out a mausoleum of a mall down there, a place of order, clean lines and polished travertine marble. Even the store signs were uniform: white letters on a black background using a font Mies designed specifically for the TD Centre.

Sadly, the building's owners, Cadillac Fairview, have since allowed each tenant to install their own vernacular signage, but some retain the elegant font created by van der Rohe, perhaps unwittingly preserving something unique to Toronto. Behind one of the walls along the corridor that leads to the TD Centre's food court (for an adventure, try a different food court each day), there's a van der Rohe cinema that has been closed for years (waiting, we hope, for Cadillac Fairview to come to their senses and reopen one of the most unique cinemas in the world). However, Cadillac Fairview is owned by the Ontario Teachers' Pension Plan, the nearly faceless behemoth fund that also owns the Toronto Maple Leafs, a fact that draws the ire of area hockey fans who rail against an organization that doesn't seem to care about whether the team wins so long as bums still keep landing in seats. Perhaps here, in the tunnels below the city, is where despondent Leafs fans and supporters of modernism can find common ground – or, at least, a common nemesis.

From here, angry Leafs fans can zig and zag south to the basement of the Royal York Hotel on Front Street, where the oldest passageway on the PATH system connects that hotel to Union Station. At rush hour, the flow of commuters here is an unstoppable force – just try to swim upstream – as people make their way to the GO trains and all points 905. When it's hockey night in Canada, the wide passage beyond the trains leads thousands of fans into the Air Canada Centre, located in what used to be the Canada Post delivery building, and past the spectacle of sports paraphernalia and virtual games that soak up whatever remaining money fans may have after breaking the bank on excessively expensive tickets. The art deco walls left over from the building's first incarnation are an example of successful façadism,

Wayfinding isn't so easy in the PATH system.

having been integrated into what is now the second busiest arena in North America, behind Madison Square Garden. While you're there, be sure to check out Micah Lexier's sculpture *Wins, Losses and Ties* just outside the east entrance, which chronicles the Leafs' history. For now, the exits out of the acc are the path's most southern ends, but as new buildings go up its reach is slowly being extended.

In *Emerald City*, John Bentley Mays' collection of essays on Toronto, the architecture critic writes of his concern that our submerged mall will have us forget that the word 'underground' once had sinister connotations: 'Moving through those immaculate and almost shadowless corridors, one finds none of those characters typically associated with the undergrounds in legend and story – sexual desperados, outlaws, mad hermits, wild boys who rule whole terrifying tracks of the dark world.' Though the PATH cowboys and girls with BlackBerrys strapped to their hips like six-shooters may be the terror of the mutual-fund crowd, both groups appear benign in the late afternoon, the latter tired, with shirttails and suit jackets wrinkled from sitting at desks all day. The Toronto underground, it would seem, is rather well-heeled and sometimes even impeccably tailored, and escapes as soon as the five o'clock whistle blows. Do visit during the day, at high noon, to see the human show, but go after dark as well, when the halls are empty and the shops and fast-food outlets have rolled down their gates and closed their doors. The piped-in muzak echoes more and competes with the hum of the cleaning machines that polish the marble floors. It's then that the PATH still holds mystery and suspicion – when any of those furtive characters in the next corridor or rounding a corner could be the desperado you were looking for.

University Avenue

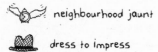 neighbourhood jaunt

dress to impress

offspring friendly

Connecting walks: Harbourfront, Nathan Phillips Square/PATH, Yorkville, Dundas.

University Avenue is Toronto's grandest street, but it's not made for walking – the scale is too big, designed more for Santa Claus parades and triumphant runs into the city by Terry Fox than for intimate strolling. Cities need big roads like this, though, and sometimes it feels good to be dominated by buildings and traffic. Imagine Paris without Haussmann's wide boulevards cutting through the tight and dense arrondissements like air ducts, letting people breathe and affording some longer vistas. Some argue the boulevards are more for cars than for people, but Haussmann designed before the car, and if cars one day disappear, we'll still require a road like University to be a kind of parade ground and linear public space.

University runs from Front Street up to College Street, where it becomes Queen's Park Crescent for the stretch around and above the provincial legislature building to Bloor before continuing north as Avenue Road. All things to all people. The character and proportion of the street are different on either side of Bloor: the street is largely residential to the north, but bears an institutional, corporate and governmental identity south of Bloor. The Royal Ontario Museum (ROM) and the Club Monaco flagship store on the east side of Bloor start the march south. The former Lillian Massey Department of Household Science, the building Club Monaco now shares with the Ontario Ombudsman, once served University of Toronto as the female equivalent of the all-male Hart House a kilometre south, complete with a gymnasium and swimming pool that are now hidden under a false floor.

The ROM's crystal addition is subtle when viewed from Avenue Road. It pokes over the top of the roof and juts off the north side but leaves the classical east side of the building intact (though still not enough to please architecture purists, who objected to the old being updated with the new). On the south end

of the ROM sits the round hump of the
former McLaughlin Planetarium, which
crouches like a neglected child. Beloved by
some and met with indifference by others
(it's described as a 'slightly phony temple' to
the stars by a character in Alice Munro's short
story 'The Moons of Jupiter'), the building
was sold to U of T in 2009 and will be torn
down to make way for a planned renovation
and expansion of their faculty of law.

Wedged in between the old Lillian Massey
building and the university's Emmanuel and
Victoria College buildings of similar age and
pedigree stands the very contemporary
Gardiner Museum of Ceramic Art, which
underwent a major expansion in 2006 by
Toronto's KPMB architecture firm. Its
concrete and glass boxes seem to float – as all
good concrete should – in orbit of each other.
It is yet another example of how very contemporary buildings can exist among their older
ancestors, a family that doesn't banish the
children when the grandparents are around.

To the south, at Queen's Park, Avenue
splits, becoming Queen's Park Crescent East
and West, and circles the provincial legislature and its very large backyard, one of
Toronto's more formal parks, which is home
to statues of King Edward VII, Lt.-Gov. John
Graves Simcoe and, most recently, a statue of
Al Purdy, Canada's unofficial poet laureate, in
repose. Purdy lived and worked in Ontario
(and British Columbia) until his death in
2000, and though this statue is an appropriate tribute to him personally, it's also important because Toronto is only starting to
celebrate its locals in such a way. Like
any good colonial city, many of our (few)
statues depict kings, queens and other British

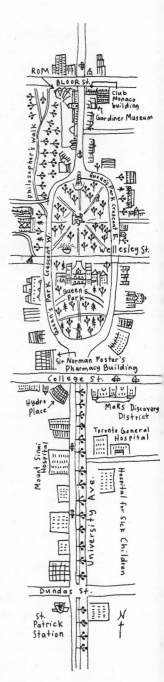

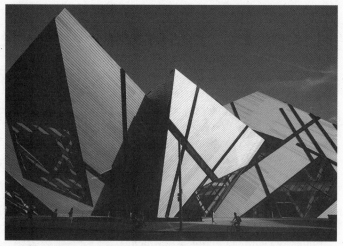

The ROM crystal rises out of the Bloor sidewalk.

military officials, rather than people who lived and worked here. More commemorations of the latter would help us think of Toronto as a place with its own history, rather than as a provincial outpost (a historical reality we're at no risk of forgetting).

The legislature itself is as big and imposing as any seat of government should (or shouldn't) be; it feels almost like an embassy for the rest of the province, where the soil is not truly Torontonian. It reminds us of the dual role that Toronto and capitals around the world play when their city represents more than just the local civic ontology. It's here that many protests against not only provincial policies but federal and even international struggles take place. During Premier Mike Harris's reign in the 1990s, this lawn was often a battleground between the not-very-Progressive Conservative government and a long list of other groups.

In 2000, after I'd arrived in Toronto thinking my future was in the provincial bureaucracy, I made weekly pilgrimages to the government human resources office on Queen's Park Crescent. One June visit happened to coincide with the Ontario Coalition Against Poverty's march and demonstration, which resulted in a pitched, hour-long battle between people and police. It was as if the air and rules changed in Toronto that afternoon. I remember only a few vivid scenes of it now: a mom with a stroller running into bushes to avoid police horses; an old man stumbling into traffic, bleeding from the head, banging on the windows of a passing minivan and asking for help; a brick flying over my head and smashing into an OPP officer's helmet, tipping him over so he hit the ground like a tin soldier. For a long time afterwards, I avoided the area, as the ground seemed to give off such a bad feeling. Scorched psychological earth in the middle of Toronto.

Follow Queen's Park Crescent East to the northeast corner of College Street and you'll find the Pharmacy Building, which British architect Sir Norman Foster designed for U of T. Foster's classroom-sized balls dangle inside the building's massive glass atrium, waiting to be filled with undergrads. These massive orbs are suspended by steel arms and contain intimate lecture theatres and open air study lounges on top. From the outside they look like white eggs stuffed into the building; they're the suspended complement to the Ontario College of Art and Design's box-in-the-sky buiding a few blocks away on McCaul. (Both the OCAD box and the Pharmacy Building's balls get the neon colour treatment at night.) Foster's indoor and outdoor concrete pillars look bare at first, but they match those across that support Hydro Place across the street. Opened in 1975, Hydro Place was heralded for being energy efficient, and for its multi-layered, two-acre plaza. 'It won't be the usual windswept plaza, but a place where you can sit down, relax and read your newspaper,' said landscape designer Keith Spratley in 1973 of the now-windswept plaza. I have a soft spot for this beast, though, because of those days when it reflects the clouds and sky perfectly, how its curves match those of Queen's Park and

One of the Pharmacy Building's big hanging balls.

The glass waterfall of the newly constructed Hydro Building in 1976.

the government building that sits kitty-corner to it and how at night the fluorescent lights on each floor are aligned in a radial starburst.

I once went into the lobby of the building, resumé in hand, and asked for human resources – always a good excuse to explore a building. I was told to leave it at the front desk and that somebody would contact me. They haven't called me yet. It's just as well: you can't see the glass waterfall from the inside from the building itself.

The old 1935 art-deco Hydro Building just to the south may just be the nicest building in Toronto. It's part of Princess Margaret Hospital now, but notice the waterfalls carved in stone out front, a reminder that Ontario's power was once supplied exclusively by Niagara Falls. For those lucky enough not to have a specific reason to visit Princess Margaret, it's worth going in through the front doors and finding the huge postmodern atrium in the rear addition to the hospital, a heavy and dark building that hangs over Murray Street (a variance bylaw was made for this specific addition so the Hydro building could be preserved) and which, unless viewed from the west, seems to disappear among the other University Avenue hospital buildings. With its the mountains of hospitals – Toronto General, SickKids, Princess Margaret, Mount Sinai and Toronto Rehab – University Avenue is

a virtual canyon of sickness, recovery and death, where the happi-
est and saddest dramas play out daily above the sidewalks.

The MaRS Discovery District, which spans College Street
between Elizabeth Street and University, is one of those places
in which the employees likely have a hard time explaining to their
parents exactly what they do. The acronym MaRS is derived from
the term 'Medical and Related Sciences,' which means to connect
science and technology to business. However, most of us civilians
think of it as the restoration of the former Toronto General Hospital, the site of Banting and Best's insulin discovery in 1922. The
most dramatic changes in the building are inside, where a vast
public atrium, complete with an underground passage to the present-day hospital, marks the transition between new and old.

Oddly, the best walk on University is down the green space in
the centre of the boulevard – it's Toronto's narrowest park, and it
affords the best views of our attempts at civic grandeur. I walked
the length of it once, passing hidden homeless shelters, subway
exhaust tunnels and close-up views of various memorials, including the ones at Queen Street for Sir Adam Beck, founder of the
Hydro-Electric Power Commission of Ontario (more waterfall
imagery and nods for electrifying Ontario), and for the Boer Wars
(the size of the statue suggests we won).

University Avenue was created in the 1820s, and was a private
road for over fifty years, with wooden gates, a gatehouse and gate-
keeper at Queen Street to prevent public carriages from entering
and (they were torn down in 1882). Horse chestnut trees were
specially imported to line the street, and a boulevard of grass was
laid in the middle of the street to provide promenades for the
general public when the gates were open. The image it conjures
is a royal one, of the Long Walk that marks the approach to Windsor Castle in England. When Charles Dickens visited North America in the 1840s, before the legislature was built, the plans for it
and University Avenue were one of the few Toronto sights he
mentioned in his *American Notes*: 'It will be a handsome, spacious
edifice, approached by a long avenue which is already planted and
made available as a public walk.' Though the avenue has fallen on
hard(er) times in the modern era, recent efforts to beautify the
boulevard have resulted in a long line of jungle-like greenery in
the summer.

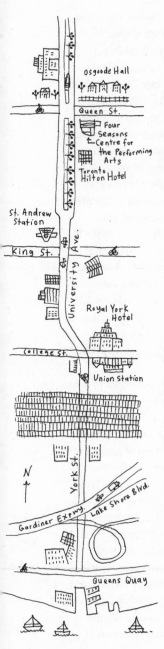

Osgoode Hall sits on the northeast corner of University and Queen, behind the heavy iron fence and odd gates said to have been designed to keep stray cows out. It's an interesting island in a district marked by much more modern buildings, and the most Dickensian (in the most positive way the term can be interpreted) bit of real estate along University. For many, Osgoode is one of Toronto's architectural gems, but I've never been particularly interested in it. It seems so overtly non-Torontonian and colonial. That is, it's of a style and grandeur that makes it seem like it was plucked from someplace else and set down here. Certainly, much of Toronto is made up of non-indigenous style mashups, so perhaps it's just the fence that makes the place seem like a museum piece or movie set (which it often is). Behind Osgoode Hall sits a more modern Ontario court building, which seems more in line with the spirit of Toronto. I recognize that my opinion is unpopular, especially considering the magnificent armoury building that was demolished in the 1960s to make way for the newer court building, but the near-abstract wing that hangs over what could be a pleasant public space – if it were cared for properly – has utopic ambitions that are hard to ignore.

University peters out at Adelaide, where it's just a foot wide. If you've walked down this garden middle, you're left exposed in the middle of traffic, protected only by an aluminum 'veer right' sign. A distracted driver gently hit me while I was riding my bike here the day in 2002 that the Pope's motorcade passed through the area. That's often the price we pay when the spectacle is bigger than the activity (at least when the Pope is in town).

Further south, through a canyon of mirrored glass, University ends after a short jog east at Union Station and the Royal York Hotel. Here, it joins York Street for the short hike under the railway tracks to the cluster of glass-point towers in and around Maple Leaf Square. Located in front of the Air Canada Centre, the square is one of Toronto's newest public spaces, and can accommodate up to five thousand people. It's easy to imagine people gathering here after a big Leafs win. Unfortunately, it's much harder to imagine the team actually winning, so for now the square is a repository for our sports dynasty dreams and a place for scalpers to sell tickets. A little further on, York slips under the Gardiner Expressway and ends at Lake Ontario, perhaps a big enough distraction to keep Torontonian minds off their team's epic losing streak.

Yorkville

 neighbourhood jaunt

dress to impress

offspring friendly

Connecting walks: Yonge, University, Dupont.

When the subway pulls into Bay station, the fine print underneath the word 'Bay' says 'Yorkville,' a reminder that Yorkville is an important enough location to warrant mention, an honour the TTC hasn't given to any other Toronto neighbourhood. Yorkville is a mythic place for Torontonians. It's where things happened, where Canadian cultural history was made in the 1960s – the place the baby-boomer nostalgia machine can't stop talking about. Today, things still happen in Yorkville, and while they're written up and celebrated as much as before – if not more – they get a fleeting kind of interest because they're mostly fashion-related, and fashion is fast and always about the next hot thing. So Yorkville is forever changing and moving, a stage where people and objects have brief starring roles and are quickly swept aside.

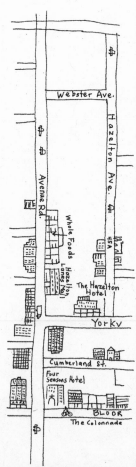

This isn't just another case of gentrification. Lots of communities going through that process in Toronto say they don't want to be another Yorkville, but there's only room for one place like this in the city (and possibly the country). It's a neighbourhood that belongs a little to Toronto, but mostly to everybody else, something all political or cultural capitals have to live with. When the Rolling Stones are in town and staying at the Four Seasons, or during the Toronto International Film Festival, when the neighbourhood's streets are as likely to appear in paparazzi shots as those in New York or Los Angeles, Yorkville no longer belongs to Toronto. Yet even as Yorkville is today about fashion, it still plays a key role in supporting Toronto's myth and ontology, so perhaps there's some style below that fashion, something deeply Torontonian that endures – something a little rebellious. If there is, it's best found on foot, as Yorkville's secrets are often down little passageways, meant to be stumbled upon randomly.

In your search of Yorkville's deepest counterculture roots, head over to Yonge, just south of the Reference Library, where the Red Lion Inn once stood. Though it was a breeding ground for the Upper Canada Rebellion of 1837, there is little indication of the inn or mention of the rebellion now, just a Starbucks on the spot where Albert Britnell's bookstore also used to be, near the inn's original site. Here, in an early example of Toronto standing up for itself, William Lyon Mackenzie, Toronto's first mayor, tried to

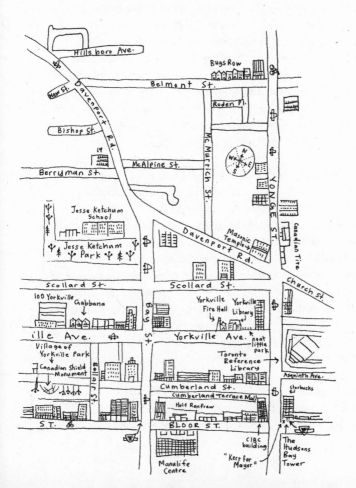

overthrow the Family Compact, Upper Canada's tight-knit ruling class. Toronto ought to send Christmas cards bearing pictures of Mackenzie to Queen's Park and Ottawa to remind them of what we're capable of when we're upset, though today an uprising would be over something like public transit funding rather than undemocratic powers.

Just south of here, at the corner of Yonge and Bloor, hulks the Hudson's Bay Centre, the kind of place that gives concrete a bad name. This complex and the buildings on several blocks west of here are connected by a PATH-like underground mall system. From Yonge/Bloor subway station, the outdoor-phobic can walk west to Bay Station and even south into the Manulife Centre without coming up for air. The first underground stop from Yonge and Bloor is the Cumberland Terrace mall, a vintage curiosity and product of the 1970s inclination to build downtown malls. Cumberland is a clunky, smaller and unsuccessful version of the Eaton Centre, running a full block along Cumberland Street, behind and under the CIBC building and Holt Renfrew. Slated for imminent renovation, complete with new tower, Cumberland, with its collection of closed stores and odd shops, a Druxy's deli and the brown-and-orange tile patterns so many Canadian second-tier malls share – the kind that have not yet become retro-cool – is at odds with the rest of Yorkville.

Back out at Yonge, near the 1837 Rebellion site, you'll find yourself standing on ground that played host to a protest more fitting with contemporary Yorkville values. In 1886, Yorkville's town council voted to move the Yonge and Bloor tollgate to the northern limit of the village because, as was reported in the town records, 'its present position in the heart of this village is an eyesore to the inhabitants and a great injury to them in a pecuniary point of view.' Nearly a century later, residents again resisted new developments when Richard Wookey, deemed a 'folk hero to the chic set' by the *Toronto Star* in 1974, assembled the properties that would become Hazelton Lanes, the mall that currently houses Whole Foods and other higher-end shops. Ursula Foster, who had lived for fifty years in the same Victorian house at 30 Hazelton Avenue, successfully fought to save her sunlight, forcing the Hazelton condos to angle backwards over her house. Her house is still there, though it has been sandblasted and turned into offices, and Hazelton's streetscape is largely intact.

With the addition of Hazelton Lanes and other commercial infill developments, Yorkville began losing the cultural venues that made it Canada's Haight-Ashbury in the 1960s. But Yorkville was a cultural hotspot even when those hippies were still teens. From the mid 1940s to 1963, Clement Hambourg ran Yorkville's House of Hambourg. Billed as 'Three Stories of Jazz,' the fourteen-room house on Cumberland hosted folks like Cannonball Adderley, Miles Davis and Louis Armstrong. In the '60s, as jazz went downtown, the folk and rock scenes took over. Dozens of coffee houses lined Cumberland and Yorkville avenues, among them the Purple Onion, Café Anglais, Penny Farthing, Mynah Bird, El Matador and Sammy's. The Riverboat, at 134 Yorkville, was where people like Gordon Lightfoot, Joni Mitchell, Steppenwolf, Neil Young and Rick James played before they went south. The Riverboat site is now the Hazelton, an upscale hotel and condo. In 1969, a proposed twenty-two-storey apartment hotel was refused on the same lot, deemed at the time to be 'clearly at variance with the spirit' of Yorkville. Fast-forward nearly thirty years and that spirit is just about gone, though physical traces remain here and there.

Older Torontonians remember the parking lot that once ran along Cumberland, in the heart of Yorkville, and which languished for over thirty years (one of many that blighted Yorkville), while even older residents recall the Victorian row houses that were there before. The houses were cleared to make way for the subway in the 1960s and, in 1991, an overdue design competition chose a bid by Oleson Worland Architects that imagined a linear park marking the ghosts of those row houses with distinct environments, including a pine forest, a marsh and an orchard. Though controversial at the time because of the cost of transportation and installation, the giant rock shipped in from the Canadian Shield that sits in the middle of that park has become a favourite meeting spot in Toronto. Next to the rock, the newly renovated entrance to the Bay subway station matches the contemporary look of some of the newer buildings in the area and is a hint of the infrastructure that lies below the park. The University Theatre, which sat between the park and Bloor Street and for many years played host to countless film festival gala screenings, was shuttered in 1986 and eventually replaced by a condo building nearly fifteen years later. The theatre's facade lives on in the Pottery Barn that now faces out onto Bloor.

Across the street from the Pottery Barn, there's the Colonnade. It provides Gucci-encrusted 'Mink Mile' shoppers a small public square in the shape of an elegant half-oval. The building was completed in 1963, and was Toronto's first combined residential, commercial and retail development. After disappearing during a recent renovation, the plaque on the unique zigzag staircase has returned. It proclaims that this one-and-a-half-turn spiral was 'the only one ever built without a central support,' adding that 'the Colonnade is a totally Canadian project' – certainly things to be proud of in the 1960s, when provincial Toronto was emerging from the shadow of the Empire.

Back up in the heart of Yorkville, Gabbana, located at 86 Yorkville Avenue, stocks oversized Dolce & Gabbana belts and other fast fashions. In the '20s and '30s, author Mazo de la Roche lived in the house that became this store, and she wrote the first of her sixteen Jalna novels here. She isn't well known in Canada anymore, but her books have sold at least 9 million copies around the world, making her one of Yorkville's first cultural exports.

Yorkville really began to change by the early '70s, when Wookey and others started building and the hippies got older. Anybody who has endured *The Big Chill* knows how this story plays out: the hippie kids grow up, give up the ponchos and the protests, switch from pot to cocktails and go shopping for Halston sheets. Though the Riverboat lasted until 1978, Yorkville denizens mark the beginning of the end as early as 1968 and 1969, when a hepatitis scare put a chill on all the free love. In 1971, the Four Seasons built their hotel at Avenue and Cumberland, establishing a beachhead for thirty years of condo and office-tower development. By the mid-1980s, Yorkville was primarily a high-end shopping district galvanized, in part, by the Holt Renfrew Centre on Bloor, which opened in 1979. The coffee houses became boutiques, salons and bars whose dress codes were a little more Dallas and a lot less *Easy Rider*.

A few doors down from de la Roche's old place, at 100 Yorkville, what was once Toronto's first Jewish general hospital, Mount Sinai, is now the aptly (if obviously) named 100 Yorkville at Bellair, a condo development that incorporated the hospital's facade into its design and, most importantly, filled in the parking lot that was behind the hotel. Many of these new developments and infill constructions replaced old surface parking lots. If you look at aerial photos of Yorkville at the height of its hippie days in the late '60s, the amount of land given over to parking is staggering. If we could be teleported back to those days, we'd likely be in shock at how open the neighbourhood was, compared how dense it is now.

Around the corner at 45a Hazelton, just up the street from Ursula Foster's former house, there's a forbidding-looking building that bears a sign that reads 'MDC Corporation.' While trying to peek in once, I met an angry security guard who refused to appreciate that the building used to be the Nimbus 9 recording studios. Producer Jack Richardson opened the studios in the late '60s and a who's who of classic rock royalty, including Alice Cooper, the Guess Who, Dr. John, Peter Gabriel, KISS and Bob Seger, made pilgrimages to Nimbus 9 to work with Richardson and his young employee, Bob Ezrin. (Ezrin went on to produce part of Pink Floyd's *The Wall* there, too.)

Further up Hazelton Avenue, hang a right on Berryman Street and walk up to No. 19. In the early '70s, Toronto architect Barton Meyers turned this former warehouse into a house-cum-showcase for his design ideas. (He also did the 1978 addition to the rear of the Yorkville Library, which still exists.) It's one of the few pieces of cool post–Expo 67 mod design in Toronto, and is the residential articulation of the change Yorkville saw in the '70s when the Victorians were either replaced by modern buildings, renovated or incorporated into other buildings. Slip down the alley next to No. 19 and walk around Jesse Ketchum Public School. On the south side of the school, there's a huge playing field that seems too vast for Yorkville and affords a great secret backdoor view of the Bloor skyline. Walk right up to the back windows of Nimbus 9 and you can finally see inside. All traces of its storied past are gone, plastered over, renovated. Like the rest of Yorkville, this building has been given a facelift that makes its history unrecognizable. Yet if you continue to wander north, to Davenport and then over to Belmont and back down to Yonge, you'll find bits of Yorkville's past tucked in between the swaths of its future: an old house, the original fire hall, the roof of a house peeking over a store or even 'Bugs Row,' a strip of townhouses along Belmont just before Yonge that were some of the first in the area to be renovated in the early 1970s – all remnants of somebody's historic Yorkville and pieces of somebody else's current one.

Metro Central YMCA

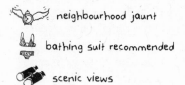

neighbourhood jaunt

bathing suit recommended

scenic views

Connecting walks: Yonge,
Downtown East Side.

On Grosvenor Street, just west of Yonge, there was, for a time, a mural painted on the pavement in front of Toronto Fire Station 314 that read 'Running the Strip since 1871.' I read it every time I walked by on my way to the Metro Central YMCA next door. I love the way it celebrated and mythologized both the fire department and Yonge Street.

The YMCA, another mythologized organization, has been a part of this city since the mid-1800s, and the Metro Central Y is its heart. Here on Grosvenor, 11,000 Torontonians of all shades, shapes and sizes come together to get ripped abs, learn English or get help finding a job. Before I joined, I thought the Y was just a gym. Now I think it's as important an institution as the Red Cross or Station 314. It's a self-contained sub-city.

The Metro Central Y is part of the YMCA of Greater Toronto and, as far as gyms go, it's a palace. Opened in 1984, the building was designed by Jack Diamond's firm, Diamond and Schmitt Architects, the same folks who also built the Four Seasons Centre for the Performing Arts at University and Queen. The Y is one of our best public(ish) buildings. Its collection of different geometric shapes are wrapped around a six-storey grand central staircase called the Athlete's Stairs, which was designed as a meeting place where people can bump into each other and chat. The building is one of the best examples of 1980s postmodern architecture, a decade and style that produced some real duds in this city.

When the Y opened, architecture critic Adele Freedman wrote in the *Globe and Mail* that it was 'tall enough to inspire heavenly thought.' Never mind that my fear of heights makes me feel like I might start rolling down those stairs, taking out an athlete or two along the way. The space soars, and being able to see other parts of the building while I'm in it makes me feel like we're all part of some kind of intricate machine.

It's that openness that makes this building great. From nearly every room, you can look into another and watch people play basketball, swim, stretch or do a weird yoga move. The running track, which is suspended over the gymnasium, passes through two or three distinct spaces depending on how the gym is divided up.

On any given day, one side of the gym might be host to a life-or-death struggle over a puck or a volleyball, while the other will house folks sweating and huffing through step aerobics to really bad circuit techno. I often wonder if their struggle would be easier if the instructor played good music – the odd times they drop Madonna or something palatable, I'm certain I run faster – but there's no place for snobbishness at the Y.

The pool room was inspired by the architecture of Roman baths and has a vaulted ceiling full of round skylights that allow beams of sunlight to pierce the water. They look brilliant underwater. The rooftop track was once a stark place of hot white light

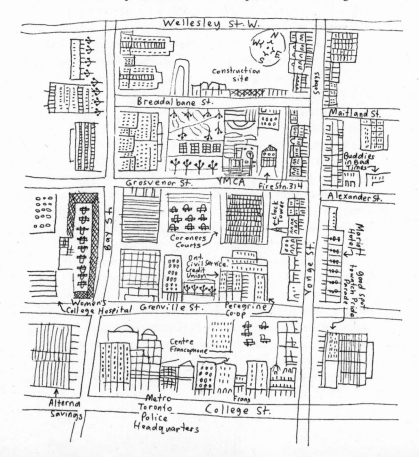

by day (but the most dazzling skyscraper-lit space by night), but that starkness has been tempered by the addition of a green roof that opened in 2009.

Inside the building, the Y's slogan, 'We build strong kids, strong families and strong communities,' is everywhere. Anyplace else, a phrase like that would give me the creeps. Not here, though. There isn't any of the moralizing here that usually goes along with those kinds of words. According to Lesley Davidson, the senior vice-president of operations, health, fitness and recreation, community service is something they're proud to do. Case in point: the Y's services are available to those who can't afford the fees. Staff assess the financial state of an individual or family and reduce or cover fees accordingly. 'About 30 percent of our patrons are on assistance,' said Davidson in 2005. 'That's representative of the poverty levels in Toronto.'

The Y's family pricing strategy also allows middle-class families to join at a lower rate. 'We noticed we were not serving working families well,' Davidson explained. 'Upper-income families were fine, and lower-income ones could apply for assistance – but [middle-class] families were left out.' Davidson said the Y worked with Toronto Public Health to identify targets like childhood obesity. They hope letting more families join will help reduce this growing trend, rendering this sub-city more healthy and equitable than the real one.

This earnestness has a long history behind it. The YMCA – then known as the Young Men's Christian Association – was founded in London, England in 1844 by George Williams, a teetotalling evangelical Christian who wanted to provide an urban alternative to the taverns, brothels and other sinful temptations of the city. Until 1984, the Metro Central Y was on College at Bay, where the police headquarters now resides. The old building included a 157-bed hotel, a service that's not provided at its current location.

It's the affordable accommodation and accepting atmosphere that gives Ys around the world their storied place in gay history, a role that declined after the 1970s when gay went mainstream. The Metro Central is still listed as a cruising spot on gay websites, but that might be wishful thinking. I've never noticed anything more there than the flirty backwards glances that make public life exciting. Once, a guy in the change room offered to show me his collection of 1972 Mark Spitz swimwear, but I'm sure he was just being friendly.

Today, the Y is a secular organization. I'm glad, because few things are as rewarding as a proper drink after a late-evening swim. On weekdays, the Y is open until 11 p.m. I usually go after 9 p.m. and wander around the machines on the main floor or read while riding a bike. Upstairs, there's a free-weights room, but all that freedom seems dangerous, and the people are more serious up there, judging by the loud grunting. Next door, the yoga room is full of an equal amount of intensity, though channelled in a different direction.

The big windows of the cardio room look across Grosvenor Street at the dark tower of the Forensic Sciences Centre. It's here that inquests into deaths take place, where tragedy becomes bureaucratic. More recently, the building has become the final stop on the 'Highway of Heroes' route that the bodies of Canadians killed in Afghanistan take from CFB Trenton. (It's possible to catch the motorcade's final few blocks along Bloor, Wellesley or Bay, where Toronto police block traffic and stand by their cruisers, saluting the hearses that sail quietly by.) The divide between trying hard to stay alive and investigation into death generally goes unnoticed.

The people at the Y are as diverse as the fabric of Toronto (it's one of the places where our diversity visibly manifests itself) and not at all intimidating (like people sometimes think gyms are). Some exercise conventionally, while others do things like roll basketballs all over their bodies. I have secret nicknames for many of the characters there: the Russian Bear, who sprinkles herbal water on sauna rocks and says, 'Good for the lungs, good for the skin'; Underwear Man, who thinks his underpants are suitable to exercise in; Stink King, who doesn't wipe his terrible odour from the equipment; Ari Fleischer, the doppelgänger of the former press secretary from early in George W. Bush's tenure, who is too serious for his own good.

They mix in with the businesswomen, computer geeks, punks and new Canadians who use the Y. In the showers, I catch glimpses of horrific-looking scars on some naked bodies – some back stories are considerably more fraught and violent than my suburban Ontario one. The Y is an oasis from all that, and it's Toronto at its best. It's also a good place to rest and be well before returning to the fine and sinful temptations of the Yonge Street strip.

Westish

Dundas Street

day trip

dress to impress

scenic views

Connecting walks: Yonge, Nathan Phillips Square/PATH, University, Bathurst, Dupont, Spadina, St. Clair, Downtown East Side, the Beach.

Few street names conjure 'Toronto' as well as Dundas does. Yet for all its iconic name recognition, it isn't an A-list superstar (in civic terms) like Queen, College, Yonge or Spadina. Rather, it's a street that snakes through many neighbourhoods, adopting local flavour like a chameleon – a street for Torontonians, not for tourist brochures. In the east, it gets rolling as a residential street that doubles as quick route downtown for cars and bikes. (Dundas boasts one of the longest stretches of continuous bike lanes in the city, even if they, like so many others, were controversial when installed.) This first bit, from Kingston Road, where Dundas begins, to Broadview Avenue, by the Don River, was a postwar creation. Look at prewar maps of the city and you'll find only an amalgam of short and non-contiguous roads that were eventually joined to form the street we now know. This explains why the street meanders, why lots sometimes flank it at awkward angles and why houses are sometimes too close to the road. Entire blocks west of Jones are all garages, as if Dundas was a really wide alley. At Broadview, it picks up its steel backbone of streetcar rails and crosses the Don Valley, becoming a proper street that was designed from the beginning.

Once past the Don River and the Mercedes dealership where director David Cronenberg filmed scenes for *Crash*, Dundas is changing fast. The rebuilding of Regent Park that began in 2009 has altered the streetscape dramatically: residential glass buildings that meet the sidewalk have replaced the dour old brick Regent

Park blocks that were set back behind poor landscaping and made the street feel dark and neglected. Surrounded by podiums and townhomes, the new towers meet the street, and can cast light out onto the sidewalk. As more of this area is regenerated, this part of Dundas will become unrecognizably urbane. By offering a mix of affordable and market housing, city planners hope to keep this new-but-old neighbourhood balanced and vibrant.

West of Parliament Street, Dundas runs through the downtown east side along the top of what was once the Moss Park estate, a space that's now home to a housing project of the same name that stretches out along Queen Street, with towers that make an M when viewed from above. Dundas curves around the exceptional neon of Filmores Gentlemen's Club, the kind of building whose shape and size and, some would argue, whose decor and services should be more common in Toronto. Dundas has many quick and sharp curves like this one, curves that awkwardly toss streetcars in a new direction, sending their tails swinging around trying to catch up. Here, too, Dundas is an amalgamation of a number of streets that were eventually joined together. It breaks up Toronto's usual grid and makes for interesting intersections shrouded in the mystery that's created when you can't see the end of the street ahead of you.

Torontonians get upset when people compare the city to New York, but Dundas does serve as our Broadway, floating loosely across the grid. Across from Filmores sit some fine but worn-out old Victorian piles that are about as rough-looking as old Toronto gets. They're an indication that the downtown east side has yet to undergo the kind of gentrification west-side neighbourhoods have seen in recent years.

If you're west of Jarvis Street at night, the glow from Yonge-Dundas Square is like an electric cloud, especially when it's humid, snowing or raining. For some people, this is the crossroads of the city, but the first block of Dundas West, just past

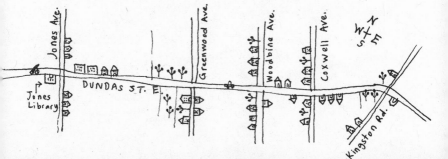

Yonge, is perhaps the city at its most boring. Here, it is dominated by the Atrium on Bay on the north side and the Eaton Centre and Ryerson University's Ted Rogers School of Management on the south side. Canadian Tire, a company whose store designs commit some of the most grievous assaults against urbanity, does try to be somewhat urban here, with windows that are almost like those seen on a traditional retail strip. Still, it's clear the inner big-box is trying to come out of the closet, as there's only one entrance and lots of dead space along the sidewalk.

Located across the street from the Canadian Tire, 600 Bay is about as film noir as Toronto gets, the kind of place where you might expect Sam Spade to have an office on one of the upper floors, his name written on the window in arched lettering. This is another type of building that should be more common in the city; dusty, wide-gauge venetian blinds still hang in some windows, suggesting the sensibility of the office behind them is retro without the chic. Behind the building, a narrow alley runs off Bay and leads to a dirt courtyard and the rear doors of other Dundas buildings, a reminder of what the area was like when it was known as the Ward, the slum that was cleared out when New City Hall was built. Next door, the bus terminal still maintains a similar noirish cinematic quality.

The destruction of the Ward also pushed out Toronto's original Chinatown, but traces of it remain between Bay and University (a handful of restaurants and old, dowdy buildings that seem out of place today). One City Hall, a fifteen-storey condo located on Elizabeth Street, just behind the back of the real City Hall, looks like a giant that's hunched over concentrating on something when viewed from Dundas. Its design invites us to walk around it and look for ourselves. The condo, by Toronto firm Hariri Pontarini Architects, bucks the trend of all-glass towers for a low-rise building with horizontal glass and concrete lines rather than vertical

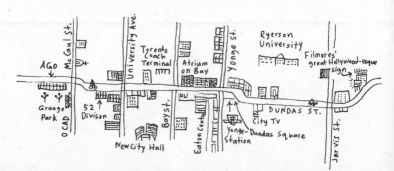

ones. It's a contrast to City Hall, likely one of the landmarks it's most difficult to build next to in Toronto, but it works, and One City Hall breathes life (and the sure sign of a real neighbourhood, a supermarket) into the old Ward, a neighbourhood that has evolved in the middle of our most institutional of areas.

A block past University sits Toronto Police Services 52 Division, a white glass-block fortress that is our homage to the *Miami Vice* style of police-station design. The concrete plaza out front has the potential to be a great people place, but it's used as a parking lot for both police vehicles and ones that quite obviously aren't, unless Pontiac Sunfires are now part of the fleet. This has been a problem since 2000, when Julian Fantino was chief of police, but the cars coincidentally disappeared when a corruption scandal broke at 52 Division in 2004. That the cars returned under the rule of kinder, gentler chief Bill Blair in the late 2000s seems like a needless PR – and urban – blunder.

The food court that all other food courts should aspire to is inside the Village by the Grange next door. The Village is made up of a series of interconnected condo buildings that stretch almost down to Queen and that boast interesting interior public and semi-public spaces, some of which seem trapped in the same 1980s time warp that gave us the wonderful neon of the facade across from 52 Division. On the main floor, a few dozen independent restaurants sell Toronto's edible multiculturalism inexpensively. You can get Jerk, Korean stew, Thai, burritos and Japanese. McDonald's is the only chain in the collection. It's a thoroughly Toronto mix that's frequented by a motley crew of Ontario College of Art and Design students and local eccentrics and workers from the nearby towers on University.

Around another quick curve, the bulge of Frank Gehry's Art Gallery of Ontario addition dominates Dundas. The Galleria Italia, as the bulge is known, gives visitors a bird's-eye view of

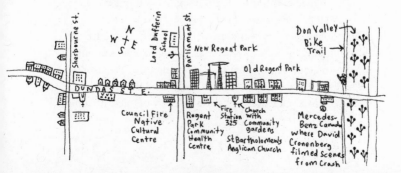

the streetscape and a second-storey view of the Victorian houses across the street. Next time you're in the neighbourhood, walk along the south side of Dundas and look at those houses on the north side. Then go up to the second floor of the gallery and do the same thing. It's remarkable to walk (nearly) an entire dense city block along the second floor of another building. It's like seeing Toronto for the first time; altering the angle by a half-dozen metres or so can radically change the perception of the city, and makes me realize how often we forget to pay attention to the upper floors of these kinds of common buildings.

The AGO is not just for looking at. The Gehry 'transformation,' as it was called, makes Toronto as much a part of the gallery experience as the art inside. The additions and alterations have opened new views to the north and south of the building. To the north, the timber beams of the Galleria Italia frame those quintessential old Toronto homes along Dundas as if they're works of art themselves. Apart from the occasional views stolen from well-positioned second- or third-floor apartments around the city, we usually don't get to see a Toronto street from this angle.

When you look out the windows on the south side of the AGO, Toronto's skyline appears all around, making it feel like you're a part of it rather than looking at it from afar. The residents of the concrete slab directly across the park now have a few thousand eyes peeping into their fishbowl lives every day. (As a friend once said when looking out at them, they're close enough to be interesting, but far enough away not to be explicit.) That slab was to be repeated in other buildings along McCaul Street, but then-alderman Colin Vaughan helped turn that proposal into plans for the low-rise Village by the Grange. To the west of the AGO, the Victorian homes along Beverley Street that face the Grange Park look like the Toronto doppelgänger of the famous Alamo Square skyline in San Francisco, where Victorian painted ladies (ours are brick) frame the park. In the other direction, architect Will Alsop's OCAD 'tabletop,' the massive floating school-box in the sky, suddenly looks even more audacious from this close up. It's the kind of building, like the CN Tower and Ontario Science Centre, that I daydreamed about when I was growing up in Windsor.

The Henry Moore sculpture that has graced the corner of Dundas and McCaul since 1973 plays a variety of roles: it's a nice

OCAD's 'tabletop' flying high over Butterfield Park and Henry Moore's Two Large Forms *outside the pre-Gehry AGO.*

piece of abstract sculpture for art lovers, a strange playground slide for children and an outdoor make-out post for ocad students. I often wonder if Moore knew that his piece would become a sort of art ambassador, introducing abstract forms to people who might not otherwise go into the AGO and see the rest of the museum's collection of his work. Toronto has a long-standing relationship with Henry Moore, and the AGO houses the biggest public collection of Moore's work in the world. Having *Two Large Forms* sitting here on the sidewalk completely accessible, without a security guard watching, is a bit of a tease. You can't climb on any of his pieces inside, even though some of them seem to be asking for it.

Though based in Calgary now, architect Fred Valentine worked on an earlier renovation of the AGO that was completed in 1973 by Parkin Architects, a descendent firm of Toronto's central modernist architect, John C. Parkin. Large parts of that renovation are still visible in the post-Gehry AGO, including the white concrete 'boxes' on either side of the Galleria Italia, one of which houses the Moore gallery. In 2008, after the Gehry addition was completed, I spoke with Valentine and he told me that he had worked with Moore himself to design the second-floor space. 'Moore had to have uniform natural light,' Valentine said of the gallery. 'He had very specific specifications for it: length, width, height, uniform light – we had proposed an oculus not unlike what Gehry [eventually] did, but Moore was very much against that and felt his pieces should be seen as they were conceived in a dull sky. We wanted to have the path of sun as it went west to east. He was a very interesting man, easy to work with, knew specifically what he wanted.' Valentine went on to say that Moore was upset at how his sculpture *The Archer* had been 'theatrically' lit in Nathan Phillips Square. When you visit the gallery today, notice how the light diffuses through the opaque glass squares in the ceiling, creating what can accurately be described as (in view of Moore's stated preferences about the conditions of his creation) 'British light.' Dull and without hard shadows, it's a most British environment in this colonial British city.

The quiet and somewhat austere space along the Dundas side of the AGO – Gehry called it a long 'front porch' – changes at Beverley, where the visual chaos of Chinatown abruptly starts. These two disparate places work well together, too, a good example of how Toronto can accommodate radically different spaces so close to each other.

The wonderful chaos continues for a few blocks, but quiets down past Spadina. (Chinatown is a north-south neighbourhood much more than it is an east-west one.) Here, the forgotten bottom of Kensington meets the Alexandra Park neighbourhood, sixteen acres of public and co-operative housing tucked between some of Toronto's most visited neighbourhoods – Kensington Market, Chinatown and Queen West – that are a psychological hole on most mental maps of Toronto. Largely built in an interesting 1960s modernist style, the neighbourhood has a space-age look, and though the grounds could and should be maintained better, it isn't an unpleasant place to walk, despite its rough

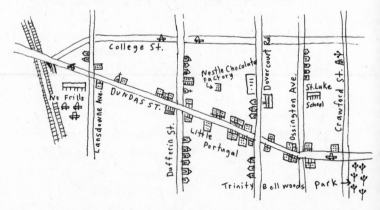

reputation. Reconnecting the area to the city around it is a complex process, but simply walking through it instead of around it can help put it back on our collective mental map.

The Dundas edge of Alexandra Park is marked by a long, black, six-foot-high iron fence that suggests somebody is either being kept out or kept in. It's a useless separation, more psychological than practical, and looking at it, the phrase 'Mr. Gorbachev, tear down this fence' comes to mind. Removing it would be a simple act that would encourage much more interaction between neighbourhoods. Another strange illusion of safety (or the lack thereof) is provided by signs that say 'Premises subject to Video Surveillance – Warning: Video Surveillance not intended to be an emergency response system.'

Around another bend and past the Toronto Western Hospital, Dundas meets Bathurst, where it becomes a mix of small retail and residential homes. Here, Dundas is the kid sibling of adjacent Queen and College streets, having recently experienced the pressures of gentrification that visited those streets in decades past. Cafés, restaurants and stores that are endlessly tweeted about have opened near old-school places like the Caldense Bakery, the Café Braziliano and 760 Dundas West, a strange and long-closed shop with (as of 2009) a funereal window display of flowers, coffin satin, a peacock statue and a fish tank. I often wonder who's behind that display. A widow? A widower? The odd campy son of the deceased owners? Displays of this type, numerous on streets where the bustle of retail has slowed down, each have a story, but maybe it's best just to admire them and wonder without knowing. It isn't clear how much longer curiosities like this will be able to survive the real-estate pressure, and the mystery makes strips like

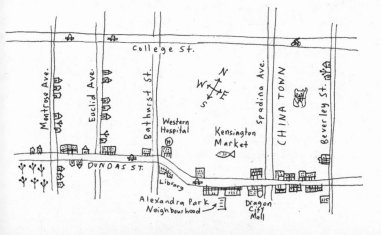

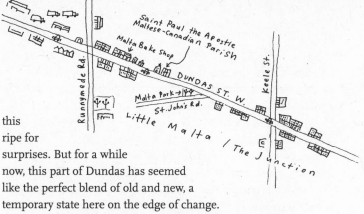

this
ripe for
surprises. But for a while
now, this part of Dundas has seemed
like the perfect blend of old and new, a
temporary state here on the edge of change.

Dundas continues like this for a number of kilometres – sometimes the typology is more residential than retail, but it's never exclusively one kind – becoming more Portuguese and Brazilian along the way. West of Ossington, Dundas veers slightly north, yet many houses and buildings along the stretch up to Lansdowne are still aligned with the grid, meeting the street diagonally as if all turning to look at something at the same time. Be sure to look back east here. Dundas is pointed straight at the cluster of skyscrapers in the core from whose centre rises the white BMO building. It's an unexpected southern perspective on downtown from a street we think of as east-west. Past Lansdowne, where Dundas rises to clear the Grand Trunk Railway line and the smell from the Nestlé Chocolate Factory often makes the air smell too sweet, the wide-angle view you get when you're looking to the southeast along the tracks presents a different Toronto altogether, making the city seem like a much more industrial-looking than the city we know it to be.

Dundas continues to curve elegantly north towards Bloor. At Sterling Road, in the middle of the two-span railway bridge, you can take the West Toronto Rail Path as a back route up to Cariboo Avenue in the Junction. Biking or walking the rail path for the first time is like seeing a remixed Toronto: heretofore unseen backyards and factories are in view, and the city seems shaped and put together differently from this new route.

For a different view, follow Dundas past where it meets Roncesvalles (where two long streetcar lines converge) and then crosses Bloor. The street there curves elegantly back west into the Junction neighbourhood. In July of 2009, the *New York Times* ran a short travel article on the Junction called 'Skid Row to Hip in Toronto.' It got Torontonians chattering, of course. For many, the 'end of hip' might be exactly the point in time when the *Times* comes calling, but if you walked through the Junction in the late 2000s, you know the article was right, even if the term 'skid row' is and was a ridiculous overstatement.

The Junction's move into hipdom (or gentrification, depending on how much analysis you want to apply) is interesting because of how slowly it happened. Compare and contrast this with the few blocks of Ossington north of Queen that seemed to transform so quickly between 2007 and 2009 that you could almost stand on the sidewalk and watch it happen. The velocity of change was so high that nobody could get a grip on what was happening, and people freaked out, which led the City to place a moratorium on new bars on that strip in 2009. The Junction, however, is a different story. It changed slowly throughout most of the first decade of this century – it's 'up and coming,' civic boosters would say – and as of this writing, it's a wonderful work in progress, poised at the temporary moment of near-perfect balance

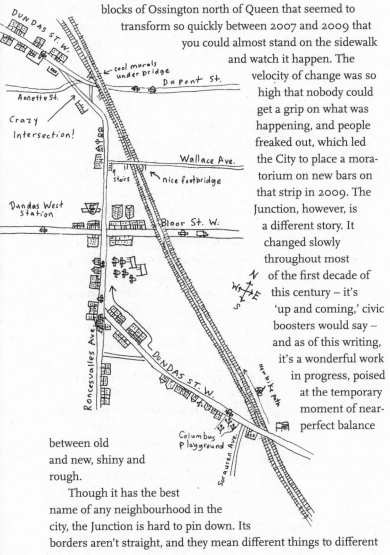

between old and new, shiny and rough.

Though it has the best name of any neighbourhood in the city, the Junction is hard to pin down. Its borders aren't straight, and they mean different things to different people. Official versions may look a bit like one of those hard-to-fit *Tetris* game pieces but, for many, the infrastructure that gives the railway neighbourhood its name is what truly defines the area. Though the centre of the Junction is at Keele and Dundas, it's good to enter the neighbourhood on foot from an oblique angle along Dundas, heading north from Bloor. The Junction being 'up there' is likely a big reason why the hipster pressure has for so long remained lower here than elsewhere: it seems so far away and past so many psychological barriers from the cool heart of darkness on Queen West.

Until 1968, the Junction seemed a lot closer to downtown and the west side because the Dundas streetcar continued north of Bloor all the way to Runnymede. (You can still see the streetcar loop there, though today the area is served only by buses.) A continuous transit line without a transfer can knit and connect disparate places together. If you walk up Dundas as it curves west, you can see retail remnants from days when this was a busier strip, though most storefronts were long ago converted into apartments.

The tracks dominate the northeast side of Dundas here, and the huge footbridge that runs along the railway breaks up this mega-block and links the Junction with the neighbourhoods to the east. Between 2008 and 2009, the clang of piledrivers sounded like the rising-action music from the *Terminator* films. If the wind was right you could hear the clanging across the city, but in the Junction it was there every day, an aural landmark as big as the CN Tower, one residents thought would never stop. The piles were being driven into the ground for a GO Transit rail overpass, and for a long time there were large fundraising-style thermometers around the Junction that showed how many piles there were to go.

During construction of the overpass, just north of the Dundas/Annette/Dupont intersection, you could slip north along an isolated bit of Old Weston Road (it once continued over the tracks north) and wander along the fence to watch the piledrivers at work. They were wrapped in a sound-absorbing material that billowed out with each blow, along with some black smoke. It was a dramatic industrial sight, the kind we don't see much of anymore in North America and a reminder of what the Junction used to be like when locomotives weren't the only big industrial things making noise in the neighbourhood.

Follow this back route along the tracks and you'll find another reason why the Junction's hip-to-straight balance is just right: here, the neighbourhood is filled with small workshops and car-repair garages. (If mechanics were an ethnicity this would be Little Mechanicville.) Things still get made and fixed and banged out in the Junction, from sausages to rubber to bumpers. Follow the tracks to Keele, past the new condos built on the old Canadian Tire site in 2009–10 and head north under the tracks to the other Junction, which often gets overlooked. Here there are more little shops, towering unused silos as grand as the ones on the waterfront and even houses. On Keele there are perfect Victorians that would be right at home in Cabbagetown, though here they're across from the giant concrete Keele Centre warehouse. (Take the centre's outdoor stairs to the second-floor roof for a Mary Poppins view of the neighbourhood.)

The area to the north of this – now home to big-box retailers and fast-food drive-thrus – was once a vast tract of stockyards, and some older Junction folk tell stories of sneaking in as kids and walking on top of a sea of cattle. St. Clair is not far away from Dundas along Keele, but it feels distant because of the railway-track barrier. Though the big-box land is ridiculously scaled, the older parts of the industrial Junction are very urban; places of stuff-making are tucked in and around places where people live. It's a very old way of living that may just be the future of cities.

Back on Dundas, west of Keele, the Junction's main strip is home to some of the most interesting retail in the city. Continuing the theme of making stuff, many of the stores here are cottage-industry outlets and furniture and building salvage shops that are sometimes fancy and sometimes downright Dickensian. Sprinkle in an abundance of cafés (fancy and not), used book and clothing stores, organic markets, electronics repair shops and restaurants and it's a near-perfect heterogeneous mix. Another mark of a good and healthy neighbourhood is that it offers both daytime and nighttime activities. Though the Junction could use a few more bars (the ban on bars was only lifted here in the late 1990s, after all), there are a handful of good places to get a drink. And unlike neighbourhoods like Dundas and Ossington and Queen West, there's an abundance of kids running around by day, and they aren't dressed like miniature hipsters either.

All this activity is housed in a remarkable stretch of some of the finest buildings in Toronto. The upside of being down for so long is that development was slow here, which has helped to preserve these buildings. Many shop windows have a film-set quality, and seem like they haven't changed since the 1970s. Change, though, is inevitable, and the Junction is increasingly becoming the place to be. What will happen to these shops and some of the long-time residents remains unclear, but perhaps the best thing the neighbourhood has going for it is the slow speed of its change. There's still time to think in the Junction.

Further, on the western edge of the Junction, the Maltese flag flies above a small patch of land between Dundas Street West and St. Johns Road. This is Malta Park, in Toronto's Malta Village, which occupies just a few blocks of Dundas. This area was once the vibrant heart of the Maltese diaspora in Canada. Though not many businesses or residents here these days

Scenes from a diaspora: Little Malta represents.

are Maltese, this part of the Dundas strip remains an important part of this small and dispersed community.

The name 'Dundas Street' resonates with all Maltese Canadians; it certainly meant something to me as I was growing up in

Windsor, where the only visible Maltese culture was in my relatives' suburban houses. Perhaps that explains why Maltese homes are full of wall maps showing the Maltese archipelago, souvenir picture plates, Malta ashtrays, Malta clocks, Malta placemats and Malta fridge magnets: the smaller the country, the louder the artifact.

The mythic Toronto of my childhood imagination consisted of three things: the CN Tower, Mr. Dressup's house and Little Malta. We would take yearly trips to see Maltese friends in Milton and make Sunday pilgrimages down to Dundas to eat at the Malta Bake Shop. If you count people like me (half-bred and second-generation), the Maltese population in the GTA is about 20,000 to 25,000. Today, most of Toronto's Maltese live out in places like Milton. University of Toronto professor John Portelli, who researches Maltese Canadians, has found there are concentrations of Maltese in west Etobicoke, Mississauga and further out in Brampton – but nothing like the visible concentration that was once on Dundas Street.

Other ethnic neighbourhoods have experienced the same suburban drain. The Italians moved from College Street, roughly following Dufferin out to Woodbridge, while Toronto's Jewish population followed Bathurst from Kensington (once known as the 'Jewish Market') to Thornhill. The first substantial wave of Maltese immigration to Canada occurred soon after the turn of the century. Many settled in the vicinity of St. Patrick's Shrine Church on McCaul at Dundas, where they held various Maltese events. The Maltese are devout Catholics, and the church exerts a strong pull. St. Paul even found time to shipwreck himself on the island – you can read all about his Maltese adventure in the Bible (in Acts, Chapter 28, if you've got the Good Book handy). New immigrants were helped by Maltese priests and later by the Maltese Society of Toronto, which was established in 1922. The society helped purchase and erect St. Paul the Apostle church just east of Runnymede in 1931, establishing the Maltese presence in the Junction. Its claim to fame at the time was that it was the only 'national church' (built by parishioners) in North America. Dundas is the street of internal Maltese migration.

I like to take people to the Malta Bake Shop, a block away from the church, not just to get them to try the pastizzi and to 'Taste of Malta's Delights,' as the sign inside says, but to show them my

secret corner of Toronto, one that has a picture of my great-uncle
Johnny Catania on the wall. My uncle was a Maltese comedian
who entertained the Allied troops in Malta while the Italian Air
Force and the Luftwaffe did their best to bomb the island into the
sea during the Second World War. In 1964, he gave up his Maltese
television show to immigrate to Windsor with my dad's family.
Each year, he made numerous trips up the 401 to Dundas Street;
he even hosted the Miss Malta of Toronto pageant in the years
before he died. That his picture is on the wall of the Malta Bake
Shop makes Toronto feel even more like home to me. I often
wonder how many other invisible, personal connections people
have to places like this. Inside, the Maltese greet each other with
an 'All right?' rather than a 'Hello' and speak with a mixture of
Maltese and English. It's the aural wallpaper I grew up with.

Since the 1920s, when Grazio Borg opened a grocery store
here, the bake shop's location has long been a centre of Maltese
life in the city. Antoinette Buttigieg, who runs the shop with her
husband Charles, is an active member of the Maltese Canadian
Business Association. She says they lobbied the city to get vertical
street banners installed that mark Malta Village: a little gesture,
but important to maintaining a small community's sense of place.
Dundas Street is 'like a symbol for the Maltese,' says Portelli,
'even though there is no new blood immigrating from Malta.'

Joseph Cini has run Joe's Barbershop on Dundas since the
1950s, and he still trims the hair of people he shared bomb shelters with back in Malta during the war. He saw a problem when
the TTC decided to terminate the streetcar at Dundas West station
on Bloor. Instead of a continuous ride from downtown, people had
to switch to a bus. 'It's not practical. We had the Dundas streetcar.
Nobody knew what the Junction bus was,' he says. Dundas is not
a sexy name or a particularly beautiful street, but the sense of
place was and is strong. Cini is one of the last holdouts, though:
his own daughter moved out to Milton.

Though most of the Maltese residents are gone, the strip still
survives. 'If you come here after church on Sunday, there will be a
lot of people,' says George Mallia, editor and publisher of the local
Maltese language newspaper, *L-Ahbar* ('The News'). 'Some come
once a month to hear a Maltese mass. Certainly, they come on
feast days.' Mallia's paper, like Dundas itself, is one of the things

that gives this now decentralized community its sense of unity, not just in Toronto, but across Canada.

The problem is that people like me aren't moving there. I like that Little Malta is there, and it's comforting, but my allegiances to other parts of the city are just as strong. When I spoke to him in 2005, Sal D'Angelo of Junction Realty hadn't sold any houses to Maltese folks returning to the neighbourhood, but for him, the culture still played a big role of the area. 'Malta Village should stay in the Junction,' he says. 'Maltese people should stay here.' I hope a few of them stay around, too; for me, losing Little Malta would be like losing the CN Tower.

Little Malta is all but done by Runnymede, save for the last tiny Maltese sign and banner. Dundas, this most everyman of streets, continues west, across the Humber, into Etobicoke and further still into Mississauga, again changing and shifting with the times and places, taking on and discarding characteristics as it goes.

Pearson Airport

 day trip

 dress to impress

 admission

Connecting walks: None, but for fun, try walking into the city someday.

Pearson International Airport is Toronto's only true international port. Sprawling into the high plains of Mississauga, it's a place that's half in Toronto, half in some distant land where the grip that familiar places like Yonge, Spadina and Honest Ed's have on us slowly loosens as we change our watches to reflect new time zones and anticipate exotic subway systems. It's a liminal kind of place – at once here and elsewhere, and a bit dreamlike, too – and a fine place to wander. If you do go there just to wander, though, try to look like a traveller or an eager relative – it's a good way to avoid the attention of those surveilling this most surveilled of places, where anything or anybody that stands out is suspect.

Completed in 2007, Pearson's new Terminal 1 gleams white, and its ceilings soar like the airplanes that taxi away from its gates. The height and arc of the ceiling is stadium-like, and the public art inside is some of the best in the city. I've been out to the end of 'Pier F,' where the big jets dock, and where there's a bar with the most expensive cover charge in the city (the cost of an international plane ticket). If you're into art, it's also the most expensive museum admission fee, as the bar has a view of a giant Richard Serra sculpture called *Tilted Spheres*, one of only two Serra pieces in the area. (The other, *Shift*, is in a field up in King City.) You can walk through its giant curved metal walls and listen to your voice echo. The spheres are so big they were installed before the walls and roof of the terminal were put up. The bar, with its overpriced drinks, is as jet set as Toronto gets (save, of course, for the lounges that are reserved for first- and business-class passengers).

As impressive as the new terminal is, old Terminal 1, now demolished, has been a hard act to follow. When it opened in 1964, Aeroquay One was this city's bold jump into the jet age. Circular in design, with a parking garage in the middle, it allowed for passengers to be whisked from Pan Am to Plymouth in two

Richard Serra's Tilted Spheres *are the last thing you may see when leaving Toronto.*

minutes. Though it was rendered inefficient by increased passenger volume, an inability to expand and the spectre of terror that lurks in the corners of our once-utopian air terminals, Aeroquay One was celebrated in aviation and architectural circles alike. Author Arthur Hailey even wrote his blockbuster potboiler *Airport* after getting a tour of the building from his friend, Aeroquay One architect John C. Parkin. The 1970 film of the book evokes the kind of analogue-techno thrills the first few decades of the jet age afforded. Journalist George Jonas once wrote a column about the indignities of modern air travel and in it recalled taking a date to Aeroquay One because, he said, it was the kind of slick and mod place you could try to impress someone with.

Once, while dropping off a friend who was embarking on one of those awful Birkenstock-and-backpack tours of Europe, we passed the time by sneaking up automobile ramps to the open roof of the centre garage. We were alone in the dark, high above the runways, feeling like we shouldn't be there, and the terrific sound of the jets moved the hair on our arms as we stood and watched like all those people did when the Beatles arrived at JFK.

In modern terminals, you rarely get to feel and hear the jets without the intervention of a thick pane of glass.

Dowdy and also-demolished Terminal 2 – originally a freight terminal but converted for passenger use in 1968 – was endlessly long, and the first place I saw moving sidewalks. Its squat, brutalist parking garage was like a futuristic ruin, with vegetation growing over the edges and guardrails that lit up from within. No one ever struck up a Save Terminal 2 committee – there really wasn't any reason to do so. But there's something romantic about old airport buildings; they're reminders of the perhaps mostly fictional days when air travel was sexy.

Few people ever mention poor Terminal 3 these days, an artifact of the Mulroney era that is itself slated for premature obsolescence in the mid-2010s when T1 expands again. Though airports lend a feeling of being somewhere else, in T3 pre-boarding, U.S. customs agents admit passengers into a zone where American laws apply, a kind of embassy territory without the ambassador. The international arrivals section at T3, as in all airports, is all theatre. Past customs, passengers are suddenly alone on a platform that slopes down in three directions, surrounded by a few hundred faces with expressions that all say, 'You're not the one I'm waiting for.' When loved ones are finally spotted, people charge up the ramp where they hug, kiss and cry before moving on in a happy huddle. It makes waiting there a pleasure, and a lovely last moment of strangeness before returning to the normal routine of the city.

Returning to the city is easiest by vehicle (car, or bus to the subway), but it's possible to walk out of Pearson on foot. At the back of the T1 parking garage, the brave and ambulatory can walk out and find Silver Dart Drive, a rather unpleasant airport service road that is at grade and underneath the flying on- and off-ramps that feed the airport with people. Silver Dart Road connects to Jetliner Road, which leads out of the airport property and into the seedy part of town that's adjacent to all airports. As port lands were to cities in the past, the shady landscape around our airports is full of nondescript office buildings and low-rise industrial buildings where the shipping and receiving, importing and exporting of things happens behind unmarked windows. Certainly most of this is legitimate, and there are Hiltons and Petro-Canadas here as well, but the nowhereland around airports is a fine place for doing things under the cover of jet noise – witness the selection of lonely-looking strip joints that dot the area.

A little farther on lie the apartment communities that house many new Canadian families, who live with that jet noise every day, their first steps into Canadian life not far from where they landed. There is no Statue of Liberty–style monument here to welcome people to Toronto or Canada, just a dowdy landscape and prohibitively expensive plane tickets that make turning around and getting back on a plane unlikely. Welcome.

Markland Wood

 neighbourhood jaunt   Connecting walks: None.

 dress to impress

 scenic views

There are islands in Toronto that aren't surrounded by water. They're communities that are isolated in some way from the rest of the city. Sometimes it's a cluster of apartment towers surrounded by ravines and a highway, where the only entrances are via bridge or underpass. Other times it's simply a railway line that divides one community from another, which, though relatively narrow, can be as psychologically dividing as the Berlin Wall (the 'wrong side of the tracks' means what it does for a reason). Toronto's neighbourhood islands aren't in complete isolation, but they lack the urban cohesion other parts of the city have, where one neighbourhood blends seamlessly into another.

One such island, on the western edge of the city, is Markland Wood. Toronto neighbourhoods tend to be known either for being superstars – the Annex, Kensington and, now, Parkdale – or for being the spots where crime happens, their names repeated too often on the evening news. Markland Wood, however, fits neither of these categories. The neighbourhood is surrounded by the Markland Wood Country Club, which follows the lowlands around Etobicoke Creek that also divide Toronto and Mississauga. There are only four entrances to the community, one of them via Bloor Street, which bisects Markland and continues into Mississauga. Like a lot of places at the end of the city, it's serviced only by one TTC line, the 49 bus, which makes a circle around the neighbourhood and returns to Kipling station, a lone bus with no connections once inside the community, almost like a rural collector bus route.

If you're coming in by bus, get off the 49 just before Highway 427 – to get a handle on a neighbourhood it's often good to walk all the way into it rather than starting at its centre. The highway is short, fast and wide here – a quick north-south route between the top and bottom of the city – and doesn't have the same identity

that the 401 and Gardiner/QEW
have. It's the route between places:
when you're on it you're either
almost at the airport or you're just
arriving back in town, and you're
wondering which lane you need to
be in to get where you're going. It's
a profound sense of nowhere standing over the 427 on the Bloor overpass, a big-sky inter-zone that
nobody owns but that thousands
pass through every hour, both
underneath and overtop, without
much thought of what they're travelling past. The West Mall, which
runs adjacent to the highway, uses
the odd British street name convention that roughly translates as 'wide
road, not much going on' (think of
Pall Mall in London – fancy, fit for
kings and queens, but boring). To
be fair, the West Mall is better than
most highway service roads (though
it's still not ready for royalty),
flanked at Bloor by a fine example
of a Toronto strip mall, filled with a
nice mix of mom-and-pop shops.

The highs and lows of Markland Wood.

Markland Wood begins a few
blocks west on Bloor. The entrance
is subtle – the ranch and split-level
homes that line the street here don't
seem much different than the ones
a few metres away. Walking through a community like this is a
challenge if you're trying to get a handle on the area without
having a reason to be there – an appointment or, better yet, plans
for visiting somebody – as it's hard to 'read' the neighbourhood.
It's private and quiet; people live behind big garage doors and
likely travel in their cars more than on foot. Not all of Toronto's
outer neighbourhoods are like this. Some postwar areas – mixed-

income and culturally diverse neighbourhoods especially – see lots of pedestrian activity even though they were designed for car use. In Toronto, the rule is that the more middle-class a suburb is, the less you'll see people out and about.

I felt extremely conspicuous walking along the residential streets of Markland Wood, alone save for a few grandmothers walking very young children from school. I was certain if people looked out the window and saw me walking slowly along the sidewalk at the end of their lawn, they'd be somewhat suspicious, at the very least. When I lived in a neighbourhood like this, a stranger walking down the street was such an odd occurrence that everybody outside noticed. 'What's that person up to? No good, certainly,' I often wondered.

Though Markland's community spirit is hidden when walking around, it certainly is there, as it has one of the oldest community papers in circulation in Toronto, the *Marklander*, started in 1963, not long after the community was established. Today, the homes in this neighbourhood are over forty years old and show the signs of a mature population: a remarkable number of porches have been glassed in, a particular quirk of retirement-living renovation.

This area along the banks of Etobicoke Creek was previously the Silverthorn farm, established in 1807 on land granted to the Loyalist Silverthorn family of New Jersey. It stayed in the family until 1958, when the 400-acre farm was sold for $3 million. This was a few years after the destructive waters of Hurricane Hazel ripped through this lowland, and new residential homes were built only on the area deemed high enough above the flood line, while the rest was given over to the low-risk golf course. The Markland Homes Association website describes the remnants of an old bridge over the creek that can be seen from the twelfth tee of the country club, though non-golfers miss out on this sight – and on many other ravines and watercourses in Toronto that are part of golf courses' private property. If liability laws allowed, perhaps right-of-ways could be established here and elsewhere.

The plaza at the centre of Markland may be the heart of the community, but apart from a McDonald's, it lacks the coffee-shop type of public-private places where neighbours can bump into and overhear each other. (Perhaps this is one of the reasons the community paper has been so successful.) North of Bloor, in

Millwood Park, the 'wood' of Markland Wood is a small thicket of forest, tamed and civilized by streetlights that keep the forest bright at night. Follow Mill Road north – the road used to lead to the Silverthorn's grist mill on the creek – and you'll see concrete brutalist towers rise above the 1960s houses, marking where Markland ends and the rest of Etobicoke begins. If the 49 bus rolls by, hop on and be shuttled off the Markland island back to mainland Toronto.

Alderwood and Lake Shore Boulevard

 pack a lunch

 bathing suit optional

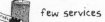 few services

Connecting walk: CNE/Western Waterfront.

I once heard someone describe Browns Line as the ugliest street in Toronto. For a long time, I didn't bother to confirm this fact; I let that idea, like many urban opinions, linger in my imagination and contaminate my impression of the place. Once you hear some place is bad, it might as well be bad.

Browns Line is rather famous, as obscure arterial roads go, because hundreds of thousands of commuters pass by its QEW and Gardiner off-ramp signs every day – it's one of those landmarks on the way in and out of the city that are noted automatically and peripherally, but rarely given any more thought. Browns Line stands out because it's not a street, avenue or boulevard – it's a line, a throwback to farm days, the kind of lonely country road where Southern Ontario gothic dramas might unfold.

On a hot, humid early-summer day, a friend and I started a walk down Browns Line at Sherway Gardens Mall. The only gothic things at this mall are some of the teenagers – this is Etobicoke's version of Bloor Street's 'Mink Mile,' complete with a Holt Renfrew and a Sporting Life. As we walked through the latter store, my ambulatory consort for the afternoon remarked that he grew up being jealous of the other Thornhill kids whose moms brought them to the shop's North Toronto location on Yonge Street. His memories, and the oddball combination of Prada, snowboards and Birkenstocks, weighed heavily on us, so we escaped into the heat of the parking lot.

Few places in Canada get as hot in the summer (and as windswept and cold in the winter) as mall parking lots, and the thin band of green at the edge of the lot served as encouragement to head south and east towards Browns Line. There are numerous tall condo towers sprouting around the periphery of Sherway and, like Square One in Mississauga and others around the GTA, this mall has turned the area into a kind of urban centre: not exactly a

downtown but more somewhere than nowhere. One condo pres-
entation centre announced: 'We're building Etobicoke's most fashionable address.' Definitive ad copy like that has to count for
something.

Evans Avenue starts just south of the mall and runs east
across the QEW's concrete trench. Standing above all those cars
here – cars filled with drivers who have just seen the Browns
Line sign – you really get a sense of how big this city is. Day or
night, the cars never stop. Just a few metres beyond the highway
there are relatively new suburban homes surrounded by grass and
garages, followed by apartment buildings that date to the late '50s
and early '60s. The semi-suburban landscape hugs the qew, but
drivers can't see much of it. The cars are harder to ignore, since
when you're on foot, the sound of the highway is impossible to
escape. These homes and apartments evoke the great postwar age
of the automobile, when Browns Line finally lost the remnants of
its rural beginnings.

Browns Line itself begins as a massive off-ramp, a southern
continuation of Highway 427 that rises out of yet another Detroit-
style freeway trench. Maybe this is why that person said it was
ugly. But beyond this place, the details tell a different story.
Perhaps it's not a story of beauty, but it's not an ugly story, either.
The car is king on Browns Line today, and the strip-mall landscape
is certainly dowdy, but it's never boring. As in Toronto's other strip
malls, the variety of stores and restaurants operating here is a
completely urban mix. The inner and outer suburbs have an
undeserved reputation for being bland and 'all the same,' but,
unlike many downtown neighbourhoods, where the chain stores
repeat every block or so like the background in a cartoon chase
scene, the strip malls here are full of unique, independent and
small-scale businesses.

Just south of the freeway interchange, Adult O'Rama (with
private viewing booths) skulks next to Veroli Ristorante, Allegro
Café and the Chesterfield Factory. In the plaza on the other side
of Browns Line, a giant Chinese Top Food Supermarket sits next
to the Alderwood Café, a golf academy and something called
'Honey World.'

This is, as one of those cafés' name suggests, the community
of Alderwood, which is nestled in a corner of Etobicoke largely

isolated by industrial land to the north and east and the Mississauga border to the west. It's also where, on a rainy Saturday night in July 2008, an suv riddled with bullets and three bodies was ditched just a block from Browns Line. Alderwood had little connection to the murders, other than being a convenient place to get off the highway when bad things happen. Browns Line was the exit.

There's lots of commercial activity along Browns Line, but we didn't bump into very many people during our walk. We saw a few folks sitting on their porches, watching the traffic, but the sidewalks were all ours. Tiny postwar bungalows, some with their entire front lawns given over to paved driveways, are mixed with the occasional monster home and commercial enterprise. A few blocks south, the east side of the street turns industrial.

The hot dirty wind was blowing, so we stopped at Timothy's Pub. It's always a bit strange to walk into a bar in the middle of the afternoon: it takes a while for your eyes to adjust, and you can't shake that guilty matinee feeling. The bar was a quarter full, mostly filled with early-retirement-age men nursing pints and watching sports on one of the many plasma screens. We sat at the bar and did the same. A couple at a nearby table talked in hushed tones and leaned into one another, and my consort that day suggested they were having an affair. Hot-and-anonymous Browns Line is where clandestine romance goes down, with eighteen-wheelers rolling by outside, golf on the television, Bryan Adams playing in the background and somebody else asking the Russian bartender if she's on Facebook. She wasn't, but the presumed adulterous couple probably didn't care.

Back outside, tipsy in the sun, we continued south, up and over the railway tracks where Browns Line comes to an end at Lake Shore Boulevard. This is Long Branch, where the 501 Streetcar route ends. The terminating streetcar loop is a little west of here, just shy of the Mississauga border. West of the loop, just before the border, there's a path that leads into a dense forest that we took back up towards Sherway Gardens following Etobicoke Creek. Typical of Toronto creek and ravine parks, signs of the city quickly disappeared, save for those new mall condo buildings peeking over the canopy. If you decide to take this route back to Sherway, when you come to the intersection of Highway 427 and the QEW, choose the dirt path on the left that leads underneath the

The former Mimico Insane Asylum, now Humber College's Lakeshore campus.

highway. The cathedral-like space down there offers an underside
view of the QEW and signs welcoming motorists to Mississauga
and Toronto. Climb the hill and you'll hit civilization again: the
mall, the Jack Astor's restaurant and acres of parking. If the natural environment isn't calling out to you, stay on Lake Shore and
head east, back towards downtown.

Long Branch could be a film set from the 1950s and '60s.
Relatively few of the low-rise commercial buildings here have been
replaced with newer and bigger buildings as they overwhelmingly
have, say, along Yonge Street in North York. Some parts of Lake
Shore even have street parking spots at an angle to the curb, which
lend a small-town feel to the strip. While walking east, take a diver-
sion south on any street between 39th and 23rd streets and walk
through the pleasant, tree-lined neighbourhood that hugs the Lake
Ontario shore. The beach is mostly private, hidden behind homes,
until Colonel Samuel Smith Park appears with its reclaimed and
naturalized waterfront. The park grounds continue on to the
Lakeshore campus of Humber College, where buildings from a
Victorian psychiatric hospital have been renovated and adapted
for use by the college, presenting a new-old landscape that, while
familiar in Toronto, is unusual in this pastoral setting.

The City of Toronto isn't very old, nor does it have much of an
empire, but east of the campus and park lies New Toronto, a post-
industrial colony that takes up 2.5 square kilometres along the

Etobicoke shoreline, and is nestled between Lake Ontario and the ten lanes of the QEW. To the east lies the community of Mimico which, like Long Branch, was an autonomous community before both were swallowed up by bigger municipalities. New Toronto was incorporated in 1913 but technically ceased to exist in 1967 when the entire Lakeshore area (as it is called today, having been rebranded in the 2000s) was amalgamated into Etobicoke.

New Toronto is a streetcar suburb, a form of development common across North America. These communities grew from the late 1800s through the 1920s, just before the automobile became the dominant factor in urban development. The houses have porches instead of garages, the lots are relatively small by suburban standards and pedestrians can get around comfortably. By the mid-1890s, streetcar service reached as far west as Long Branch (a fine name for the still-operating termination point of Toronto's longest streetcar line). Many New Toronto residents still use that same transit route to get in and out of the city.

New Toronto was, and still is to a large extent (though demographics are changing), a working-class town, one planned for industry from the beginning. The main intersection, Islington and Lake Shore, resembles the four corners of a small Ontario town. Numbered streets spread out in grid formation toward Mimico and Long Branch. The south side of town is largely residential, while vast tracts of land to the north were given over to huge industrial concerns. The factories had mythic-sounding names, some familiar, some just impressive: Anaconda American Brass Limited, Goodyear Tire and Rubber, Continental Can, Gilbey's Distillery, Lake Simcoe Ice, Campbell's Soup, McDonald's Stamping. The town was so focused on industry that Campbell's Soup shared the excess steam it generated with Continental Can, piping it between the plants. At the height of the postwar-production good times, from the 1950s into the 1970s, Goodyear alone employed over 3,000 people.

Wendy Gamble, president of the New Toronto Historical Society, described a time when factory whistles sounded around town and workers would walk to work. On 6th Street, the original Gothic revival and bay 'n' gable workers' cottages still exist. The streetscape is unexpectedly similar to that found on Oxford, Nassau or Wales in Kensington Market. Town lore has it that the Beer Store on Lake

Shore used to be the busiest location in Ontario due to all the factory workers heading straight there after work.

The prosperity of New Toronto made it a desirable place to settle. Large numbers of immigrants came from Eastern Europe, primarily Poland and Ukraine. Today, a large Polish population remains, and the Polish consulate is located in a lakefront mansion just east of New Toronto. Some of the restaurants have Polish writing in the windows and Zywiec beer on tap. Lots of immigrants came from Atlantic Canada as well, including a large number of Newfoundlanders, some of whom frequented the Newfie Pub, a rough-and-tumble draft joint on Lake Shore that closed in the late 2000s. New Toronto was a town that worked. Residents were highly unionized and there were a number of strong credit unions. Service clubs were popular, and there were four active legions.

New Toronto's luck ran out in the 1980s, a time that saw a general industrial decline and the introduction of free trade. In 2005, Bill Worrell, then program manager (now director of Healthy Communities) at the Lakeshore Area Multi-Purpose Community Health Centre, described New Toronto as being like a Bruce Springsteen song: 'When all was said and done,

10,000 industrial jobs left, and that shook this place to its foundation,' he says. 'It was a very stable community until this time.'
Many of the companies not only closed but tore down their
buildings as well. Today these former industrial sites, known as
brownfields, cover much of the northern half of the neighbourhood. Behind hundreds of metres of barbed-wire fence, chunks
of concrete and twisted steel are scattered in the prairie-like grass.
Many of these brownfields are waiting for redevelopment, but the
high cost of the massive environmental cleanup these sites require
means they're still empty and languishing.

Worrell pointed out that much of the postwar generation
picked up and left in the prime of their lives, leaving behind a
community that was economically unstable with a large older
population and some very young families. With the core gone,
the entire Lakeshore area is now experiencing a shortage of
programs for youth and older teens. You can see the economic
distress in the storefronts along Lake Shore. While there's an
incentive to shop in the area because it's a short walk from home,
it's served by too many dollar stores, flea markets and used clothing shops. (Note to downtown thrift-store enthusiasts: go west!)

However, not all of the brownfields are vacant. The Goodyear
site is among those that have been redeveloped, and in the 1990s
it became home to Toronto's largest co-operative housing project.
The pastel and earth tones of these tall buildings provide a strange
backdrop to the traditional storefronts and remaining industrial
structures. The residents of the co-ops are largely new Canadians
who have changed the face of New Toronto. At the same time,
many of the worker homes are being bought up by well-off families who renovate, commute to work and shop outside the community at nearby Sherway Gardens.

Worrell saw New Toronto's future in terms typical of many
other inner suburbs: it's either going to go urban or suburban.
'Are we a Port Credit or the Beaches, or are we a diverse urban
community with all the mix? Do we want more Starbucks or do we
want to keep the Newfie Pub?' While the Newfie Pub is now gone,
Starbucks hasn't shown up yet as of this writing. Neighbourhoods
like this, away from the trendiness and development pressures
found downtown, gentrify more slowly than those closer to the
core because they don't become super-cool super-fast (a blessing

more than a curse). Change can take its time, and yet, as people are priced out of downtown, New Toronto's solid and more affordable housing stock is beginning to look appealing.

New Toronto has also had a thriving arts community. The area's relatively low rents and easy access to the city have attracted many artists, and more will settle here as the downtown becomes too expensive. Wendy Lilly, a mixed-media artist who's lived in New Toronto for over thirty years, likes the variety of environments. 'We're away from the city, but connected to it by streetcar,' she said. 'I don't consider it suburban, but there is a bit of cottage energy here.' The arts out here are located in places like the Islington-Lakeshore Mall, a dilapidated-looking building that rents rehearsal space to between sixty and eighty bands. Rock 'n' roll lives in unexpected places.

Not being in the middle of everything can offer a unique perspective. Cliff Lumsdon Park, at the foot of 7th Street, has the most stunning view of Toronto's skyline: a perfect cross-section of the city as it rises Oz-like across Humber Bay. In one quick, unobstructed glance, you can take in the city from Hanlan's Point all the way up to St. Clair Avenue. New Toronto and the rest of Lakeshore may be far out, but being here, at the edge, can give you good perspective on Toronto – both literally and figuratively – now that these inner suburban neighbourhoods are changing in ways that may become a model for many other parts of Toronto.

The CNE and the Western Waterfront

 day trip

 bathing suit optional

Connecting walks: Harbourfront, Bathurst, Alderwood/Lake Shore.

admission

Toronto's western waterfront doesn't have an official beginning, but for me it starts somewhere just west of Bathurst. The Tip Top lofts, housed in an old building with a modern top hat, are the last of the close-to-the-water condos, and they give way to a fairly continuous greenbelt of waterfront parks disrupted only by Ontario Place and a few other buildings. Coronation Park, the first named park to the west, is built on landfill and has a baseball diamond that's lit up bright on summer evenings, when games compete with the adjacent skyline for attention.

The unlikely lighthouse on the strip of Coronation Park between Lake Shore Boulevard and Fleet Street seems to be directing cars rather than boats. Built in 1861, the Queen's Wharf Lighthouse was originally located at the end of the Queen's Wharf, which ran 215 metres into the lake south of where Bathurst and the Gardiner cross today. In 1912, as infill extended the shoreline south, the lighthouse was moved to its present location, and was then deactivated and almost destroyed before it was eventually renovated to its current working condition in 1988.

The Princes' Gates on Strachan Avenue provide a grand white beaux-arts background to this entire area, and serve as the entrance to the vast Canadian National Exhibition grounds. There are two times to visit the CNE: when the fair is on, and when it's not. When it's not (or when other events like the Grand Prix aren't on), it has a forlorn, empty and lonely quality. Like amphetamine users, places of celebration seem to crash when the party's over. These grounds seem extra lonely, and walking easily through the gates seems wrong: there should be somebody here taking my ticket. During these down times, cars routinely use the CNE grounds as a shortcut in and out of Parkdale, but driving on this kind of civic sacred ground seems like a sacrilege to me.

The place changes in late August when the CNE opens. Even far from the grounds, up Dufferin or Bathurst, you can tell the Ex is on by the increase in bus and streetcar service. (It's the best time all year to wait for the TTC, as there's always a vehicle in sight.) The first time I went, in 2005, I was surprised to find out that the CNE is a lot of fun. For the past twenty years, people have questioned the value of its continued existence as anything more than an antiquated curiosity. The Ex is irrelevant, little more than a stop on the Conklin carnival circuit, they say. While it's true that the midway, with its requisite toothless carnies and creaky old Zipper and Polar Express rides, is the flashy focus for a lot of people, I've yet to attend any event in the city that slams together so many disparate elements into one sweaty, loud, kitschy package.

The other way to get onto the grounds is through the Dufferin Gates. They may be less grand, but I think they're more interesting, and they're the way I made my way into the Ex one year. The city and the fair almost touch here, and the gates signal an abrupt shift from normalcy to festival. Unlike most places along the waterfront, the Gardiner and railroad tracks are hardly noticeable, sunken below grade in a trench.

Once inside, the farm smell from the Ken Jen Animal Stars and Petting Zoo was strangely inviting, in the way gasoline sort of smells good. Every day during the fair, some of the most formidable ducks, donkeys, goats and pot-bellied pigs you'll ever see endure twelve hours of heavy petting from some very enthusiastic kids.

Over at the Farm, Food and Fun pavilion there was less fun frottage and more reality. The Pig Mobile charted the life of the average Ontario pig from start to almost-finish. (Even meat eaters don't want to see the last step.) In some of the most honest market-ing I've ever seen, the big banner above said, 'Ontario Pork: From Farm to Fork.' There were other signs around that read, 'If you ate today, thank a farmer,' along with nice

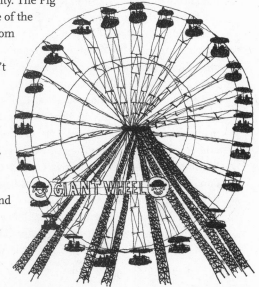

pictures of the kings and queens from various county fairs. The Ontario hinterland comes to Toronto during the Ex, providing a connection to the rest of the province that goes unheralded. Visitors to this booth were also faced with aggressive signs that said, 'Farmers Feed Cities.' Well, no guff. Imagine if Toronto did the same and sent out ambassadors to those county fairs with signs that say, 'If you enjoyed the economy today, thank Toronto.'

The strangest place at the CNE is the massive trade show. It's part flea market, part international bazaar, part Dufferin Mall. Every booth is like a live infomercial, with a guy in a golf shirt giving his sales pitch. It's an intimate version of capitalism that's both swashbuckling and desperate. At one of a dozen or so hot-tub displays I visited, I stared at a tub that had four built-in speakers and a plasma TV. 'This is the premier tub in North America,' I was told. I asked if it had a sub-woofer. 'Two hundred watts,' answered the salesman. 'You can really feel the bass in the water.'

In the early part of the century, the CNE constructed its beaux-arts buildings in the tradition of the 1893 Chicago World Fair, which started the City Beautiful movement. The structures had official-sounding names like the Ontario Government Building (now known as the Liberty Grand event hall) and the Arts, Crafts and Hobbies Building (now Medieval Times). Toronto architect Alfred H. Chapman built the Princes' Gates in 1927. They're made up of eighteen columns, each set of nine representing the nine provinces of the day. The gates were supposed to be called the Diamond Jubilee of Confederation Gate, in commemoration of Canada's sixtieth birthday, but they were instead named after Edward, Prince of Wales, and his brother, Prince George, who were good enough to pay it a visit when they were in town. Though grander than the Dufferin Gates, the Princes' Gates

The Princes' Gates give a beaux-arts welcome to CNE visitors.

seem almost forgotten – entering from this side, it's a bit of a walk before the excitement starts – and now seem more a landmark for motorists into and out of the city.

After the Second World War, a new generation of optimistic buildings were constructed here, this time in the atomic style of the day. We still have wonderful structures like the Better Living Centre, complete with its multicoloured Piet Mondrian/De Stijl–inspired ornament, as well as the Queen Elizabeth and Food buildings nearby. The displays inside don't live up to their grandiose names, though. There's a casino inside the Better Living Centre (strangely, the quietest part of the grounds), and the build-ing has housed events during the Ex as varied as an extreme-sports exhibition adjacent to a bunch of vendors selling tube socks. I don't think this is the kind of better living the builders had in mind, though the occasional rave parties that happened here in the 1990s and early 2000s may be closer to that mark.

The greatest blow to this optimistic age was the 1985 destruc-tion of the Bulova Clock Tower (originally known as the Shell Oil Tower), which was the first example of a welded steel and glass structure in the city when it was built in 1955. The clock tower was destroyed because it stood in the way of the Molson Indy. In fact,

Molson paid the $150,000 demolition costs. Many didn't see any architectural value in the structure, including then mayor Art Eggleton, who told the *Toronto Star*, 'I think the money could be better spent on the other fine old buildings on the site.' Though Eggleton now speeds toward the dustbin of history, we're still without our tower and stuck with the Molson (now Honda) Indy. It's because of the Indy, and its need for empty space for grandstands, that there is so much empty, treeless, underused space at the CNE.

Rising above acres of paved and barren CNE parking lot is BMO Field, the new soccer stadium where the quickly beloved Toronto FC play. Its construction was certainly a good thing – the sounds that come from the open-air stands full of supporters are dramatic – but the new stadium resulted in the demolition of the Canadian Sports Hall of Fame, another handsome, mid-century building that even had heritage status. Too bad we couldn't have preserved a modern gem and put the stadium in one of the many other parking lots.

Near here, Exhibition Stadium used to fill up what is now a parking lot. For a time, just to the east of the Better Living Centre, a plaque in the ground showed the footprints of the old grandstands next to some old seats that were salvaged from the stadium, but they disappeared when BMO Field went up. In 1988, on our Grade 8 class trip to a Toronto Blue Jays game, the bus dropped my classmates and me off at this spot. We sat in the outfield bleachers, right behind George Bell playing in left field. The Jays lost that day, but I was in awe of it all. Others have memories of seeing Duran Duran or U2 at the Ex when they played in the huge bandshell-on-wheels that was moved into place for shows. This whole site is a landscape of our collective memories, the best days of all of our lives memorialized in a parking lot.

At the back of the Direct Energy Centre, the location of trade shows like the Royal Agricultural Winter Fair and the One of a Kind Show, there's a fairly big historical exhibit that's curated new every year. It's the smartest part of the CNE, and serves as its memory. One year, the theme of the exhibit was 'Boomers and the Ex: 1947–1980.' A car from the old Flyer roller coaster was set in front of an old CTV video projection of the ride. Just like being there. What these exhibits do well is show how much the Ex has

been a barometer of the times, and a part of Toronto's – and even
Canada's – cultural life over the years. The NORAD band even
played the fair in 1962.

The CNE should stick around because it's fun. What's disap-
pointing is some of the decay and those tube socks and hot tubs
and the vast underused space. The buildings were meant for better
things. Back in 1893, when the Chicago World Fair was winding
down, a writer from *Cosmopolitan* magazine envisioned what might
happen to those grand buildings: 'Better to have it vanish suddenly,
in a blaze of glory, than fall into gradual disrepair and dilapidation.
There is no more melancholy spectacle than a festival hall, the
morning after the banquet, when the guests have departed and the
lights are extinguished.'

I felt that melancholy in full one quiet night when a friend
and I were wandering around the empty grounds after the CNE
was over. Channelling Ninjalicious, a.k.a. Jeff Chapman, the urban
explorer and founder of the *Infiltration* zine who passed away in
2005, we climbed up the back of the Music Building, one of the
few older structures that sport a glass dome. We sat on the roof for
a while, looking at the city rise above the empty land, listening to
the hum of the Gardiner. I'm not ready for a blaze of glory here,
but if we could come up with a way to make the CNE a 'place' all
year round, I think Toronto would be better off.

From the Music Building, wander back out the Dufferin Gates –
there used to be a sign here that said 'Welcome to Parkdale' – and
follow Springhurst Road west as it runs just north of the railway
corridor. The city feels artificially cut off here, so dense and then so
empty. Springhurst eventually curves north and meets King Street,
which itself soon skirts the top of the railway, above the corporate
topiary ads spread out on the embankment that drivers and train
passengers see when entering the city. King ends at the end of
Toronto where there is, fittingly due to their ubiquity across the
city, a Coffee Time. This corner of Parkdale, where Queen, King,
Roncesvalles and the Queensway terminate in an impossible urban
tangle of streetcar tracks and wires, is the most dramatic end of
Toronto. Somewhere up in Vaughan, Aurora or Newmarket the
city starts to come together, rolling south, getting thicker and less
suburban, acquiring subways, streetcars, more people and then,
suddenly, nothing. A freeway followed by Lake Ontario wilderness.

This is a good place for the Katyn Memorial, a monolithic slab of steel cracked in half that's just east of this intersection, on King. The memorial was built 'in rememberance of 15,000 Polish prisoners of war who vanished in 1940 from camps in USSR ...' Over 4,000 were later discovered in mass graves at Katyn, murdered by the Soviet State Security police. This very Polish part of town is home to another memorial a few blocks up Roncesvalles, where a statue of Pope John II looks down on the eastern sidewalk.

Parkdale wasn't always estranged from its lake. However, the construction of the Gardiner resulted in the destruction of 170 homes near the lake, where most of Parkdale's north-south streets ended as wharves. Parkdale was once posh and mansion-filled, and many streets are slowly poshing up again as a result of gentrification.

The Palais Royale sits across the tracks and the freeway, a seemingly lonely lakefront outpost despite being only a two-and-a-half-minute walk from two major streetcar lines and the Roncesvalles pedestrian bridge. Built in 1889, the Palais Royale was originally home to Dean's Sunnyside Pleasure Boats, and the original frames for the boat doors are still visible in the Royale's basement. It was converted into a dance hall in 1922 and drew all the usual big-band names, including Tommy Dorsey, Duke Ellington and Count. In a 1988 *Toronto Star* article on the building, Basil Dolan recalled that 'there were [once] so many people here that you weren't allowed to break into jive. You had to stay close or the bouncers would come over and warn you. "No breaking or you're out."'

After big bands fell out of style, the Palais went downhill, host only to occasional shows like the 'secret' Rolling Stones gig in 2002, for which a temporary air conditioner was installed onstage to keep the millionaires from overheating. In 2006, the Palais underwent a $3-million renovation and reopened with regular live-music bookings and a huge lakeside patio. The renovation also busted one of Toronto's long-held myths: the legendary sprung dance floor wasn't sprung at all, it just had a little give to it. No matter, legends aren't always built on the truth, and it's good to have the Palais Royale back.

West of the Palais, there's another legendary Toronto spot. On hot summer days from the 1890s until August 1950, streetcars would rumble along Toronto streets, stopping for children in bathing suits carrying towels. They could climb aboard for a free ride to the intersection of Queen, King and Roncesvalles, where the car would turn south, pass over the railway tracks and head west down a gentle slope. The destination was not the middle of the Gardiner Expressway, as it would be today, but the Sunnyside Beach area. Toronto provided this free 'bathing car' service to children in order to bring them to Sunnyside – or to three free 'bathing ferries' to the Islands – so they could cool down in Lake Ontario. An added bonus: the land adjacent to the beach was home to an amusement park.

To feel truly isolated from the city today, sit on one of the benches in front of the Sunnyside Bathing Pavilion and look directly north. It's like being inside a primitive 1980s video game: two lanes of cyclists, eight lanes of Lake Shore Boulevard, six lanes of the Gardiner Expressway, and, finally, the railway tracks. This is a more formidable barrier than the alligators and floating logs players dodged in *Frogger*. It's not such a far-fetched idea that there could be floating logs here, actually, since the area up to the railway was once all lake. In the early twentieth century, the Toronto Harbour Commission started the Sunnyside Reclamation Project, which extended the shoreline with topsoil that was shaved off a ninety-six-acre Pickering farm through which Highway 401 now runs. By 1922, nearly 197 acres had been reclaimed from the lake between the Humber River and Bathurst Street.

Cut off from the city it still serves, Sunnyside has become a sort of gateway landmark that commuters note peripherally on their way into the city. Sitting on that bench out front, High Park (to the north) and Parkdale (to the east) seem much further away than they actually are. Yet despite being nearly paved over by modernity and progress, Sunnyside is alive and still a part of everyday Toronto, especially in the summer.

When you stumble upon relics like this one in other cities, they often have a melancholy feel of faded glory, as nothing seems more faded than festive architecture. The bathing pavilion was designed as a Roman bath by Alfred H. Chapman, the architect who designed the Princes' Gates. The Sunnyside Bathing Pavilion must certainly have stirred up exotic thoughts in staid and provincial Toronto the Good when it opened in 1922. While it was under construction in 1921, an article in the *Globe* suggested the new building would 'look like a compromise between a pseudo-classical villa that should be perched on the steep slopes of some hill looking over olive gardens to the blue waters of the Mediterranean, and a casino at some ultra-sophisticated watering place, through the doors of which should stroll a smartly dressed throng of smart women and blasé men bent on a little turn at the tables.'

As immodest as Toronto the Good could get at Sunnyside in the 1920s.

Archival photos suggest reality was often a little more down-to-earth and fun: they show huge crowds of people in itchy- and hot-looking bathing suits packing the beach around the pavilion. The photos of the beach here are always jam-packed with people until about the early 1970s, by which point pool culture and the Gardiner (the Sunnyside-area stretch was completed in 1958) had sucked the life away from this most magical of public spaces.

The nearby Sunnyside Amusement Park entertained visitors from 1922 to 1955, when it was demolished to make room for the Gardiner Expressway. At the time of the demolition, Metropolitan Toronto Chairman Frederick 'Big Daddy' Gardiner (for whom the highway was named) said, 'We can't have this honky-tonk at the main entrance to the city on both sides of the main expressway.' But Sunnyside is interesting precisely because it exists somewhere between those high-class Mediterranean looks and a honky-tonk sensibility. During the Depression, Sunnyside was known as the 'poor man's Riviera' – it had been built in a manner that suggested even the common man or woman deserved to feel glamorous. It's fitting that the first Miss Toronto contest was held here in 1926.

After falling into disrepair and having been threatened with demolition in the 1970s, the Sunnyside Bathing Pavilion was designated a historical site in 1975. The city renovated it in 1980, and when you stand in front of it today, it's easy to conjure up the pavilion's old sense of grandeur. Staircases sweep upstairs to the open-air dance floors, where wedding photo shoots and occasional summer electronic-music parties have replaced the big-band swing that you can almost hear echoing up in the rafters, where these imaginary sounds compete with the constant hum of the traffic nearby.

Wandering inside and out on quiet summer days, you get a sense of the people who have passed through this place. What if their ghosts returned to walk the courtyard and dance floor? It's likely they wouldn't notice much change, as the essence of Sunnyside remains, all these decades beyond their heyday. If they went down the front steps, the shock of Lake Shore Boulevard and the Gardiner would probably rattle them – who knew the automobile would go on to change the landscape quite so much? – and the skyscrapers to the east and west along Lake Ontario might seem like a World's Fair dream.

Still, the interior courtyard continues to feel 'exotic,' even if some of the decorative fountains have been filled with cement. Originally, both sides of the pavilion were open-air changing areas for men and women, with 7,700 lockers. Today only the east side serves this purpose – and does double-duty for both sexes – for the massive Gus Ryder outdoor pool next door. Added in 1925, the pool was built to attract more paying customers and people who felt the water in Lake Ontario was slightly too cold for comfort. The concrete breakwalls built off-shore were also an effort to keep the water warmer for swimmers. Though good for rowers and dragon-boat enthusiasts, they have the unintended consequence of reducing the circulation in the water, leaving it murky and stale.

Toronto has swimmable and even clean beaches, but Sunnyside isn't one of them. Nobody swims here except the swans, who watch, with their patrician aloofness, the beach-volleyball players on the sand. In the café and on the lively patio, Toronto's citizens – now more multicultural – still mix, though some details at Sunnyside aren't quite right. The café uses too-cheap plastic garden chairs, tacky catering equipment is stored in various corners, and the iron railing that runs around the building is flimsy. But the thing about a honky-tonk is it's a wonderful spectacle and great fun that doesn't discriminate. And despite Big Daddy Gardiner's opinion, all the varied activity around Sunnyside is good and should be encouraged. Sunnyside puts on some strong regal airs, but it's not a relic. If our ghostly visitors from the past had some time to spare, they might change into shorts and T-shirts, spike a few volleyballs and then order a pitcher of beer.

If you walk west from sunnyside, you'll come upon Sir Casimir Gzowski Park, complete with its modish memorial. The park is named after the engineer who served as acting lieutenant govenor of Ontario from 1896 to 1897, and who worked on some of the province's most notable pieces of infrastructure, including the Grand Trunk Railway and the Welland Canal. (He is also the great-grandfather of late cbc broadcaster Peter Gzowski.) Near the memorial, there's also a concrete lion that used to sit in the middle of the qew before the Gardiner was built, back when highways were called parkways and bits of the City Beautiful movement made their way into their design. This end of the old City of Toronto's western waterfront also doesn't have an official end, though the white bike-and-pedestrian arch bridge that crosses the Humber River into Etobicoke has become a major landmark since it was installed in 1994. It's adjacent to the twin Palace Pier towers that for many mark the entrance and exit points to the city (with apologies to the rest of Etobicoke). When the first of the two towers was built in 1979, it had, true to the spirit of the day, a discotheque in the penthouse. (Today it's merely called a 'party room.') The decision to put a disco here is not without historical precedent; the towers are named after another lost landmark, the original, and actual, Palace Pier, which jutted out 300 feet into Lake Ontario and included a dance hall that was also popular during the big-band era. The pier was destroyed by a fire in 1963, ending Toronto's version of amusement piers, which were once a feature in many waterfront cities. A monument at the site, just past the bridge, contains one of the original concrete pier footings. Beyond, there's more parkland along the Etobicoke shore, and a new lakefront high-rise community that has made the Palace Pier less lonely without diminishing its landmark status.

Bathurst Street

 day trip

 dress to impress

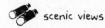 scenic views

Connecting walks: Harbourfront, Dundas, Dupont, St. Clair, Eglinton, Sheppard, CNE/Western Waterfront.

At first glance, Bathurst is not a pretty street. You don't see it on tourist postcards, and when people think 'Toronto,' it likely isn't the first corridor that comes to mind. But it's a street that means a great deal to the city. It's the line the Jewish community has roughly followed as it migrated from downtown to the suburbs, just as other ethnic groups followed other streets from the traditional inner city 'heart' to the open spaces and bigger houses outside the city limits. Bathurst is a long road that extends north into rural areas, but its urban delights are often subtle and easy to overlook when you're not on foot.

Today, Bathurst begins at the Toronto Island Airport dock. Though Mayor David Miller swept into power in 2003 on a pledge to stop a bridge to the airport, the great unmentionable secret among the downtown chattering classes is that the Island Airport stopped being a political issue shortly afterwards. Porter Airlines started up once the taxpayer-funded bridge was killed, and the company seems to have won over the guilt-ridden hearts of many Torontonians who were previously against it. Whispers of admiration for an airport and airline experience without the usual indignities are overheard in cafés, on blogs and in Facebook and Twitter updates. Though there still may be no love for the Toronto Port Authority, the rogue agency in charge of the airport that we love to hate, Porter has quietly become just another part of the city. A new terminal has been constructed for the airline, but the original airport building can be seen just beyond the ferry terminal – it has a design similar to the first Pearson Airport building, back when that international landing strip was still known as Malton Airport.

Down here at the foot of Bathurst, this is all new land, part of Toronto's massive and long-running effort to extend its waterfront southwards. At the water's edge, hundreds of metres south of the original shoreline, the passage between the mainland and the Island is often rough and choppy. The airport ferry, especially in winter, has a maritime-workhorse air to it, fighting a constant battle against the elements, even if the crossing takes just two minutes. Looking backwards, it's nearly impossible to see the original shoreline: Toronto came a long, long way, and stopped in a very straight line.

However, to avoid politics, let's pretend Bathurst appears out of the Lake Ontario fog down by Little Norway Park on Queens Quay West. The exiled Norwegian Air Force had a base here during the Second World War, but only the white flagpole at the southwest corner of Queens Quay and Bathurst Street remains today. A few very wordy plaques commemorate the occasion; in fact, half of one plaque is dedicated to explaining that there is another plaque nearby with more information. Maybe the plaque editors were on strike in 1987 when His Majesty King Olav V was in town for the dedication. After the Norwegians left, and until 1967, this was also the site of Maple Leaf Stadium, home of the Toronto Maple Leafs baseball team that now plays at Christie Pits Park.

These days, Little Norway Park is like a museum to various kinds of playground equipment, some of it unlike anything found in other parks. There's a wire mesh 'ship' that's built into the side of a small hill, complete with what looks like a twisting cement slide. How you're supposed to slide down it is unclear. Bums won't work on the gritty material, the curves are too tight for skateboards and inline skates weren't yet invented when it was built. If it was just put in for whimsy's sake, Toronto must have been doing all right in the mid-1980s. There's also a large maze for

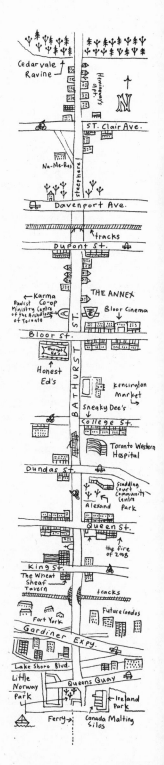

toddlers that dates to about the same time, as well as a newer addition: a slide that's constructed into the head of a giant concrete lion. Nearby, there's a promenade that extends along the western passage and offers scenic views of the Porter Airline buildings.

Turn to face north and you'll see a condo building on the opposite side of Queens Quay. This building is remarkable in that something so big comes right down and meets the sidewalk at a scale that isn't overwhelming. Waterfront condos get a bad rap – and some are indeed atrocious – but at this end of Queens Quay, many of the buildings are quite urbane. Walk a hundred or so metres north on Bathurst and the half-kilometre-long crossing of Toronto's most intense transportation corridor begins. First up is Lake Shore Boulevard, with its wide, two-stage crossing on which the usual rules of traffic don't seem to apply, as cars come from many directions, obeying traffic signals not visible from sidewalk level. It isn't a fun crossing on foot, and the cozy urban feeling of Queens Quay quickly evaporates.

On the northwest corner of Bathurst at Fleet Street, you'll see two giant toy soldiers, public art created by Canadian author and designer Douglas Coupland. They're cheeky and potentially inflammatory to tourists from Buffalo, as the British soldier is standing, while the American is lying down, defeated. The outcome of the War of 1812 is always a point of debate, but here on a Toronto corner it's been decided in high relief.

Look west on Lake Shore and you'll see the beginning of a relatively new condo corridor that's turning the area around Fort York into one of Toronto's newest neighbourhoods. Though controversial when they first started sprouting up – many thought the towers were going to ruin the historic surroundings of the Fort – they've breathed new life into the National Historic Site by turning it into the green heart of the new community. One of the new condos, the Malibu, is part of a somewhat unfortunate Toronto tradition of giving buildings names that have nothing to do with the place they're in. Toronto's original downtown residential tower cluster, St. James Town (on Parliament Street north of Wellesley Street), did the opposite, with buildings named the Halifax, the Winnipeg and even the Toronto, evoking a connection to the rest of Canada in a city whose residents come from across the country. I wonder on how many occasions people moved to Toronto only to end up in a building named after their former home. Still, the

Malibu, named after a California beach town, has roots that are tangled in old Toronto: when excavating the foundation, crews found the logs from the Queen's Wharf, which had been buried by fill at the turn of the century, when the shoreline started crawling south from its original position just south of the Fort.

The original, much shorter version of Bathurst Street began near here and was named after Henry Bathurst, 3rd Earl Bathurst and secretary of war for the colonies. Though he never had the courtesy to visit Canada, he's the guy who granted the University of Toronto (then King's College) its charter while waging distant wars from the Home Office. North of Queen Street, Bathurst was known as Crookshank's Lane until 1870, when it too became Bathurst as the city grew up and around it. The first bit of old Bathurst we can still see is the bridge that runs alongside Fort York.

Though the city's identity doesn't embrace them, Toronto is a city of bridges. Some cities, like San Francisco and Vancouver, are known for their iconic bridges, but our only famous bridge is the Prince Edward Viaduct – the one Michael Ondaatje wrote into our collective consciousness in his novel *In the Skin of a Lion* – which leaps across the Don Valley, affording magnificent views few cities can match, whether you're on it or looking up at it. We think of our other workaday bridges only when they're being repaired and aren't available when we need them, or when some cataclysmic bridge collapse occurs in another city and we cast a wary eye toward the cracks in the concrete holding up the Gardiner. All around Toronto, there are unsung bridges that cross the city's ravines and, while perhaps quotidian on top, they're often works of engineering beauty when seen from below.

The Bathurst Street Bridge, one of the city's oldest, is one we never worry about letting us down. Its 680 tonnes of solid steel and concrete are not hidden behind euphemistic or sexy architectural forms more pleasing to those with delicate sensibilities. So much visible structural metal seems too industrial and almost obscene, but this is what old Toronto the Good looked like. To David Spittal, an archaeologist with the City of Toronto, the bridge is a sort of living museum: 'There used to be dozens of these old truss bridges around town, down along Spadina and other places,' he says. 'But fewer and fewer remain. It's part of our cultural landscape, like overhead wires and wooden poles. People want to bury them, but that alters the historic look. It's a conundrum – we want

The Bathurst Bridge in 1917 (top) and in 1931.

to improve the city, but we want to preserve things, too.'

The Bathurst Street Bridge is about as solid as anything in Toronto gets. Take a walk along it and hold on to the handrail as a streetcar crosses the bridge. This is what Toronto feels like when streetcars roll over its civic body: your hands vibrate from a direct connection to those heavy steel wheels. When large trucks go by, the bridge gently bounces and sways, making it seem awake, responsive, alive. Built in 1903, the bridge originally crossed the Humber River, where Lake Shore Boulevard is now. In 1916, the trusses were taken down and reassembled in an expanded fashion at the Bathurst location to replace an earlier truss bridge that dated to the 1860s.

In 1931, the bridge was realigned twenty-two degrees to allow Bathurst a straight slope down to the lake. In 1985, it was designated a historic structure, worthy of preservation. Though it is structurally sound, the bridge suffers from a lack of maintenance; up close, you can see that the metal is rusty and the paint is flaking off in places. The iron handrail is ornate and as solid as the rest of the bridge, but children would be wise not to run their hands along it lest they embed chunks of old Toronto in their soft palms. Stand under the bridge and you'll realize that what's underneath is as important as what's on top: this bridge, which was designed to get us over the railway land, is the best place to see that Toronto is still very much a rail town. The main span of the truss floats over ten sets of tracks that make up a disconcertingly empty view as you look east towards downtown.

From here, you really get a sense of how much land the railroad takes up; suddenly the Gardiner seems like a patsy, not the barrier to the waterfront it's made out to be. The Bathurst Street Bridge continues south beyond the truss section as a standard-issue, steel-plate-and-concrete structure that dates to 1930. A smaller pedestrian bridge connects the sidewalk to the west gate of Fort York. This was once the main entrance to Toronto's birthplace, but it has been rendered a mere backdoor entrance by modern development.

At Fort York Boulevard, a ramp takes you to the base of the fort walls. The walk down to the fort lands gives a sense of the enormous earthworks that American soldiers so desperately wanted to scale during the War of 1812. Here there's access to the underbelly of the bridge, the part you're not supposed to see. The southern section of the bridge is cathedral-like below, with a series of concrete pillars holding up the roadway. Though the ground is littered with what one expects to find under an urban bridge – assorted garbage, the odd condom and dirty Y-front underpants – a mid-afternoon visit I once took there turned out to be a bucolic and nearly rural experience. A cooling wind blew through the pillars as the

The Bathurst Bridge today.

faint sound of the fifes and drums played by volunteer soldiers at the fort drifted underneath, making the perfect place for an illicit daytime nap had the ground been a little more gentrified. David Spittal pointed out that 'people have been living under there for generations, it's not a new phenomenon.' He recalled that during his university days, he saw folk singer Murray McLauchlan sing a song called 'Under the Bathurst Street Bridge.'

Though the land was deserted on this particular visit, there were signs of life everywhere. The pillars tell fragmented stories through the graffiti painted on them. 'Stop doing drugs.' 'Mensa almost died here.' 'Tri-force Sucks' and, most curiously, 'The best feeling is standing naked in the wind and trying to feel every cell in your body at once.' Stained clothing was strewn around an open suitcase that looked like it had been left there only hours ago. Nearby, an unused ticket to the Art Gallery of Ontario and a Centre for Addiction and Mental Health appointment reminder lay on the ground surrounded by dozens of business cards from outreach workers, lawyers and plumbing and drainage contractors. This area has much to reveal, and these recent visitors from the transient fringe of society are just one layer of many that extend back through railroad, colonial and First Nations history. Spittal considers it one of the most dangerous sites he has ever seen a dig take place, as it's also the site of the original mouth of Garrison Creek, which still runs underground. 'As soon as you dig a hole,' he said, 'it fills with water.'

From the mouth of the original creek, by the concrete pillars that hold up Bathurst Street, walk west along the south side of Fort York's ramparts and the Gardiner Expressway. From here, eyes wide shut, it's easy to imagine Lake Ontario only a few metres away. The hum of the Gardiner even sounds like the surf. But open your eyes and the freeway looms on its concrete columns, and you must look between condominiums to catch a glimpse of the distant water.

On the north side of the fort you see hints of why we have Toronto terra firma where the shoreline once was. Nearly a dozen rail lines cross Toronto here; one branch heads along the lake towards Hamilton, the other curves northwest towards Weston and Georgetown. The latter follows part of the route of the historic Grand Trunk Railway, Toronto's first railway and a piece of infrastructure responsible for much of the city's early development.

The name Grand Trunk still sounds expansive; it is a reminder that after the War of 1812 it was railways, not armies, that started to decide Toronto's future. The Grand Trunk grew, as planned, into a main trunk line – becoming, for a time, the world's largest railway system – and finally morphed into CN. But when it was first built, the Grand Trunk didn't even cross what is now downtown Toronto. It swung down toward the lake from the northwest and stopped at a terminal on the south side of Fort York. Evidence of the railway remains in impressive earthworks that are visible between the fort and Strachan Avenue. In the shadow of the Gardiner nearby, there's an old trench that stretches west to Strachan, where it curves north and now disappears, with few traces, under modern Liberty Village.

The Grand Trunk was originally chartered under the name Toronto & Guelph Railroad Company, and became part of plans for a railway between Toronto and Montreal and southwestern Ontario. Between 1853 and 1856, lines were built in two sections: Toronto to Montreal and Toronto to Sarnia. Engineer Casimir Gzowski was the contractor who worked on the western section, and the lakeside park west of Sunnyside bears his name. The large terminal yard for the Sarnia line was constructed in front of Fort York on eight hectares, about half of which was landfill, thus beginning the shoreline's slow move south to its current point across from the Toronto Island Airport.

More than anything else, the railways were responsible for the extension of Toronto's waterfront, because the rail companies had the political and financial muscle to get what they wanted. (The term 'to railroad' means what it does for a reason.) There was a gap between the Sarnia and Montreal sections of the GTR for only a short time before the railway bullied Toronto city council into letting it lay tracks across the front of the city along the newly created Esplanade, a development that marked the beginning of the city's estranged relationship with its waterfront. In the late 1850s, the view from the fort's bastions was still of the lake, but also of a busy Victorian industrial scene.

The Fort York yard was formed when workers dumped fill behind a line of sixty-two massive timber 'cribs,' which were then filled with dirt also from Garrison Common, a vast tract of land that included what is now Exhibition Place and the residential neighbourhoods to the north of the fort, and from the GTR itself. Archeological issues were not considered then, so Grand Trunk was able to carve the railway's trench through the heart of the 1813 battlefield. That's the equivalent of paving the Plains of Abraham in Quebec City or Gettysburg in Pennsylvania, and it's probable that the fill still contains cannonballs, artifacts and even human remains. The site is so historically important that the City of Toronto began a campaign in 2009 to have Fort York recognized as a UNESCO World Heritage Site, a process that's likely to take years. As for the railway itself, we tend to either take it for granted or else complain that the tracks cut the rest of the city off from the lake. According to David Monaghan, curator of the House of Commons and former curator of the land transportation collections at the National Museum of Science and Technology, 'One of the great tragedies of Canadian industrial and transportation history is that so little remains of the original infrastructure that played a critical role in the development of the first railway networks in Canada.'

With this sentiment in mind, that lonely trench under the Gardiner suddenly echoes loud with meaning, as it was one of the reasons Toronto grew as a city. The Grand Trunk connected Toronto to Sarnia, where a ferry (enhanced in 1891 by a rail tunnel) crossed the St. Clair River to Port Huron, Michigan, allowing cargo to connect by rail to Chicago, a big market for Toronto's industrial might. Though there is a huge rail enthusiast community (just

Google anything railroad and see for yourself), the heritage here has not yet been interpreted for the public on-site.

North over the bridge and a block east of Bathurst sits Victoria Square. Though it looks like a pleasant grassy square, as unassuming as the ground under the bridge, it's Toronto's first military cemetery, holding nearly 400 graves of people connected to Fort York who died between 1793 and 1863. Designated a National Historic Site in 2003, it's one of the few sites outside of the fort that maintains a connection to the War of 1812. That history isn't buried very deep either – in the 1930s, while installing a wading pool in the square, city workers horrified onlookers when they accidentally unearthed human remains.

Bathurst continues north as a mostly residential street, albeit a busy one. There are a few stores and restaurants along the way, as well as landmarks like the Oak Leaf steam baths and the massive Toronto Western Hospital, but it is mainly lined with a jumble of houses, from high Victorian homes to worker's cottages. North of Dundas Street, Bathurst meets Nassau Street at Kensington Market's ugly back door. Stand here and imagine Toronto's Jewish population pouring out of their traditional neighbourhood and heading north.

In the 1920s and '30s, Kensington was known as the Jewish Market, and some 60,000 Jews lived in and around the area, worshipping at over thirty nearby synagogues. After the Second World War, people wanted their own versions of the Canadian Dream: more space and a better life. In turn, Bathurst became an extremely long ethnic strip, as the Jewish community moved up along it towards Thornhill.

Bathurst remains remarkably uneventful up to Dupont. Except for places like a Beer Store, Reg Hartt's strange Cineforum private screening theatre and a small retail strip south of Dupont, Bathurst is a private kind of street whose address doesn't come up much as a destination even though it's a road often travelled. It can be hard to live on a busy route like this. The little front yards tend to be treeless and paved, and this stretch has a batten-down-the-hatches look, as if it's taking the hit of pollution, traffic noise and graffiti taggers so the leafy streets to the east and west can keep real estate agents salivating. Even grand Central Tech High School, located a block and a half south of Bloor Street, lines

Bathurst with an seemingly endless chain-link fence along its playing field. A low hedge and a few trees could transform this stretch
from its current prison-yard-like self into something more akin to
U of T's serene Philosopher's Walk.

Under the tracks north of Dupont, Bathurst softens into a
more genteel, quieter and leafier kind of urbanism. The white
building at the northwest corner of Davenport Road and Bathurst
is the Tollkeeper's Cottage. Recently used as part of a nearby residence, it was returned to near its original location by the Community History Project, a volunteer group that has been restoring the
circa-1835 building. Now a museum, the cottage is a reminder that
Davenport is Ontario's oldest road, originally a trail that ran along
the shore of ancient Lake Iroquois and was used long before European settlers arrived and gave it its current name.

Past the top of the Davenport hill, Vaughan Road splits off
from Bathurst, heading diagonally to the northwest. The wonderful – and rare – V-shaped intersection could be home to a stunning flatiron-type building, but instead an atrocious thirty-storey,
poo-brown building with triangular balconies rises out of a giant
cement toilet bowl of a base. High-rise haters have nightmares
about this exact building multiplying and destroying the Annex
like an army of architectural Godzillas. With a little work, though,
this boring pedestal could be fixed up and become a people place.
The brown colour could even remain. For a visual pick-me-up,
look across Bathurst and you'll see the lovely Wychwood branch
of the Toronto Public Library – possibly the city's cutest branch –
which was built with a Carnegie grant in 1916.

Bathurst enters its golden stretch north of St. Clair, where
it's lined with a few blocks of walk-up apartments and beautiful
modernist high-rises. Just before Bathurst flies over Cedarvale
Ravine, it's home to 1599, the building where Ernest Hemingway
lived for a few years in the early 1920s writing for the *Toronto
Daily Star*. In the *National Post* in 2003, Robert Fulford explained
that Hemingway originally 'came to Toronto as the male version
of a governess, hired to babysit a young fellow whose rich parents
believed he needed a masculine role model.' The Connable family
lived a few blocks southwest of St. Clair and Bathurst. Their son
Ralph walked with a limp and they hired Hemingway, says
Fulford, to give their son 'the right slant on life, especially as

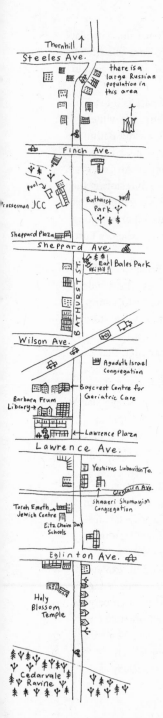

to his sports pleasures.' He goes on to explain that Hemingway's mentor, Ezra Pound, held a certain disdain for Toronto, and addressed his letters to Hemingway 'Tomato, Can,' while Wyndham Lewis suggested he was toiling away in a 'sanctimonious icebox' of a city. Hemingway shared his own view of Toronto in verse he penned for the *Star*: 'I like Canadians: They let women stand up in the street cars / Even if they are good-looking. They are all in a hurry to get home to supper / And their radio sets.'

Just past Papa Hemingway's place, the Holy Blossom and Beth Tzedec temples, two massive synagogues built in 1938 and 1950 respectively, are the first major indications of Jewish life on this street. This stretch also marks the beginning of a nearly continuous string of large cardboard signs for 'Operation Security Blanket' and 'Project Northern Recovery' – campaigns to raise money for Israel. It's one of the few places in Toronto where there are visible connections to world events, daily reminders of war and terror.

At Shallmar Boulevard, a few blocks north of Eglinton, there's a collection of brilliantly white buildings fronted by huge Caesars Palace–style fountains. They all hold many stories. In one of these buildings lives Sidney Raykoff, whose family owned Raykoff Hardware in Kensington Market (where European Meats is now) until the 1950s. Raykoff remembers neighbourhood boys Joseph Berman (his family owned a chicken store down the street at Augusta) and Eph Diamond joining the navy during the war and 'every night getting the hell kicked out of them as they were the only Jews on their ship.' He also remembers them each borrowing $2,000

The house on Lyndhurst Avenue where Hemingway lived.

from their grandmothers after the war to build their first house, founding the Cadillac Fairview development empire and eventually erecting the building Raykoff lives in today. (Raykoff, too, is part of that Jewish migration up Bathurst.)

The area between Eglinton and St. Clair avenues was the site of a very public 1970s battle between the car lobby, who wanted to widen Bathurst, and those who supported more urban-friendly visions like the Stop the Spadina Expressway movement. An editorial in the *Star* from that year was firmly on the side of automotive progress: 'the city politicians are so blinded by their opposition to cars that they vote against virtually all road improvements ... City council may be comfortable with its narrow-minded view of the role of roads but Metro Council owes it to all Metro citizens to recognize that some road improvements are necessary to improve the efficiency of transit and preserve neighbourhoods.' Over thirty years later, the arguments sound very much the same, and the hyperbole is just as intense.

North of Glencairn, the signs of Jewish migration, and the references to Kensington Market, increase. In Lawrence Plaza, which Queen Elizabeth II visited in the 1950s, lives United Bakers Dairy Restaurant. A Toronto institution since 1912, it first opened at Bay and Dundas, then moved to 338 Spadina in 1920, where it stayed until it relocated to this plaza in the 1980s. Behind it is the Barbara Frum branch of the Toronto Public Library, named after the legendary Canadian broadcaster who lived nearby before she moved to to the York Mills and Bayview area with her husband, dentist-turned-developer Murray Frum.

The Baycrest Centre for Geriatric Care, a bit farther north on Bathurst, is a sort of bookend to Kensington in the south. Though it's true that there are thousands of Jews living in this area and well into Thornhill – the Holocaust memorial in Earl Bales Park at Sheppard West is a powerful spot – the sprawling collection of buildings that make up the Baycrest Centre is a storehouse of memories of Jewish life in Toronto like no other. Inside the heads of the residents here lives a library of memories that detail a lost Toronto. There's even a re-creation of an old-time Kensington peddler scene here, complete with chickens, produce and a sign that says 'all the bones you want for free.'

Established in the early twentieth century, Baycrest was originally located are at 29–31 Cecil Street, where it was then known as the Jewish Old Folks' Home. In the 1950s, the home purchased ten hectares of farmland north of Toronto, and Baycrest has been expanding there ever since. With halls full of contemporary and abstract art – even some Andy Warhol prints – it feels more like a big public gallery than old-age home. Hang out by the papier mâché peddler long enough and a resident is bound to tell you his or her Bathurst story, too.

North of Baycrest, the wonderfully named Neptune Drive winds through a treeless, 1960s apartment development along the south bank of the gas, steel and rubber river that is Highway 401. There are old bus shelters scattered throughout the area that still say 'North York Transportation Department.' There must not be enough revenue potential to convince the city to replace these relics, left over from North York, a city that technically no longer exists, with the new shelters that have space for ads. Throughout the city, just off the main drags, you can find bits and traces of pre-amalgamation Toronto. The details of what was, it seems, are difficult to completely erase.

From here, you can walk north up Bathurst under the sixteen lanes of the 401. It's a tight squeeze – the sidewalk is wedged between the 401's supporting wall and a little steel fence. Pedestrians almost have to rub up against people coming the other way. The underbelly of the 401 is like a cut tree with its growth rings exposed: you can see the original overpass, left over from when the

401 was the King's Highway and carried my mother and countless other Maritimers to Windsor during the 1960s, and the lanes that were added later, turning it into the bloated express-and-collector-lane beast it is today. This mythic Canadian highway can make a pedestrian feel very small.

Continue up Bathurst, past mini-malls and the 1960s apartment buildings on the west side of the street that overlook Earl Bales Park. This street would have done well with a subway, but instead the trains run a few kilometres west in the middle of low-density freeway corridor. Toronto's ravines are celebrated for giving the city deep fissures of mystery, but at Earl Bales Park, one ravine – part of the west Don Valley – is also home to the North York Ski Centre, complete with chairlift and rope tow. Though folks in the Rockies might scoff, it's an impressive slope in a city that's often thought of as flat. Earl Bales Park was previously the site of York Downs Golf and Country Club, and the ghost shapes of tees and greens can still be seen around the park. The snow machines here keep pumping as long as the cool weather will allow, and a strips of dirty glacial-like snow often last weeks into the warm almost-spring weather.

North of Sheppard Avenue, Bathurst thins out even more, crossing the west Don Valley before it enters Bathurst Park. At the bottom of the valley you'll find the Bathurst Jewish Community Centre, a sprawling complex that's partially on stilts over the flood plain. It meets Bathurst at grade with a rather impressive pedestrian entrance into the Holocaust Centre of Toronto, though few people other than transit riders likely ever use this entrance, as the main entrances are down in the valley near the parking lots.

Nearing Steeles, Bathurst exits Toronto's limits as it started, with a collection of residential apartment towers, including some remarkably modern white towers on Antibes Drive that rise high above the nearby bungalows. Once in Thornhill, residential subdivisions were allowed to 'turn their back' onto Bathurst, so the streetscape is a topology of backyard fences. It's no way to honour a street as important as Bathurst, but this treatment doesn't last long, and Bathurst is soon semi-rural, eventually meeting up with Yonge Street near the village of Holland Landing. Henry Bathurst, 3rd Earl Bathurst, ought to be pleased at how long the street he never knew grew.

Dupont Street

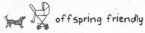 neighbourhood jaunt

dress to impress

offspring friendly

Connecting walks: Yorkville, Dundas, Bathurst, Spadina.

Dupont is the back street/alternate route of western downtown Toronto. For drivers, it's a shortcut across the city that avoids busier routes like Bloor and St. Clair. Cyclists and pedestrians trying to cross mid-block will tell you it's fast, maybe too fast. Like the servants' side of a British manor house, things get taken care of on Dupont: it's a working street that keeps the prettier parts of the city running. Though this has been its role for years, Dupont is changing, and its current look is a heterogeneous mix of styles and uses sometimes referred to as 'messy urbanism.'

My favourite approach to Dupont is to walk north on St. George and meet it at a rare-for-Toronto T intersection. There, the sign for People's Foods seems bigger than the diner itself. Next door, the giant Victorian pile that is the Pour House pub – almost-old-timers will remember it as the former home of the Red Raven – is a perfect example of a storefront extending out from an old house and meeting the street, residential transformed into commercial. Finding hints of the former 'houseness' inside buildings like this one provides some amateur archeological amusement.

Nearby, there's a giant LCBO liquor store (people from small, compact European countries will find it amazing and endless, or perhaps obscene), an interior-decorating store, the oft-recommended Nick's Shoe Repair shop, various dry cleaners and a suburban-style 'Tiger Convenience' Esso store whose design is so generic and inappropriate that its south-facing doors and windows are blocked by a fence along the sidewalk. This is about as mixed up as a Toronto street can be.

Dupont begins just east of here, at Avenue Road, in another T-intersection that faces the Hare Krishna Temple. The little sign for the temple always seems to stand out on the old stone building, but it's a high-traffic example of how old British Toronto adapts and accommodates the new. The temple has been a local landmark since the 1970s, in a very un-'70s building. Built in 1899 by Toronto firm

Gordon & Helliwell (builders of many a local church, such as the Anglican one across the street, as well as the West End YMCA), the building held a Presbyterian congregation until 1941, when it became the Avenue Road Church of the Nazarene, founded by famed Canadian evangelist/politician/broadcaster/cartoonist Charles Templeton. (Templeton later declared he was agnostic.) The Nazarene's congregation is now part of the evangelical Bayview Glenn Church in Thornhill. On summer days, you can hear the Krishna chants float out of the open windows here.

This first bit of Dupont west of Avenue, is a rather nice residential street that has evolved into a busy thoroughfare. A dip in the landscape marks where the now-buried Nordheimer reach of Castle Frank Brook once ran. A bit further west, downtown-bound cars heading east on Dupont whip around the corner where it meets Davenport; the streets don't meet at a right angle, and a few degrees can mean a lot to a car. It's one of those places where you can stand still and feel why big streets are called 'arteries.' This intersection collects traffic – both automobile- and human-powered – and feeds it into the city like an asphalt aorta. Trains moving along the CPR railway tracks just to the north seem almost airborne, and make the urban layers here seem almost like a movie set.

It's worth it to detour from Dupont and head up Davenport, past the tracks and, after a quick right, north on Poplar Plains. It's all uphill here as you climb the shores of ancient Lake Iroquois. At this point, Toronto's street grid gets wonderfully disorganized – analogous, in a way, to the twisting streets of the Hollywood Hills above L.A.'s street grid. Take another short detour up Glen Edyth Drive where there are fine views when the trees are bare of leaves. Glen Edyth climbs high rapidly, with only a steel crash barrier on one side keeping the Saabs and Audis from tumbling into the ravine below. Up at the top, you can see a cross-section of midtown Toronto – the Four Seasons Hotel, the Manulife Centre – all from a weird, unexpected angle and height. Directly below, trees and houses spread towards Avenue Road. During the day, when the area is deserted save for the few tradespeople working on lonely homes, you can feel like the only person in the city, which is laid out in front of you almost too perfectly, like a Currier & Ives lithograph. Nobody seems to live in these big houses – I never see the owners, that is – but they're always being fixed up.

Walk back down – Glen Edyth has no outlet at the top (but there really should be a pedestrian passage over to Casa Loma) – and around to Russell Hill Road. Here, there are modest mansions and immodest ones. I secretly covet the immodest ones because some of them are perched high above the road and have grand lawns that lend them a *Great Gatsby* look. (The electronic gates let me know I'm not invited.) 'The rich are different from you and me,' and all that, but living behind walls and gates has a perverse anti-urban desirability. To get back to Dupont, walk north to St. Clair, west to Spadina Road and then back south using the Baldwin Steps by Casa Loma. Once back down, you'll see the unique plexiglass entrances to Dupont subway station. If you'd rather not take the steps, you can simply backtrack to the LCBO block of Dupont.

The two Dupont subway station bubbles, located kitty-corner from each other, invite us into a subterranean 1970s fantasy land where there are no sharp edges and everything is rounded and soft. The station interior is the architectural manifestation of the tail-end of that laid-back decade. Opened in 1978, the orange interior includes a somewhat hippy-inspired lush and flowery tile mosaic by James Sutherland called *Spadina Summer Under All Seasons* that starts at track level and grows up into the mezzanine. Remarkably, the thousands of bits of glass that went into the mosaic are still intact. Dupont station is one of the last stations built into the urban fabric rather than on it: two buildings were removed for the bubbles and everything else was kept underground. Today, subway stations seem to require vast spaces and terminal-like surface buildings.

Beyond the station, Dupont turns into a heterogeneous, sometimes ugly, sometimes pretty street that runs parallel to the railway tracks all the way to the Junction. Much of the industry that once lined Dupont is gone, most of it from an era when a 'mixed-use neighbourhood' meant a factory could be next door to home. This is the Dupont that Alfred Holden so wonderfully evoked in his 1998 *Taddle Creek* magazine essay 'Dupont at Zenith,' in which he wrote 'Enterprises, as great as Eastern Airlines or as lowly as a corner store, will often die pathetically, with no ceremony or celebration of their achievements. Dupont Street in Toronto at the close of the twentieth century is an open graveyard of such industries, most of which collapsed without so much as a pauper's funeral. Their skeletons lie exposed. They are the parking lots, warehouse loft condos, and retail joints of the post-industrial age.' As though itemizing a hero's feats in an elegy, Holden goes on to list the industries that had left Dupont in the 1990s, after the Free Trade Agreement of 1988 sent manufacturing jobs out of the city en masse.

In the decade-plus after Holden wrote 'Dupont at Zenith,' Dupont has started to sprout again. It hasn't experienced the wholesale makeover that Queen Street West has; rather, it's as if the high-ended Yorkvilleness of Avenue and Davenport has seeped west and collected sporadically along Dupont. Little shops selling small, cute middle-class things dot the street now, sometimes sprouting up between lumberyards and luxury car dealerships. The lovely Faema Café at Dupont and Christie is just a couple blocks from a ramshackle store that sells industrial cleaning products and is known to more people than I ever expected. (A fire in 2009 here revealed that fact.)

The fancy and fey places become less frequent the further west you go, and the 1970s Quaalude bubble entrances of the Dupont subway station seem a distant memory. Brick homes give way to ones with cheaper siding as the Annex and Seaton Village neighbourhoods become places without such widely known names. Just east of Ossington, peek into auto-shop windows to see a Ferrari on the hoist and a showroom full of Lotuses (you can even buy an Aston Martin if you want), while further west there are little European shops where old vw beaters go for life support.

We celebrate innovation-incubating institutions like MaRS (College and University) and the Centre for Social Innovation (Spadina and Queen), but this part of Dupont is another kind of incubator for small businesses, a natural one that passes under the radar. Behind many of these old industrial facades – inside the old subdivided warehouses on Lansdowne Avenue and even in the hardscrabble Galleria Mall at the corner of Dufferin Street – there are start-ups that can't afford rents elsewhere in Toronto.

As the gentrifying flow from Ave & Dav moves west, this low-rent incubation will move on, as transient as it is necessary to the city. Even in the Junction, where Dupont ends in a complicated five-point intersection, much of this kind of space is now priced out of reach. Dupont remains a series of snapshots representing disparate views of Toronto, a sort of theme park of its various forms of cityness. Walks along Dupont don't feel like an isolated back route, but rather dense and almost humid, like being in the thick of where things happen.

Northish

Spadina

pack a lunch

dress to impress

scenic views

Connecting walks: CN Tower, Harbourfront, Dundas, Dupont, St. Clair.

Spadina is a strange word. Say it. *Spa-die-nah*. Now repeat it a few times. You'll soon wonder how we use it in conversation without pausing in curiosity. Yet we say 'Spadina' easily, and it means 'Toronto' just as much as the Ojibway word it's derived from, *Ishapadenah* (the word has various spellings), which means 'hill' or 'rise in the land.' To get a perfect view of the street, climb the Baldwin Steps at Davenport, stand next to Casa Loma and look south over Toronto and the southern, downhill length of Spadina (a 'road' at the north end and then, south of Bloor, an 'avenue') to its glittery, skyscraper end. It looks as if somebody cleared a wide swath of land through Toronto to make the street – the 'spine of Toronto' as the late writer Matt Cohen called it – and, in a way, that's true.

Spadina's girth is due to William Baldwin who, in 1818, cleared a royal-scaled driveway from the lake, through what was then a forest, to his 'Spadina House.' (The word is pronounced *Spa-dee-nah* in reference to this house on the hill, which is now a city-owned museum.) Baldwin's family got a clear view down to the lake, but the effort also gave the city a rare street that matches the proportions of today's Toronto.

Toronto was never supposed to be a metropolis, and its infra-structure is forever catching up. It's why we've got wooden hydro poles (which some of us think of as nice artifacts of our industrial past) and, less romantically, small sidewalks. Even Yonge Street – Toronto's main drag – can't match Spadina's wide sidewalks. Strolling on Spadina's broad concrete walks is like being in another city, because sidewalks, and their comparative size, affect how a city behaves.

In an entry in his *Moscow Diary* dated December 17, 1926, philosopher and urban observer Walter Benjamin wrote, 'It has

Spadina meets Lake Ontario with a wave.

been observed that pedestrians [in Moscow] walk in "zigzags." This is simply on account of the overcrowding of the narrow sidewalks; nowhere else, except here and there in Naples, do you find sidewalks this narrow. This gives Moscow a provincial air or, rather the character of an improvised metropolis that has fallen into place overnight.' He could have been writing about most places in Toronto.

On Spadina, however, Torontonians can walk proudly, like world-class pedestrians. Yet as Spadina starts near one of the most intense development zones in the country, it also seems to, as Benjamin writes, 'fall into place overnight.' We hardly notice skyscrapers going up anymore until somebody moves in and flicks a switch, at which point a light glows in the sky where it didn't before. The city was shocked (shocked!) in 2008 when Waterfront Toronto opened the Spadina Wave Deck at the foot of the street, on the shores of Lake Ontario. Not only did it bend the rules of what a sidewalk can look like, but it confused people who were adamant in their belief that waterfront development would never move forward. The wooden waves at the water's edge cause people to stop, look and linger, where before they may have carried on without noticing that this is the beginning of Toronto's spine.

The first leg of Spadina, which stretches north to the Gardiner Expressway, might not make Mr. Baldwin proud. It may be our worst connection to the water, as pedestrians can pass only on the east side and have to 'wait for the gap,' as the signs say, to cross a

busy expressway off-ramp – an unexpected and speedy yield in a part of town where people on foot generally have critical mass over cars. Rough crossings aside, this has become a crystal entrance to the city for those coming off the Gardiner, in an area that less than a decade ago was either parking lot or urban scrubland. West of here lies a vast cathedral-like space, hidden underneath the Gardiner. While not particularly pretty right now – it's mostly covered in mud, rocks and highway detritus that includes everything from stuffed animals to pieces of truck tires – it's another part of the underside of this hated highway that has much potential. At the very least, basketball courts with a fifty-year-old concrete roof overhead could be easily installed.

The Concord CityPlace condo development – which is made up of nearly two dozen buildings – is clustered on both sides of Spadina. Skyscraper- and condo-haters have derided CityPlace since the first towers started going up. Part of this sentiment is certainly due to Toronto's fear of heights, which, when applied to places completely appropriate for towers, becomes ideology rather than good city planning or thoughtful opinion. The other reason for the hate seems to be a kind of underlying misanthropy. Phrases like 'Ugh, more condos' are often heard, but rarely interrogated. Are we talking about condos in general, or just the badly designed ones? Replace 'condo' with 'people' and suddenly we have one group – presumably made up of those living in tidy two- or three-storey houses – sneering at another group of people who want to live downtown and don't seem to mind spending their money on glass perches in the sky. 'Condo dweller' is the new sloppy epithet for 'bourgeoisie' or, worse, for 'uncool.'

It's true that at ground level, the east side of Spadina, the one closest to the SkyDome (or the Rogers Centre, as they now call it), is imperfect, and feels too much like a Supercentre entrance. But take a walk through the newer development on the west side and you'll see fountains, townhouses, pathways and a Sobeys store. Here, CityPlace has learned from its mistakes, and has created a completely urbane neighbourhood where it's easy to forget there are dozens of floors overhead.

The extension of Fort York Boulevard that connects Spadina to Fort York – only a few hundred metres west at this point – passes Canoe Landing Park, designed by Douglas Coupland and landscape architects Phillips Farevaag Smallenberg of Vancouver in collaboration with Landscape Architects and the Planning Partnership of Toronto. The park continues Coupland's Canadiana theme with giant fishing lures, a pathway named after Terry Fox and a new Toronto landmark: a big red canoe on a hill that points directly at the Gardiner traffic – certainly an unexpected site for motorists passing by. Coupland has been busy in Toronto lately: nearby at Front and Bathurst, his War of 1812 soldiers are in front of a condo while up at the Shops at Don Mills, his 'exploding bungalow' piece is a scrambled take on postwar suburban Canada.

The vast scale of the CityPlace development can be seen along the rail corridor that runs across from the dowdy *Globe and Mail* building at 444 Front Street West. (Consider this building alongside the *Toronto Star* building at 1 Yonge and the *National Post* building in Don Mills and you'll notice that our major newspapers have less-than-flagship-worthy headquarters.) There, a massive concrete wall containing a honeycomb of hidden parking garages rises out of the ground. Like in many parts of Toronto, the ground we walk on may be real or human-created. A new pathway here extends underneath Spadina and will become part of the east-west bike-trail network.

Watch out for Ayn Rand at the Morgan.

At Front, across the tracks, old Spadina begins to appear with familiar turn-of-the-last-century warehouses. The Toyota dealership and surface parking lot here are remnants of a time when cars ruled the area and there was near-contiguous pavement from the CNE to University Avenue. Today, much of the space in and around those old warehouses has been filled in with new buildings. Some, like the Morgan, which sits on the northwest corner at Richmond and boasts a massive penthouse that looks like the lair of an art deco villain from an Ayn Rand novel, match the older form. Others, like the District Lofts just east on Richmond, with its soaring catwalks that link mid-rise towers, are completely contemporary.

Old and new Toronto coexist in this ever-changing neighbourhood, and not always easily. Walk Rush Lane, the alley west of Spadina between Queen and Richmond, and see how the Morgan resists becoming part of Toronto's celebrated 'Graffiti Alley' with what must be weekly sandblasting. Back down at King, the parking lot that stood for a long, long time on the southeast corner has been filled in by an LCBO location.

The Queen and Spadina intersection is, for many, the heart of Toronto. It was an early Toronto landmark for me as a visiting kid – I worried that the thick web of streetcar wires hanging overhead would electrocute lost skydivers – but half of it needs a facelift. The east side, with the CIBC and Lettieri café buildings, is Toronto at its most beautiful. Go to the northwest corner and you'll see the world's ugliest McDonald's housed in a brown turd fortress. Knowing this was once the Mary Pickford Theatre, built in 1908 but demolished in the uncaring 1950s, doesn't help attempts at appreciation. The TD Bank on the south side is also bunker-like, and it smothers sidewalk life. It's a symbolic marker for the less-gentrified strip of Queen between Spadina and Bathurst, and it's very Toronto: the exceptionally good and the exceptionally bad, right next to each other.

The Cameron House bar a block west of Spadina on Queen has served as Toronto's largest canvas for three decades or more. The lower facade regularly receives paint treatments by different Toronto artists, and ten giant ants crawl over the upper floors. The ants are by Napoleon Brousseau, a co-founder of Toronto art collective Fastwürms, and were in part a response to the City of

Toronto inspectors who routinely visited the Cameron House to check on the ten 'illegal dwellings' that housed a variety of artists. The ants were installed in advance of the Pope's 1984 visit to Toronto, and also symbolized the tenants – or ten ants – of the aforementioned dwellings, who were eventually allowed to legally stay in the building. In late 2009, the owners of the Cameron House placed the building and business up for sale, and it was ultimately sold to other family members. It's unclear as of this writing if the artistic tradition of the bar will be maintained, but the new owners have made it clear that there will be changes.

North of Queen, Spadina becomes a relatively quiet zone. While still busy, it's an in-between space, tucked just south of Chinatown and just north of condo-land. Both sides of the street have some fine old warehouse buildings, some of which have been renovated and modernized into loft offices, while others still wait for the same treatment. Of note is the Robertson Building at 215 Spadina. It's the one with the Dark Horse Café on the main floor (part of Toronto's full-on commitment to coffee culture) and the green wall in the lobby (the building is open during the day, and passersby are welcome to go in and look at it). In the winter, your eyeglasses will fog up immediately when you walk in due to the humidity created by the wall. Urbanspace Property Group, the company that owns and runs 401 Richmond Street just a few blocks south, owns this building too. These two buildings are, to use an overused word, some of the best-curated buildings in Toronto, with a tenant mix of social and arts organizations.

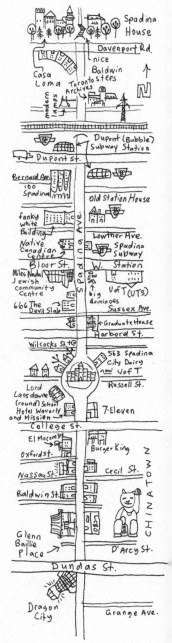

The Chinatown Centre across the street is one of Toronto's more interesting malls. Inside you'll find shops, cellphone accessory boutiques and other hard-to-categorize businesses. Unfortunately, the white facade is perpetually dirty and the large open courtyard – a space that could be Chinatown's public square – is an unhappy, treeless and often garbage-strewn area. To get an idea of its squandered potential, go inside and find the original Chinatown Centre architectural model on display, complete with trees, crowds of miniature people and open second-floor patios.

The Dundas and Spadina intersection has a mild Yonge-Dundas Square look, mostly due to the other Chinese mall located on the southwest corner, which routinely has advertisements on it. (The mall replaced a Hungarian church as the area gave way to the influx of Hong Kong money that poured into Chinatown during the 1980s.) On the northeast corner there's a standard-looking Royal Bank branch, but look behind it and notice the graffiti-covered fly tower, which betrays the abandoned theatre within. This was originally the Standard Theatre, which operated from the 1920s onwards and hosted Yiddish and Vaudeville productions. In the 1940s, it became the Victory Theatre and, by the 1970s, morphed into the Victory Burlesque, where strippers often mixed with the likes of Rush, the New York Dolls, Peter Frampton, the Soft Machine and Iggy and the Stooges. Its last incarnation was as the Golden Harvest Cinema, which showed Hong Kong films until the cinema finally closed in the 1990s. It's spooky to stand nearby and imagine that vast, empty theatre space behind the bank, a portal to a lost and dead world.

Chinatown peaks north of Dundas, where it's strewn with the overlapping signage and bustle commonly found in Chinatowns everywhere. On the northwest corner of the intersection, Chinese guerrilla grandparent-types sell herbs and vegetables on the sidewalk. The City has tried to remove them, as they don't have permits to sell food, but they always return. We expect a little bit of permit-blurring and disobeying in a Chinatown; it's necessary to its existence. The Bright Pearl Restaurant, on Spadina at St. Andrews Street, is one of Chinatown's more recognizable buildings, but few people know that behind the Chinese facade and main-floor luggage store is what was once Toronto's Labour Lyceum. From 1928 to 1968, the Lyceum was the centre of Toronto's labour movement. Famed anarchist Emma Goldman once gave a speech called 'The Youth in Revolt' here during the time when she was exiled from the United States and living in Toronto. (After her 1940 death, her body lay in state at the Lyceum.) Slip down tiny Glen Baillie Place west off Spadina and follow the alley behind the Lyceum for a secret entrance into Kensington Market.

Chinatown continues north to College Street and fades out by the venerable old El Mocambo nightclub, a legendary Toronto dive and yet another historic local venue where the Rolling Stones have played. A recently separated Maggie Trudeau attended one 1977 performance, and a recording of that show was released as the album *Love You Live*. Their opening act that night, April Wine, also recorded their performance and released it as *Live at the El Mocambo*. There was a great fanfare in the mid-2000s when the El Mo's palm-tree sign was relit, though it has since returned to its familiar half-working state.

Beyond College, 1 Spadina Crescent is the bubble that makes Spadina (the road) interesting. Without this building – built in 1875 and formerly known as Knox College – sitting in the middle of the street, the Spadina streetcars wouldn't need to make their wild and graceful arcs. One Spadina gives our eyes somewhere to rest when scanning the urban horizon – another rare terminating vista – and is also a resting spot for eyeballs in a more literal sense, as it houses the Ontario Eye Bank. Look for the *Pole Colonnade* public-art piece by Stephen Cruise on top of the streetcar poles just to the north at Willcocks Street; the one entitled *Bottle/Mold* refers, in part, to the period when the Connaught Laboratories produced penicillin at Knox College. Until the pedestrian crosswalk was installed, the only way to get to the building was by crossing the street mid-block. The history of this building is rife with ghost stories: a U of T professor was murdered here in the early 2000s and, in 2009, a woman trying some amateur (is there any other kind?) urban exploring was killed when she fell from the roof.

Lord Lansdowne Public School, located on the west side of the circle, is sometimes known as the 'crown' school due to its round modernist design. (It so evokes the postwar era that parts of the 2007 remake of the movie *Hairspray* were shot here.) The huge Precambrian boulder in its front yard was unearthed during excavation of the lot, and takes Toronto's new-old theme to the extreme.

The Graduate House hangs out over Harbord Street.

Around the top of the circle Spadina becomes a mix of residential and institutional, with the U of T lining the east side of the street. The old part of New College (north of Willcocks Street – a new New College is to the south) was built in 1964 and presents Spadina with a nearly blank brick wall. That barrier seems like a mistake now, but in 1964, this part of Spadina was slated to become an expressway, so building a wall between cars and students seemed like a good idea. An interior courtyard is hidden inside, protected from whatever the city might do outside the walls.

The U of T's Grad House hangs out and over Harbord Street at Spadina, the architectural equivalent of a loud and bold grad student elbowing his or her way into a conversation. When it opened in 2000, the building, by Los Angeles–based and Pritzker Prize–winning architect Thom Mayne, was controversial because of that un-Torontonian overhang. Yet as the following decade passed, one rarely heard a word about it; buildings of this average size tend to fade into the background, even if they're bold. A block away, the much higher and chubbier Robarts Library still has the lovers and haters nattering away more than forty years after it was built. I've always thought that all the concrete poured into Robarts keeps the books safe. When I'm in a library, I like to feel that I'm in a cocoon where I can't hear the outside world, kept safe and sound in a place where the books can take over.

Just north, on the southeast corner of Bloor and Spadina, a small parkette was formed when the underground Spadina street-car line was installed in 1997. The giant granite dominos by Susan Schelle and Mark Gomes are an homage to the checkers and dominoes players who would gather here before the intersection was re-engineered to accommodate the streetcar line. Behind the dominoes there's a grassy knoll surrounding a TTC vent that bears metal leaf imprints – a reminder of the Carolinian forest that once grew here. Just south, there's a small parkette named after writer Matt Cohen, who lived and worked along Spadina and who wrote a short story called 'Spadina Time' in 1972.

A block east of here, on the other side of the University of Toronto School, sits a concrete high-rise that's one of Toronto's most unsung landmarks. From 1968 to 1975, what today is the Senator David A. Croll apartment building was known as Rochdale College, Toronto's 'vertical Haight-Ashbury.' An experiment in alternative education and communal living, its baby-boomer idealism degenerated into a culture of bad drugs and squatting bikers, culminating in a massive police-led eviction in 1975. The only physical vestigial remnant of the Rochdale days (there are other cultural and individual echoes throughout Toronto today) is the *Unknown Student* sculpture out front. The statue originally faced towards the building, but it was reoriented to face the street when the building reopened.

North of Bloor, Spadina becomes a mix of homes, low-rise apartment buildings and a couple of very tall landmark towers by late Toronto modernist architect Uno Prii, whose curving buildings can be found around the city. Along Spadina Road, some of the 'tower in a park' quality of these buildings has been corrected with townhouse and low-rise tower infill, so what was once a somewhat uninteresting stretch of street is now home to many more people. Though a bit of green space was lost, it wasn't ever used as a true public park since it belonged to the apartment buildings and was largely empty. Toronto's most homey subway station entrance, formerly a grand Annex home, can be found at 85 Spadina Road. Once you pass the automatic turnstiles, you'll find Joyce Weiland's huge and sprawling quilt, called *Barren*

Ground Caribou. It's puffy-soft public art from 1978 that furnishes
the soul with the warm feeling that Trudeau is still in power and
offers the fantastic illusion that the Spadina Line extends all the
way north into the Canadian Shield and the caribou-land beyond.

A few blocks north of here, take Bernard Avenue to Jean
Sibelius Park, which is tucked away by Kendal Avenue in the deepest Annex, a neighbourhood named as such because the part east
of Brunswick Avenue was annexed to the City of Toronto in 1883
along with Yorkville. Three years later developer Simeon James
named his new subdivision 'Toronto Annex.' Jane Jacobs lived a
few blocks west at 69 Albany, and it's worth the walk to see the
inner parts of her neighbourhood.

Jean Sibelius Park is named after the Finnish composer, and
his bust can be found to the north end, where it was regularly
surrounded by packs of dogs until the park's leash-free-area status
was revoked. The site of predictable discord between Toronto's
fiercest warring factions, dog owners and parents, the park also
includes an elaborate children's compound where fur-free
offspring can play in a fenced-in enclosure. The most remarkable
thing about the park is the number of communal toys that are
always scattered around the compound, making the area seem
more like a backyard than a public park. Toronto often functions
so perfectly well on micro-levels like this (toys left out) while so
poorly on others (dogs and kids).

At Dupont, Spadina dips under the railway, and here you'll
find *Spadina Line*, a public artwork installed in 1991 by Brad
Bolden and Norman Richards. It consists of various references to
the railway, including a clock that tells time both digitally and by
the sun, and a stainless steel archive. North of the underpass, a
series of light standards illuminate bronze words inlaid into the
sidewalk that mark the development of both the adjacent City of
Toronto Archives and Spadina Road, and which refer to Casa
Loma builder Henry Pellatt with the word 'Power'. (Pellatt made
his money electrifying Toronto.)

Toronto has its share of great museums and great libraries,
and straddling the line between the two is the Toronto Archives.
Housed in a postmodern fortress on Spadina Road, underneath
the Davenport escarpment, the archives contain Toronto's official
memory, which is deep and extensive. You can research your

house there, look at sewer photos from the 1920s, read past council debates and browse reports on just about anything city-related. The best part of the building is the large atrium, which hosts rotating year-long exhibits, curated by in-house archivists, that ensure that even when you're not looking for something in particular, you'll find something interesting. The building is set back from Spadina, a remnant of zoning rules that created a right-of-way for the Spadina Expressway, which would have burst out of the escarpment here as it headed south through the heart of the Annex. This part of Spadina ends at Davenport, and though the road jogs west and continues on further north as a narrower road, pedestrians can use the Baldwin Steps that start here to climb up the steep hill. Once at the top, winded or not, don't forget to turn around and look down the wide swath of Spadina, just as Baldwin once did. (That's his house on the east side of the street, while Casa Loma is on the west side.) The view is now more electric and packed-in than he'd ever have imagined. Spadina, like Yonge, belongs to all of us now; it just has more elbow room on those sidewalks.

St. Clair Avenue

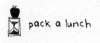 pack a lunch

 dress to impress

 offspring friendly

Connecting walks: Yonge, Dundas, Bathurst, Spadina.

St. Clair Avenue is a street in two acts, with the Don Valley as entr'acte between the lesser-known St. Clair that starts in East York and heads east into Scarborough, and the more familiar part of the street that starts in upper Rosedale by Mt. Pleasant and heads west. The folks along the Scarborough stretch likely carry the burden of always saying, 'No, we live along the other St. Clair' when they're asked where they live.

The St. Clair most of us think about, which begins a few blocks east of Yonge at the Moore Park Ravine and continues west, is initially the highrise edge of Rosedale and Forest Hill, boasting a long row of upscale pre- and postwar residential buildings. Most meet the sidewalk in a 'big-city' way, though the sidewalk seems smaller since the addition, between 2005 and 2010, of the street-car right-of-way between St. Clair subway station and Gunns Loop. One of Toronto's most controversial public works in decades, many see the St. Clair transit right-of-way as an example of how not to go about installing such things. As space was made for the streetcars, cars and car turning lanes, the sidewalks became too narrow in places and aren't at all 'big-city' anymore. There's no on-street parking along this first stretch, nor is there a buffer between

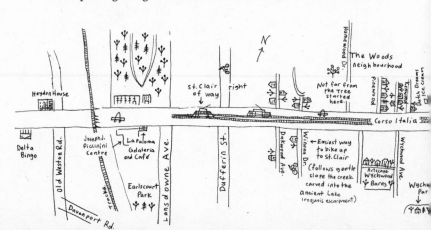

pedestrians and traffic, and that proximity can feel uncomfortable. Cars often hug the sidewalk as if they're driving along a mountain-side road.

The Park Lane apartments at 110 St. Clair, between Yonge and Avenue Road, are notable because of their streamlined deco look, but also because pianist Glenn Gould lived in the penthouse here, when he wasn't at his perch at the nearby twenty-four-hour Fran's Diner (now a Hero Burger restaurant and pub). Toronto could be called Glenn Gould City. In addition to the statue of Gould by the cbc building down on Front Street and the studio inside that same building named after him, there is also Glenn Gould Park, at the corner of Avenue and St. Clair, which is often known as 'Peter Pan Park' due to its statue of the pan pipe–playing boy in it. Just across the street is Amsterdam Park, named when that city's burgomaster met then Toronto Mayor David Crombie here when the two cities were twinned in 1974.

Toronto has little in common with Detroit, but for a time both cities had at least one abandoned skyscraper. Toronto's rare example was the 1957 Imperial Oil Building on St. Clair west of Yonge Street. Imperial moved their headquarters to Calgary in 2005, but passersby can still see York Wilson's massive mural the *Story of Oil* in the lobby. Originally a contender in the New City Hall design competition in the early 1950s, this building was designed to double as a hospital in the event of a nuclear attack (its hallways were built wide enough for beds).

At Avenue Road stands the unoriginally named the Avenue – not a road, but a condo that was billed as 'Distinctly Forest Hill' and 'The ultimate address' when it was being constructed. Clad in stone and brick, it's tall but nondescript enough that it fades into

the Toronto wallpaper, as most good buildings should. Here, especially, where there are lovely pre- and postwar buildings as far as the eye can see, being subtle is okay. The rub is that the marketing language used to woo buyers to the Avenue was distinctly not Forest Hill, where the older money usually likes to keep a lower profile behind high hedges. The stretch of Avenue north of here will lead you to exclusive Upper Canada College, a private boys' school. Follow the road towards its fine terminating view of the school's preppy, private and privileged clock tower, but don't forget to look around you as you go: this part of the road has some of Toronto's best stock of mid-century apartment buildings (and a few from later on too).

Further along St. Clair, at Spadina, two unique 1960s apartment towers rise out of green Nordheimer Ravine like supermodern white monoliths. Though large and indeed monolithic, the Tower Hill buildings seem ready to float into the air due to their white iron wraparound balcony rails (and the 100 percent glass walls behind them), which make the buildings seem honeycombed and light. Another tower complex here on the north side of St. Clair, next door to the giant Loblaws grocery store, has an indoor pool building designed, intentionally or not, to look like a flying saucer. In the summer, these buildings rise out of the green fabric just like those utopian science-fiction cities in *Star Wars* or *Star Trek* do.

At Sir Winston Churchill Park, on the southeast corner of the St. Clair and Spadina intersection, you'll find one of Toronto's hidden lakes. Though it looks like a standard park, with tennis courts and dozens of fancy Forest Hill dogs romping around, the park sits atop one of Toronto's ten water storage reservoirs. The reservoir was completed in 1931, at a time when we built public works with great style. The pumphouse buildings towards the southwest corner of the park are miniature versions of the famously grand R.C. Harris Filtration Plant out in the Beach. Stand on top of the south 'cliff' to see the magnitude of the structure, and then look down into Nordheimer Ravine, under which is buried Castle Frank Brook.

To the right of and below this look-out you'll find the Spadina Road Bridge. Near the base of the bridge, notice the 'Russell Hill' subway escape hatch. It was through this passage that the victims of the 1995 Toronto subway crash escaped the superheated tunnels (three were killed and many more were injured). It's quiet now. Every few minutes the sound of the subway rushing by some-where deep inside will echo up this unnatural cave and, if you stand close enough, you can feel the warm air blow through the grate. Though it seems as though you're immersed in nature here, deep below the city's surface, Toronto's artificial arteries are pump-ing people through the city like blood droplets. There is a bit of wetland regeneration here too, and the long-buried creek surfaces in some areas. The path leads up north to the Loblaws supermar-ket on St. Clair, past a locked subway station exit through which people could go directly from train to forest, or south to Poplar Plains and Davenport roads. This is the zenith of Toronto's urban ravine system, with green passages in many directions.

Back up at St. Clair, take a short walk north on Spadina to Forest Hill Village. Once the hub of the autonomous town of Forest Hill, it's now an exceptionally cute enclave that feels a bit like a summer cottage town, its small and intimate scale over-whelmed by people jockeying too many cars into position in front of the Starbucks or the grocery store. On a stroll there once, the elderly widow of a flamboyant Toronto millionaire was pointed out to me by a long-time Forest Hill resident as she walked along with her rhinestone-encrusted dog, anonymous to most – Forest Hill Village feels like a soft place to land when the bold-face society columnists no longer want to write about you. Contrary to Forest Hill's manse-filled image, there's a remarkable number of old walk-up apartments here, too, complete with vintage light poles that bear the old Forest Hill insignia.

Further west along St. Clair, the street dips low by the Loblaws and St. Clair West subway station, a sort of land bridge of fill between Nordheimer Ravine to the south and Cedarvale to the north. The giant underground bus and streetcar bay – a dreamy 1978 disco-era palette of gold, brown and orange – would be above ground had the ravine not been filled in. Getting the Bathurst bus from here is one of the most awkward transfers on the TTC: riders must walk a few hundred metres on St. Clair to get from the station to the bus. There's often a northbound crowd waiting by the Petro-Canada for the number seven bus, as if in perpetual protest that the Spadina subway goes up the middle of an express-way instead of up Bathurst, where the people who use it are.

West of Bathurst, St. Clair's retail strip comes alive, at first without a discernable character – a typical Toronto jumble – to eventually become Corso Italia. The neighbourhood to the north of this stretch has been called 'the Woods,' as its streets include Humewood, Pinewood, Wychwood and Kenwood. Laura Reinsborough, founder of the urban fruit-gleaning organization Not Far From the Tree and a resident of this neighbourhood, sees these woods through her 'fruit goggles' – her group harvested 3,000 pounds of fruit from the neighbourhood's trees in 2008. Reinsborough got into the fruit-picking business by accident when she volunteered at the nearby Wychwood Barns farmers' market and was asked to pick apples from the heritage orchard at nearby Spadina House, near Casa Loma. Back at the market, they were sold with a sign that read 'This was biked here from 1.3 kilometres away – trying to put to shame the 100-kilometre diet.'

NFFTT's fruit-picking activities have spread to other neighbourhoods – Reinsborough estimates there are 1.5 million pounds of 'edibles' growing around Toronto that could be harvested. She has a theory that there is such good fruit growing around St. Clair because it's up on the escarpment, just like the Niagara peninsula and its vineyards.

Thankfully, Toronto doesn't welcome gated communities (as long as condo buildings don't count), but Wychwood Park, just south of St. Clair, is the exception we can live with. This bucolic historical anomaly is hidden between Christie and Bathurst streets, climbing up the shore of ancient Lake Iroquois, the escarpment that runs across the city just above Davenport Road.

Unless you look for the 'Wychwood Private Road and Park' sign, you're likely to mistake the two entrances to the neighbourhood for somebody's driveway. The circular road climbs up the old Lake Iroquois escarpment from Davenport through a forest of old trees and multimillion-dollar homes. When it's icy, I've slid down the steepest part of the road, by the only ultra-modern bungalow in the park, with its low, horizontal windows, which afford a perfect view of the owner reading in bed. Designed by Toronto architect Ian MacDonald, 4a Wychwood Park won the Governor General's Medal for Architecture in 2008. It sits upon the footprint of the site's original house and carries on this city's tradition of successfully mixing old and new.

Marshall McLuhan's house in Wychwood Park.

Wychwood Park was settled in the 1870s as an artists' colony by Marmaduke Matthews and George A. Reid. It's the only place where Toronto's long-buried Taddle Creek is still visible. A pond, thick with algae and quicksand, was created by damming the creek. Descendants of goldfish deposited by Matthews' grandson on the eve of his departure to fight in the First World War are said to still swim it. Toronto's finest have lived here, including Marshall McLuhan, at No. 3. Just outside the north gate, at 41 Alcina Avenue, lived York Wilson, the artist behind the Seven Lively Arts mural that is in the lobby of the Sony Centre for the Performing Arts and the mural in the Imperial Oil building mentioned earlier in this chapter.

Unfortunately, some of Wychwood's residents seem to have forgotten the neighbourhood's artistic heritage. When Artscape proposed turning the TTC streetcar barns to the north into the complex that's now known as the Artscape Wychwood Barns, a group called 'Neighbours for a 100% Green Park' mounted a ruthless campaign against the plan. Their true colours became visible when Elaine Waisglass, a Wychwood resident, told the *National Post* in 2002: 'What if my friend Fran wants to have a dinner party? Where are her guests going to park?'

There must be something about the altitude up on St. Clair that makes people go into a car-crazed frenzy, opposing artists and streetcar rights-of-way. While some of Wychwood's current residents might be out of touch with what it means to be a Torontonian, the rest of us are free to walk around their patrician neighbourhood and pretend it's still full of McLuhans and Marmadukes.

Back along St. Clair, the street does have the feeling of being high up above the rest of the city. There are fewer buildings on the skyline and no hills in view. Further west, closer to the heart of Corso Italia and just before Oakwood Avenue, there's another dip in the road, this time where the headwaters of the Garrison Creek once flowed. Though the ravine is now filled in, its legacy is seen in the gentle slope of Winona Drive, which is the easiest way to bike up to St. Clair from the south.

Corso Italia works differently than College Street's Little Italy does. By day, the stores are busy, but at night, if you're driving or on transit, it doesn't appear to have the life that Toronto's other Italian neighbourhood does. There are no lineups at bars or wild packs of tiara-wearing brides-to-be out on a last rampage. St. Clair moves at a slower pace, which may be the most Italian thing about it. Cafés, restaurants and bars are quieter; you know you're coming up on one when there is a cluster of folks standing around, smoking or talking, a human trickle that spreads down the sidewalk. Kids, too, will sometimes be with their dads at bars, running around while the adults talk. I grew up partially in Canada's Maltese diaspora, a culture with a similar Mediterranean sensibility, and for me these were the most magical times to be a kid, extended ultimate freedom while parents nursed their highball glasses. Corso Italia ends at Earlscourt Park and La Paloma Gelato. People line up around the block for La Paloma gelato on hot summer nights. Several years ago, on a trip to Wales, I met a journalist from the BBC who had been to Toronto only once and whose memory of the city was La Paloma. For some, food is as strong a memory and landmark as the CN Tower is for others.

St . Clair continues beyond the railway underpass, and though this stretch certainly won't win any urban design awards, it might yet be the most exciting part of the street in the coming years. It's an under-the-radar Wild West of evangelical storefront churches, automotive stores and bingo halls, not unlike Ossington Avenue was until the late 2000s when it became the epicentre of hipster gentrification. Heydon House, at Old Weston Road, is a secretly beautiful Gladstone-like hotel that was once on the frontiers of Toronto. Rundown, beat up and carved into numerous unglam-orous uses (such as a convenience store), it's hard to imagine it getting the kind of loving renovation treatment that the Gladstone Hotel on Queen Street West received. Yet the rapidly changing Junction is only few blocks south of St. Clair at this point – a geographic proximity that is a bit of a surprise if you're used to the distance between Dundas and St. Clair downtown – so an Ossingtonization of St. Clair could happen. Being this far from the pressure of Queen West, the process would likely be a lot slower, allowing for more thoughtful change free of the neigh-bourhood freak-outs that were common along Queen in the 1990s and early 2000s.

Further west, St. Clair gets big. Like the part of North America we call the West, this is big-sky country and big-box land. Some of the giant retail operations here are built on former railway lands and stockyards. There are still some meat-packing plants near Gunns Road, but housing tracts have replaced many of these operations. The mix of large-scale retail, light industrial and some scattered, misplaced-looking residential homes continues until St. Clair ends at Scarlett Road, not far from the Humber River and the suburb of Etobicoke.

Eglinton Avenue and the Borough of York

 pack a lunch   Connecting walks: Yonge, Bathurst.

 dress to impress

 scenic views

Toronto is built on York. The word, that is. It's everywhere: there's Fort York, York University, even the landmark Royal York Hotel. Names and nicknames like Yorkville and Muddy York are splashed all over our mental maps of Toronto. But the one place that probably isn't on that map for most Torontonians is the former City of York. It is, and was, Toronto's forgotten borough, an underdog of a municipality that lived in the shadow of its bigger, richer neighbours Etobicoke and – there it is again! – North York until all were amalgamated into the Toronto megacity in 1998.

York is not easy to find: it's completely landlocked and asymmetrically shaped, and displays very few overt signs to help you realize that you are, in fact, there. It stretches roughly between St. Clair and Eglinton avenues, and extends west from Bathurst Street to the Humber River and Weston area, with a few municipal tentacles reaching in various other directions.

The name York originally referred to the township established in 1850 that stretched from the Humber River east to Scarborough Township and from Lake Ontario up to what is now Steeles Avenue. As Toronto grew, it annexed communities in the township like Parkdale, Deer Park and Yorkville, continually encroaching on York until the Municipality of Metropolitan Toronto was created in 1954 and established the City of York out of what was left over. In the final edition of the York Municipal Code – a sad book, now without a city – the preface boasts, 'York is a pleasant surprise in Metropolitan Toronto, with a future that holds promise!'

Though the Heath Street entrance to St. Clair West station is just inside the borough's boundary, York is without its own subway station, perhaps a comment on the former municipality's economic fortunes. York's poor financial lot was due in part to the fact that its southern border with Toronto was established just north of the lucrative tax base of the St. Clair retail strip. There's a

Arthur Erickson's Eglinton station spaceport.

similar shift in wealth starting from Eglinton West station, again just outside the borough's boundary.

If you approach the station from the east, Eglinton Avenue does a gentle Forest Hill fade-out as it rolls out from Yonge Street, where it is dotted with upscale boutiques and shops. The affluent neighbourhood of Forest Hill's main street and spiritual heart is nearby Spadina Road, but this part of Eglinton fills out the rest of the area's proximal needs. The low-rise retail is on a relatively wide sidewalk (a welcome change from Toronto's tendency for narrowness in this regard), which makes the area feel like a neighbourhood despite the width and busyness of Eglinton. Just before Bathurst, Eglinton crosses over the Beltline Park, the former rail cut that is now a diagonal park and trail through Forest Hill. (The park provides a quick route southeast to Yonge and Davisville or, to the northwest, deeper into York.) Around the Beltline there are modish and deco-inspired apartments, much like those on St. Clair to the south. Though known as a neighbourhood of mansions, Forest Hill has some of Toronto best pre- and postwar residential apartment buildings. Between Bathurst and the Allen Road Expressway (and Eglinton West station) the Forest Hill–ness of Eglinton is still evident, and there are obvious signs of its Jewish character, but the north lanes of the street begin to seem like the freeway on-ramp they become as they get closer to the Allen.

The TTC's best advertisement to entice motorists out of their cars and into public transit may be Eglinton West station, which is more spaceport than subway station, with a floating concrete roof and glassed-in platforms. It's one of a handful of buildings in Toronto that were designed by Canadian architect Arthur Erickson – a starchitect long before that term existed – and a vestige of the heady days in the late 1970s when subways were built not just to transport people from here to there but to inspire futuristic utopian visions. Erickson's work, here and at Yorkdale subway station, Roy Thomson Hall on Front Street and the King's Landing condos on Queens Quay, still feels like a future we've yet to reach. Below this odd island in the middle of the planned Spadina Expressway, which was cancelled before it was to be extended south in 1971, lies another future Toronto didn't get: the first tunnels for the planned Eglinton subway line, which were dug out in the early

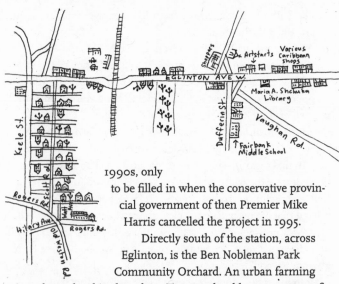

1990s, only to be filled in when the conservative provincial government of then Premier Mike Harris cancelled the project in 1995.

Directly south of the station, across Eglinton, is the Ben Nobleman Park Community Orchard. An urban farming project, the orchard is also where Toronto should erect a statue of Jane Jacobs if it ever decides to do so. This patch of land is where the Spadina Expressway, which the legendary Jane Jacobs and hundreds of other activists campaigned against, was stopped in its bulldozer tracks after the province, under the leadership of Bill Davis, bought up a small strip of land, effectively blocking the proposed road. Here, on a nondescript part of Eglinton, the province has both given and taken away subway and freeway megaprojects. Now you can quietly pick fruit here. Walking the residential streets to the south is like being on death row after the governor calls to pardon everybody. These roads were spared when the expressway was called off, and somewhere deep below the subway rumbles along, roughly following the diagonal path of the Cedarvale Ravine, which begins a block south of Eglinton. Formed after the last ice age by the Castle Frank and Cedarvale streams, the ravine eventually leads back to Forest Hill Village.

The Glen Cedar Pedestrian Bridge south of Ben Nobleman Park is designated under the Ontario Heritage Act, and was the first bridge over the ravine. It was built as part of Casa Loma–builder Henry Pellatt's development scheme for the area. (Called 'Cedar Vale,' his plan imagined the construction of a 300-acre exclusive subdivision.) For years, the bridge was closed and

condemned, but it was renovated in 1989 as a pedestrian-only crossing with commanding views of the ravine below.

Back on Eglinton, west of the station and orchard, you cross the old border between the City of Toronto and the City of York. Here, Eglinton's upscale character is quickly replaced by the jumble of independent businesses that characterizes many of Toronto's less glamorous streets. This is also where Toronto's Caribbean community has established its own ethnic strip, which begins in earnest with the Celebrity Tough hair salon and Celebrity Roots and Culture Supplies next door, and which is as dense as Chinatown or Little Korea, but much less celebrated.

This area wouldn't win an urban-design award for beauty – nor would most of York – but like those other jumbled-up strips, Eglinton provides cheap rent for all sorts of small-scale economic activity, some good (like the store selling 'Church dresses, suits and hats!') and some not so good (the inevitable cheque-cashing services that blight all lower-income neighbourhoods).

There are still traces of the old city around, most often in the form of vertical 'York' signs in parks, which are often coupled with Toronto's 'A City Within a Park' signs. At the corner of Eglinton and Dufferin streets, where tiny St. Hilda Square gets the double-signage treatment, Vaughan Road stops just short of what was once a five-point intersection. Previously known as the Vaughan Plank Road, it used to connect Davenport, one of Toronto's earliest roads, with Vaughan Township to the north of the city, following an early aboriginal trail. Davenport crosses York on a diagonal, like Rogers Road does just to the west, breaking with the standard Toronto grid just enough to throw off those with an untrained sense of direction.

The intersection of Eglinton and Dufferin streets marks what was once the centre of Fairbank, one of the many hamlets that were eventually consumed by Toronto's growth. The name survives on a few buildings like the New Fairbank Hotel, a stucco-clad 'gentleman's club' just north on Dufferin. It sits next to the Universal Church, an architectural atrocity best described as a suburban Roman Coliseum. The part of Dufferin that runs north from here is one of Toronto's ugliest stretch of streets, one you don't want to show visitors. Many of Toronto's high-end interior design shops are hidden here in York's old light-industrial land-scape, well-known to all those Forest Hill homeowners.

All along Eglinton, a handful of surviving Italian businesses hint that this was once a third Little Italy, behind the celebrated College Street Little Italy and St. Clair's Corso Italia. Italians have been slowly evacuating this area, just as they have the two other ones, travelling up Dufferin to Woodbridge, a northern migration parallel to the one of Toronto's Jewish population.

The area west of Dufferin south of Eglinton is one of Toronto's most unique yet uncelebrated neighbourhoods. Though it has no defining style, and even the most passionate Toronto booster would not call it beautiful, the topography makes this area charming. Built on a series of hills and valleys, streets make sharp turns and dead-end abruptly, sometimes at a grade that looks too steep for cars. Toronto has been called 'San Francisco upside down' because of its many deep ravines, but this part of Toronto could easily be 'Little San Francisco.' Instead of multimillion-dollar Nob or Russian Hill homes, though, York is made up of treeless lots dotted with brick bungalows, rusting Buick Centuries and Pontiac Fieros, and recycling bins overflowing with copies of the *Toronto Sun*. I'm sure there are numerous Mary Poppins–style views to be had if you're floating above the rooftops and chimneys, and many parks with secret escapes up outdoor *Exorcist*-like staircases.

Back on Eglinton, before it slopes down into the Humber Valley toward the Etobicoke skyline, there's a break in the continuous streetscape: a large plaza that includes a Canadian Tire and Shoppers Drug Mart. A busy café there with a proper espresso machine looks across the street at a rise in the land that exposes a strip of residential backyards in an almost obscene manner, as if the houses have been caught with their pants down. Below, in a space carved out of the ridge, an Adult Video Plus does business next to the Ready Lube, itself adjacent to the Aromatic Sensation Massage Parlour – an accidentally appropriate combination. It's a typical Canadian landscape, but perhaps one we don't like to talk about.

At Keele, just before the Black Creek lowlands, 'main-street' York continues south and passes through the kind of nondescript but still functioning commercial block that York is full of. At Rogers Road, there's a strange architectural oddity, a multi-coloured apartment building on top of a huge concrete parking garage. It's a little bit of Holland in Toronto, or someone's Dutch nightmare, depending on your tolerance for kitschy landmarks. There's an edge feeling here, where the Grand Trunk Railway cut and Black Creek Drive create an informal border.

A left on Rogers Road leads east, back into deep York. The complex five-point intersection where Rogers meets Old Weston Road and Watt Avenue is a chaotic, European-style mess of traffic that somehow works. On one corner, the Nova Era café overlooks the traffic flow, as do a Pizza Pizza, a Petro-Canada and a Portuguese restaurant. In so many upscale suburbs you can walk kilometres without finding services like these, but York, despite its dowdiness, is still a walkable city. Had York developed sufficiently before the age of the automobile, this could be one of Toronto's greatest intersections, maybe even marking the centre of York. However, like the Caribbean strip up on Eglinton, York – or the idea of York – lives quietly tucked away in a corner of Toronto only the locals know about, asking to be discovered.

Yorkdale Mall

 neighbourhood jaunt   Connecting walks: None.

dress to impress

 offspring friendly

Some of us might not want to admit it, but the best place to see Toronto might be at the mall. Where else does a nearly complete cross-section of the city exist in one spot? On those rainy, overcast Sundays when melancholy blankets the city, I like to ride the Spadina subway line to Yorkdale Mall and walk in circles with some of the 70,000 or so people who head there on weekends. Apart from being anonymous in the only crowd available on that kind of day, I see all sorts of Torontonians I don't run into on Queen West, the Annex or Harbourfront – all those places downtowners might prefer to bump into them. Women in hijabs parade past shellacked Holt Renfrew–bound ladies, who brush by the guys who wear baggy shirts that go to their knees, who follow the teenage girls with impossibly visible thongs, who are being dragged away by weary moms into the Gap to 'buy something nice.'

You can see this at any mall, but Yorkdale is extra special because it also helped vault Toronto into the modern age when it opened in 1964, a year before our iconic City Hall was built. This was the largest indoor mall in the world for a time, and the first of its kind in Canada. With Eaton's and Simpsons department stores and a Dominion supermarket as anchors, Yorkdale was an Emerald City on the fringe of Toronto. It was designed by John Graham and Company, the Seattle architecture firm that did the Space Needle and, two generations earlier, the Ford factory and showroom at Dupont and Ossington that now houses Faema Café on its ground floor.

Adam Sobolak, an activist in Toronto's modern preservation movement, speaks in glowing terms of what some see as just a mall: 'Yorkdale always seemed more ample and luxurious than the usual Graham fare ... what intrigues me is, from photographic evidence, how astonishingly Kennedy-era suave, stylish and timelessly fresh their graphics and accoutrements were.' Sobolak also

points out that the interchange of
Highway 401 and the Allen Expressway
that fed into Yorkdale's 7,000-car lot
was called, in the space-age parlance of
the day, a 'turbochange.'

From the outside, that suave style is
now hidden by various additions and
inconsistent tacked-on facades. Yet
inside, the utopian modernism is still
evident: the ceilings are wider and
higher than in most malls, and light
floods nearly all corridors through
nearly continuous windows above
all the stores. Even the latest addition,
carved out of the hulk of the old
Eaton's store (whose white rectangle
you can still see rise above the rest of
the mall from the edges of the parking
lot), has a massive glass atrium that
hangs from an exterior skeleton and
'floating' benches made of smooth
Jatoba wood.

In the tradition of Iain Sinclair's
book *London Orbital*, which gives an
account of his walk around London's
M25 ring-road expressway, a fellow
mall rat and I did what you're not
supposed to do one summer day walk
around the outside of the mall. We

Yorkdale then and now.

started at the former Simpsons (now the Bay). Up close, the big
concrete building has details few malls would bother with today,
like lovely tiny orange tiles above each entrance.

Unlike the rest of Yorkdale, the Simpsons Building was
designed by CN Tower architect John Andrews while he was at
Toronto's legendary modernist architecture firm John B. Parkin
Associates. In an essay on Yorkdale she wrote for the 2007 book
*Concrete Toronto: A Guide to Concrete Architecture from the Fifties to
the Seventies*, architect Veronica Madonna writes that the building
'demands to be seen while driving at rapid speeds. Its repetitious

Lester B. Pearson addresses the crowd in the Simpson's Court in 1965.

vertical piers stand like a fortress holding thousands of eager shoppers inside [where] the concrete vaulted ceilings made Yorkdale a shopping cathedral.'

Parishioners at this cathedral of commerce can still pay indulgences in the ruins of the old Simpsons Court. Once one of the best rooms in the city, the lamps that hung from each 'stalactite' are long gone, and the fountains there were reorganized and partially covered as the Bay colonized more space. The old Simpsons restaurant once overlooked the Kresge's across the court, which sold giant helium balloons to children whose slippery hands let many escape up to the ceiling. 'My parents always refused to buy me the balloons,' recalled Miriam Verberg, who went to the mall as a child in the late 1970s and early 1980s. 'So when we ate at Simpsons, I would stare at the balloons above me and wonder how many people the size of my dad would have to stand on each other's shoulders to reach one for me.'

Back outside, you can walk among some of the 70 percent of Yorkdale patrons who drive to the mall rather than taking transit. There are few places more sinister than the lawless Wild West of a shopping mall parking lot, where even the Ontario Highway Traffic Act doesn't apply and cars battle for choice spots. There always seem to be lone men sitting in idling cars, the streams of runoff from their air conditioners pooling together in the middle of the pavement. The sun and asphalt conspire to create a blast-furnace microclimate, the solar opposite of the controlled environment inside.

Yorkdale's paved wilderness is mitigated by a twenty-foot-high sculpture with amusingly obscene genitalia called *Universal Man*. Created by Gerald Gladstone, the sculpture was originally located by the CN Tower to 'give balance of human scale' to Andrews' more famous freestanding masterpiece.

Continuing our orbit, we found bits of the intricate brickwork patterns from the original Yorkdale hiding between the garish Las Vegas-style add-ons.

As Yorkdale has aged, it has progressed from middle- to upper-middle class. The Dominion gave way to Holt Renfrew and the everyman's Eaton's and Kresge's became stores a rung or two up the ladder, even as the mall's visitors still range across class lines. It's worth the walk across the parking lot and south down Dufferin a block to Orfus Road, where Yorkdale's working-class slack has been taken up by outlet stores with giant block-letter signs that advertise liquidation blowouts and 'urban wear' 50 to 75 percent off. If Yorkdale and the turbochange are the utopian future of the 1960s, Orfus is the hinterland that feeds off the commerce the mall lets get away, as remora suckerfish do with shark leftovers.

Back in Yorkdale's orbit, we stopped at the Moxie's for lunch. The restaurant's facade attempts to make it look like a separate building, the kind of comforting hyperreality – 'the authentic fake' – that Umberto Eco wrote about while he was travelling America. Our nice waitress introduced herself by name, we drank huge, suburban-sized beers, and the only problem we had in the world was the kitchen's prolific use of iceberg lettuce. (We pretended it was an homage to the weird food people ate back in 1964.) We had intended to eat at one of the old department store cafeterias, but most have left Yorkdale.

Tipsy, we continued on, stumbling through the bushes behind Holt Renfrew, where the sidewalk abruptly ends, and into the GO bus terminal below the mall. Signs direct people to buses bound for Barrie, Gravenhurst, Sudbury and even 'Western Canada,' making Yorkdale seem like a centre for more than just shopping. Malls like Yorkdale were often built in what was the middle of nowhere, and the city eventually surrounded them. With its bus

station, Yorkdale (like other Toronto area malls) has become a regional hub.

Not wanting to face more empty sidewalks and a daunting parking garage, we cheated and went back inside. Our initial, near-euphoric urge to buy things had waned, so we enjoyed the crowds and let their flow take us around for another circuit. With its recreated streetscapes and multicultural and class mix, Yorkdale's hyperreality may be where the reality of Toronto's celebrated diversity actually exists in one place.

The eastern wing of the mall leads to a glassed-in tube of a walkway that connects shoppers with Yorkdale subway station. Opened in 1978, the Arthur Erickson design originally included 158 colourful neon glass tubes along the length of its 570-foot-long transparent ceiling. When trains arrived and departed, a computer connected to the TTC's signaling system caused the lights to pulse, reflecting the speed and direction of the train, like a launch pad from a science-fiction film. Designed by artist Michael Hayden and called *Arc-en-ciel* – 'rainbow' in French – it was dismantled in the early 1990s and remains in storage, neglected and un-electrified, because the TTC's public art budget doesn't cover maintenance costs and, like many of Toronto's 1970s-era future-forward elements, the future has become the past.

The subway can take you right downtown, but if you're leaving the mall on foot, you face a task nearly as challenging as walking out of the airport and into the city. You need four (or more) wheels to do it comfortably. But strolling is possible.

On different walk, this one at night, a few of us walked around the noise barrier at the south edge of the parking lot and into the residential community below it. Two hours later we were on College Street. (Yorkdale seems a lot farther away when you take the subway.) Another time, I arrived on my own for a walk into North York. I first stopped by the Rainforest Café inside the mall – I figured it might be a long time before I'd have another chance to get a gin and tonic. The maître d' sitting in the giant elephant head out front directed me to a frog barstool next to duck, parrot and zebra stools. The bar in the Rainforest Café is made of glass and has bubbling water and, at times, the whole restaurant becomes a rainforest, complete with falling rain and flapping robotic butterflies. One more dose of Umberto Eco's hyperreality before re-entering the real Toronto. But after spending time in Yorkdale, it's hard to tell the real from the fake. Perhaps it's all just Toronto.

The Sheppard Line

 neighbourhood jaunt   Connecting walk: Yonge.

 dress to impress

 offspring friendly

The city constantly creates, devours and recreates itself, and the velocity of this cycle is quickest in Toronto's inner suburbs. If you stand at Yonge and Sheppard in North York, you can see the change happening in one 360-degree glance, as everything big, shiny and new quickly gives way to tiny mid-century bungalows and front lawns. If urban planning were like a game of chess, these older homes would be the pawns that only a few generations ago were the first line of Toronto's expansion into Ontario farmland.

As they do in many areas of the city, long-time residents quibble with the boundaries and proper definitions of the neighbourhood. This isn't actually Willowdale, they might say, but Lansing. They've got signage on their side – the city has marked area streets with this historic designation – but neighbourhood boundaries (and even the idea of a neighbourhood) change as populations shift. It's easy to forget that neighbourhoods we think of as historic are human creations that have evolved over time.

Historic Lansing was centred at Yonge and Sheppard, and its last immediately visible vestige, Dempsey's Hardware Store, stood on the northwest corner until 1997, when the store was moved a few blocks north. A local landmark, the store was a symbol of old North York, a place whose civic ontology was made up of a

number of small hamlets and villages like Lansing and Willow-dale. Today, the site is an empty lot, one of two on the west side of Yonge that sit on Sheppard subway station, the point of inter-change with Toronto's newest, and most debated, subway line. These lots are remnants of a time, in the early 2000s, when Yonge Street was diverted while the new Sheppard line subway station was being built underneath the intersection. Once they, along with the parking lot of the Metro grocery store on the southeast corner, are filled in with development, Yonge and Sheppard will have much in common with Yonge and Eglinton just a few kilometres south of here, which followed a similar development pattern a generation or two ago.

To head east on Sheppard is to walk above Toronto's great 'subway to nowhere,' the five-station line that runs from Yonge Street to Don Mills Road. That term was (and still is) used by detractors because, at the time of its construction, Sheppard Avenue passed through a part of Toronto where density was relatively low. However, it's important to remember that when the Yonge line opened between Union Station and Eglinton in 1954, density along parts of that line was not much greater than it is along Sheppard today. And those who still refer to this area as 'nowhere' either haven't been here in a long time or hold a grudge against the newer parts of Toronto.

Only a few blocks east of Yonge, the office-and-condo land-scape fades into the familiar bungalow landscape that many North Yorkers grew up with. Yet urban growth is more like *Monopoly* than chess, ruled by a market that decides what has value and what can be discarded. Some of those bungalows along Sheppard are showing signs of these market effects, now sitting

uncomfortably close to streets that have grown fat and eaten up their front lawns. The nuclear families they were intended for have long since departed, and now some are offices for dentists and lawyers, while others offer shiatsu and psychic readings. People, it seems, don't like to live in a tiny house on a big road.

Directly south of here, between Yonge and Highway 401 – an area that's three to five blocks wide – the transition from postwar to postmodern development is stark. Small, single-family homes sit across the street from thick new townhouse developments and condominium towers. The houses on the front lines tend to look a little battered and worse for wear, as if their owners saw the approaching development and decided not to bother fixing the roof. Around Yonge and Eglinton, where the line between towers and homes was fixed decades ago, stability has been returned to the neighbourhood, but up here change continues to seem inevitable.

The land immediately adjacent to the 401 and Yonge was once slated for the Toronto Maple Leafs' new arena, but when a more appropriate downtown location was chosen, the land was developed as residential. From the highway, the condo towers seem to hug and almost lean over the road, leaving those who have never been there on foot to wonder if the situation is too close for comfort. While the view from many units includes the 401's express and collector lanes, it's likely the unencumbered city view to the south that makes it tolerable to live there. Still, when viewed from above, this stretch of the 401 is impressive, a twenty-four-hour river of steel. It has a beauty in both its contrasting rhythms and gentle curves. Those constantly worried about Toronto's world-class status can take solace; our main expressway is bigger than most.

On the ground, wandering between the towers, the experience is typical of many new developments: everything seems new. Jane Jacobs said neighbourhoods take a generation or two to grow into themselves, a sentiment first expressed a century ago by landscape architect Frederick Law Olmstead. Trees grow, people make subtle alterations to their properties and the place acquires a patina that only comes with age, the one that makes buildings seem like they belong. Though new-seeming, there's the foundation for a good community here, with a mix of buildings and townhouses that,

perhaps most importantly, are not dominated by the car. Unlike
the traditional landscape of North York, parking is hidden underground in this area, and much of the public space around the
buildings is car-free and dense, the spaces in between the townhomes often sidewalks rather than roads. Borrowing ideas from
the New Urbanism movement, these smaller developments may
actually work because they are located within walking distance of
the shopping and entertainment locations on Yonge. This area is
a nice change from many New Urbanism communities like it,
where services are all a drive away and urbanity is only an illusion.

For two weeks in October 2009, the transition from not-so-old
to new was explored on Leona Drive, two blocks east of Yonge.
The street hosted the kind of public art project that Toronto needs
more of, one that is ephemeral rather than permanent, and which
explores and raises ideas and then disappears – an arts event
staged as much for the local community as it is for people who
come from elsewhere to experience it. The *Leona Drive Project*
was a temporary, large-scale art installation that took over six
1940s bungalows that were slated for demolition to make way
for newer, slightly-more-dense housing. The vacant houses, interpreted and transformed by over a dozen artists, explored the territory of this suburban landscape, the one we're led to believe (at
least by popular mythology) has no worthwhile stories and isn't
interesting. What was most striking on the block was a bungalow
painted entirely green, like a real-life *Monopoly* piece waiting to be
bought, sold and replaced by something bigger.

The remarkable project was organized by the collectives Public
Access and L.O.T.: Experiments in Urban Research. The green
Monopoly house was by artist An Te Liu, and though it was made
of solid brick, wood and plaster, a simple paint job rendered the
house plastic-seeming, as if it really were as disposable as it was
being treated. Next door, Daniel Borins and Jennifer Marman
impregnated a living room window with a white Honda Civic,
evoking a common late-night news story where an errant car
drives up over a lawn and crashes into a house, a David Lynch
Blue Velvet view of the tranquil suburbs, where the very instrument
that gave rise to this kind of development later destroys it.

Janine Marchessault, one of the project curators and a professor at York University, cobbled together various small arts grants

(to a total of around $50,000) and many in-kind donations to make the project happen. Marchessault and her colleagues' greatest work of art may have been getting a developer to agree to the project. As Marchessault explained, 'The risk for him was if this project caused people to take too much of an interest in these houses.'

Leona Drive was part of the first wave of residential development that took place after farmland here was subdivided and most indications of rural life were bulldozed and covered up. The head-

The Leona Drive Project.

waters of Wilket Creek used to flow at Leona Drive, but the watercourse has been long buried and entombed in concrete tunnels. You can follow its path south along a slight depression in the land; it meanders through parks and in between bungalows to the giant 401 sound barrier. There, a metal grate blocks access to a culvert under the highway, beyond which this nearly lost vale continues to meander through middle-class neighbourhoods to York Mills and Bayview, where the stream finally sees the light again. Along the way, there are oversized drains that, coupled with the vast size of the 401 culvert, give a spooky sense that this infrastructure is waiting for the flood, a kind of semiotics of potential disaster.

Here and elsewhere, following Toronto's lost and buried streams and creeks is like navigating the city with an old, outdated map written in another language, where only vague symbols and signs guide the way. Many of the bungalows along the Wilket's path have been replaced with monster homes, another way the stability of a neighbourhood can be thrown off. Many down-town residential neighbourhoods have historic designations, meaning a walk down the street today feels like it did in the past and, if the bylaws hold up, what it will feel like decades in the future. Younger neighbourhoods don't have this kind of protection, so something that has been the same for over fifty years can quickly change.

Back on Sheppard, by the Leona Drive TTC escape hatch –
a small brick building that leads deep below the buried creek to
the new subway – Sheppard dips slightly, marking where Wilket
Creek passed. Cross Sheppard and follow the vale north all the way
up to the Empress Walk mall on Yonge, site of North York's first
municipal buildings. The streets around here – a royal quartet that
include Empress, Duchess, Princess and Kingsdale – are part of
an early North York suburban development. Kingsdale was billed
as a place of fresh air and open spaces only thirty-five minutes
from King and Yonge by electric streetcar. Today, the streets are a
mix of new monsters and old craftsman homes that date back to
the 1910s and '20s – a sense of history not often associated with
North York.

The *Leona Drive Project* dug into some of the ideas and
assumptions we have about our suburbs. Of the six houses used,
only one was open to visitors. Crossing the threshold into the tiny
home felt transgressive, as if you were invading somebody's actual
home – perhaps this level of intimacy came as a shock because,
unless we know someone in a particular neighbourhood, we don't
get to see the domestic side of that place. The rooms of the house
were small and compact, radiating from a central foyer where a
narrow staircase led to the second floor (a half-storey where each
bedroom had a slanted roof). However, the house didn't feel small
in the way a similarly sized open-concept condo does. Compart-
mentalization can make spaces feel bigger. A front room was
covered with thousands of pennies artist Ryan Livingstone had
painted white, an ode to both the 'save a penny for a rainy day'
ethos and, he told me, the polka-dot dress his grandmother wore
when greeting company. Upstairs, artist Christine Davis had
painted the bathroom 'Victory Red,' a shade of lipstick from the
era. How can this place be 'nowhere' when somebody's wearing
Victory Red?

Saddest was the kitchen, where Shana MacDonald and Angela
Joosse used artifacts left behind by Ruth Gillespie, the home's
owner, first with her husband and later as a widow, for fifty years.
After she died, the relative who sold the property didn't bother to
clean out all her personal belongings, which included diaries and
a book of poems written to her by friends and classmates that
included the line: 'Dream lofty dreams, and as you dream, so shall

you become.' Back out on Leona Drive, every one of the near-identical bungalows suddenly seemed filled to the rafters with stories of so many Ruths who dreamed quiet dreams and lived quiet lives but weren't boring and did matter. Nothing seems to happen in the suburbs because the stories haven't been told as much, and the *Leona Drive Project* started to tell some of them. For some of the people who visited the project, those stories will remain written on the street forever.

The mishmash of converted bungalows and small apartment buildings continues east along Sheppard, a distinctly modernist typology that, like the stories inside the surrounding neighbourhoods, hasn't been celebrated much yet. As change comes to Sheppard, buildings are disposed of without challenge. Perhaps many don't have value, and it's smarter urban planning to replace them with more density, but the net waste of energy that comes with demolition is a hidden but large factor in what's happening up here. How to preserve these bungalows while acknowledging what the market wants is a tricky riddle to solve.

At Willowdale Avenue, a planned subway stop was nixed by neighbourhood opposition that predicted that the speed of change would overwhelm them. At Bayview, where there is a subway stop, it's evident their prediction was correct. Like the area around Yonge, Sheppard and the 401, North York's constant, skyward transition is evident here. Bayview Village, once a small neighbourhood mall, has evolved into an upscale shopping centre, a kind of indoor Yorkville but without whatever grit Yorkville has left in the corners. There's an interesting vibe inside; it's the kind of place you might expect to see Dustin Hoffman's parents shopping in an updated version of *The Graduate*. Out in the parking lot, by the new subway station, an oval blue-and-white condo tower sits like a cross between a cruise ship and Phillip Johnson's famous Lipstick Building in Manhattan. All this on land that, during the Second World War, was used to grow potatoes.

Starting in the 1950s – a decade or so later than the homes on Leona Drive were built – the farmland here was turned into a meandering housing development that gave the mall its name. Designed by Eugene Faludi – the planner responsible for much of the postwar low-density development in cities across Canada – it's quintessential suburbia, a sort of utopic museum for a Canadian dream. South of the mall, Faludi's landscape collides with more of the change brought by the so-called 'subway to nowhere.' A 1950s-style ranch house (not the sight you generally expect when exiting a subway station) had white development signs out on its lawn in the spring of 2009, complete with the familiar bureaucratic poetry describing the proposed tower that would be built there soon. It's as if these houses are on death row, each carrying their white-sign stigma. There's still

New York or North York: these NY Towers grew because of the Sheppard subway.

a handful of these houses on streets running south of Sheppard, before you bump into the development known as NY Towers.

It's a startling transition, as if the sets from two different movies are sitting next to each other. The NY Towers hug the 401 and look vaguely like the Chrysler Tower in NYC. In fact, one is called the Chrysler, while others are the Waldorf and the Chelsea, correcting any thought that the NY part of the name might stand for North York. The name and style may be embarrassingly un-Torontonian, but even in New York there are buildings that are supposed to look like somewhere else. (Think of all those European-looking courthouses and museums.) Walking through this area isn't unpleasant; townhouses and their barbecues, hedges and patio doors wrap around bases of the all towers. It's still a version of the Canadian Dream, just packed in a little more tightly.

Back on Sheppard, the buildings soon give way to a landscape of mod walk-up apartments and attached homes, the kind of places so many baby boomers started out in in the second half of the 1900s, when this was Mel Lastman's North York. Sheppard starts to slope downwards here, and there are dramatic views a few kilometres west to Don Mills Road. This is a valley as vast as the Don River Valley to the south, but the development here hides the topography well. For many Torontonians, the intersection of Sheppard and Leslie means only one thing: Ikea-land! The hinterland disappears at this goal-oriented intersection: get in there, buy exotically named furniture, get out. Ikea is like the sun: stare at it and you can't see anything else. However, if you do succeed in looking away from that Swedish sun, you'll notice there's lots to see.

Named after a short road nearby, Bessarion subway station is a lonely outpost on the way downhill, one of the least busy of the TTC's sixty-nine stations. This may change, though, as the Canadian Tire distribution warehouses here are replaced by a glass-tower community very much in the style of the CityPlace development that's adjacent to the Rogers Centre. It's the kind of place that the Ikea next door seems destined to furnish.

Let's return to that Swedish sun for a moment. Ikea seems to be the only big-box store that can evade the heat of the urbanist anti-big-box attack, safe because everybody secretly likes it. Though it's on the subway, the North York location's connection to Leslie station is still awkward: shoppers who come by transit either have to walk about ten minutes from the subway or take an odd little Ikea shortbus that waits by the station. The walk isn't much in urban terms, but the scale of the roads and the underpass tells you you shouldn't be here on foot.

If you are, though, you'll see the entrance to the East Don Parklands at the intersection of Sheppard and Leslie. Head south along the trail and you'll come upon a cathedral-like passage underneath the 401. Walk north and a path leads down under the humid tree canopy to the Don River, whose rushing can't drown out the sounds of traffic coming from Sheppard and Leslie. Further north, a network of trails expands octopus-like into northern North York. Most of this Sheppard walk is scored by a long motor symphony. Yet walking the trail north of Sheppard on the trail is a bucolic experience punctuated by the the smell of trees, the chirping of birds and little footbridges that cross the stream, all of this below the soaring railway bridges crossing everything else up above. As wilderness-like as this all is, it too was once farmland, and dotted with mills. But during redevelopment, trees were allowed to sprout up rather than homes. The landscape here has long been altered and is untrustworthy (is this real or human-made?), but the bigger picture is true: this is a river valley. Twists in the river or sugarloafs in the ravine wall, though, may be natural, or they may not.

Not far from Sheppard, a staircase leads up to Villaways, a public housing project wedged in between Leslie Street, the GO train tracks and the valley. It's almost like an island, isolated from the rest of North York. Just four streets of 1970s townhomes, the Villaways feels like *A Clockwork Orange* meets *Sesame Street*, only more natural, as backyards open up into communal spaces and some homes sit on the top of the ravine, a setting that would likely be worth seven figures across the valley. The streets – Ocra, Grado, Tomar – all end with the street designation Villaway. At 20 Adra Villaway, there's a tiny community house that's used by a few agencies, including Art Starts, an art-based community development organization.

Sarah Bothwell, an Art Starts project manager who worked here in 2009, chatted with me in front of their 'garage front' operation one day. Bothwell ran what they call 'the rec,' an initiative that got youth from Villaways to work on projects that included building soap-box racers, treasure hunts in the creek and even field trips to Interaccess, a gallery on Ossington, for robot-building workshops. 'I think of this as sneaky art,' she said, 'I just tell them to just come to the rec. This neighbourhood is fantastic, but we work with youth who have a rap for being bad kids.'

By getting the kids involved in art projects, Bothwell was working to flip that image, to connect these kids not just with the rest of the city (or the cool kids on Ossington), but with their immediate neighbours. It isn't as easy as it sounds. Bothwell said that when they held a community yard sale on Leslie, hoping to attract people from the middle-class suburb just metres away, only one person came over.

Back at Ikea, inside the great machine of commerce, Villaways seems far away. With some shame – but I know I'm not alone – I came up here on one walk with only one thing in mind: to eat at the Ikea restaurant. It's an odd experience, unlike most dining experiences today, and it plays on our nostalgia (much like some of the furniture sold here). Cafeteria-eating was once more common – most famously in New York's Automat locations – and it's sometimes comforting to slide a tray along stainless steel rails and eat food from the Swedish machine. Ikea also offers interesting people-watching opportunities: tragic and heartbreaking domestic squabbles are routinely fought in public here, a good counter-balance to the romantic North York nuclear-family ideal that may blossom on this walk.

From the restaurant's windows, you can glimpse a fine view of the valley around Ikea-land, an area that's home to the Ontario Naturopathic College building – a perfect specimen of 1970s concrete architecture surrounded by the requisite institutional pine trees that were the style then – and North York General Hospital, which was one of Toronto's ground zeros during the 2003 SARS crisis.

The walk up out of the valley east along Sheppard is decidedly boring, as the adjacent neighbourhoods were allowed to turn their backs on the street, so it is lined on both sides with backyards. Only near the crest of the hill before Don Mills Road do things improve, where a corner of the Henry Farm neighbourhood provides Sheppard with more than just a fence to look at. Though the whole neighbourhood here is known as Henry Farm – it was named after Henry Mulholland, who settled it in 1806 and whose great-grandson, George Stewart Henry, was Ontario's tenth premier – the area spreading out from the southwest corner of Don Mills and Sheppard is most interesting. Unlike the typical detached homes of the surrounding area, this corner is a multi-layered maze of townhouses. It is a wholly pedestrianized commu-nity, where the residences have been built into the hills and parking is hidden in a lot underneath. It compares favourably with the apartment tower and townhouse community on the east side of Don Mills, where caretaking is not at the same level.

On the northeast corner of Don Mills and Sheppard sits Fairview Mall, the terminus of the subway line. Though many Torontonians' subway dreams would see this line extend to the Scarborough Town Centre, where it could connect to the Scarbor-ough RT, for now the station is a kind of exotic transportation hub, with buses to the most distant corners of North York and Scarbor-ough. To ride one of these bus lines is to realize just how big Toronto is.

If you opt not to board a bus, getting into Fairview Mall is a little odd. The subway doesn't offer a particularly glamorous route, letting passengers out into the parking garage, where they must walk briefly outside (interrupting what could be a completely indoor experience from the downtown core to this mall), and through the Sears women's underwear department before finding the busy corridors inside.

On cold or rainy Sunday afternoons, it's good to take a ride to Fairview and wander around the stores and food court to see a slice of Toronto that isn't visible on the street. Though North York sidewalks are far from desolate, they don't have near the amount of pedestrian traffic you find downtown, and thus far fewer conversations to overhear. As a result, you may come away from this walk without a sense of who lives here. At Fairview, the aisles are just like Bloor or Queen on a Saturday afternoon. To distort the lyrics of a Neil Young song, everybody knows this is somewhere.

The Finch Hydro Corridor

pack a lunch   Connecting walk: Yonge.

rough terrain

few services

If you look at a map of Toronto, you'll see that two bands run across the top of the city. One is the fat and wide Highway 401 that all Torontonians and most Canadians are familiar with. The other is the Finch Hydro Corridor, which runs across the city just north of Finch Avenue, and looks like a continuous green line on maps, bisected at predictable points by longitudinal streets. In Google Earth, the corridor seems like a linear park, though you can make out the steel hydro towers and follow the line of them right out of the city. I once started a walk of the corridor at Finch station at about 2 p.m. on a nowhere, no-time Sunday afternoon. (Days like this are often the best time to walk, a much better way to spend the day than sitting around a cramped brunch hot spot.) I was going to exit the station at the kiss 'n' ride passenger pick-up area because I've never done that, but that seemed presumptuous. (Who exactly can you kiss and ride?) Instead, I exited on the east side of Yonge.

The hydro corridor extends to the horizon in both directions, but I decided to walk east. Just outside the northern exit of Finch station lies the expanse of the TTC commuter parking lot, so vast that it rivals the one found at the Canadian National Exhibition. If it weren't for the power lines, an Airbus A380 could land there, or at least crash without much collateral damage. The scale is more airport than urban. Except for the spots closest to the subway, this lot is nearly empty on a Sunday afternoon.

There's much to notice in an empty parking lot, like the tight black rings of rubber tire tracks (what else is there do with a small, front-wheel-drive car with an overpowered four-cylinder engine in an empty lot but make doughnuts?), the massive footprint of power towers (about the size of a downtown duplex) and the puddles of broken safety glass (smash-and-grab surprises at the end of the day). Perhaps most striking is the skyline to the south. Here, Toronto's Yonge Street skyscraper spine, which begins at Lake Ontario, begins to sputter out. To the north there's nothing but a low bungalow horizon.

After the parking lots ended, I continued east along Bishop Street, which runs parallel to the grassy hydro corridor. It's impossible to get lost on this walk: just follow the lines. The grass here is taller and wilder than a lawn, though it's still not quite a prairie. The houses nearby all have garages with opaque glass transoms over the door. So many Toronto subdivisions have a subtle, admirable trait like this one that shows that some unsung architect cared. Like a lot of places in Toronto, this place has a small-town-Ontario, almost exurban feel. A braided metal wire fence attached to rough wooden posts marks the perimeter of the hydro area. If these old fences could talk, they might express surprise that they are, in fact, part of a giant metropolis now. This far from the city's core, Toronto has grown so quickly that traces like this, things that suggest this wasn't supposed to be a big city, are common. It's hard to tell if I'm allowed to walk here or not, but the fence is passive and Canadian-looking enough to not scare anybody off. We're taught to think power lines and corridors are dangerous or private – like railways – but they are so inviting.

After passing some community gardens, I moved into the middle of the corridor, walking along the beaten path through rolling hills. This is about as close as I've ever come to feeling like one of the early Romantic peripatetics like William Wordsworth who wandered through the rural Lake District in England. That this place so close to the action of the city feels so shockingly rural makes it seem more rural than true rural places, where ruralness is expected. However, Wordsworth never had the buzz of the power lines above to keep him company as he ambled along. Though mine was a mostly solitary walk, there were other lone hikers – mostly dog walkers – out along this natural passage through the cul-de-sacs. We greeted each other with hellos like people do on trails in Algonquin or the Bruce Peninsula (and not like on most Toronto sidewalks), so perhaps it's more like a bucolic Wordsworth ideal than not.

There's quite a bit of hilly terrain in North York that former mayor Mel Lastman's boosterism didn't celebrate much, if at all.

After climbing down a muddy path, I was blocked by a somewhat-raging brook that I couldn't cross, something that also isn't supposed to happen in a city. Had I been wearing rubber boots, I could've made it across. However, that would have required wearing rubber boots within the city limits, which just seems wrong. I retreated and headed south along the top of the ravine, but soon found myself on a manicured lawn with Costco-style lawn furniture. Figuring I had wandered into some kind of suburban backyard annexation of public space (there was no fence suggesting I was on private property) I backed out before somebody could see me from their kitchen window and get upset. After feeling like a creep for lingering in the northern bushes on the edge of a playground, and then trying unsuccessfully to find a makeshift creek crossing, I made my way around the ravine by walking along Gustav Crescent, where I noticed, by way of the name of a public school, that this area is called Cummer Valley.

I found a passage back to the hydro corridor and was suddenly in the middle of a huge dog park with what seemed to be the largest dogs in Toronto. (They grow everything big in North York.) Once across Bayview Avenue (about the only place commercial activity was in view during most of this walk), I followed a nearly continuous single-track path past abandoned Esso gas stations, Swiss Chalets, familiar Toronto 1960s apartment clusters and chains of backyards. The rhythm of the path was broken only where it intersects with the other north-south Don Valley trails, and comes to a full stop at the Old Cummer GO Station, where I broke the law and crossed the train tracks so I didn't have to break my stride. I then found myself at a giant power substation just off Leslie Street, where that electric hum buzzed as loud as the planes in the Pearson flight path above.

My walk ended after I'd ambled through more vast parking lots – an eastern bookend of sorts – and ended up at the Seneca College campus and the sound barrier of Highway 404. A few pine trees, some lawn and a giant wall kept me safe from the no-person's-land of the speeding expressway. Though the wall is ugly, its presence conjures up thoughts of other walls around the world of a similar look that have much different meanings, so perhaps there's little to really complain about here. The power lines carry on east, over the 404, but I backtracked through the Seneca campus to Don Mills and Finch, where I sat with a Tim Hortons coffee and waited for the bus down to Pape Station. I was 8.4 kilometres from Finch station, where I'd started, having walked through some of the best countryside Toronto offers.

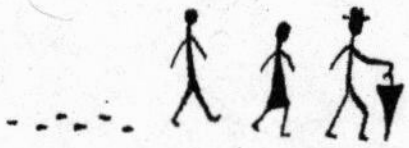

Eastest

Rouge Park

 day trip

 rough terrain

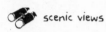 scenic views

Connecting walks: None.

The opening lines of Robert Frost's poem 'Stopping by Woods on a Snowy Evening' read, 'Whose woods these are I think I know / His house is in the village, though; / He will not see me stopping here / To watch his woods fill up with snow.' Though he's writing about a semi-rural area, there's something about the proximity of those quiet woods to the nearby village that makes Frost's poem seem cozy and urban – a quick escape into the wild but never far from civilization. How wonderful it would be to walk through a forest on the way to a friend's house, or to a tavern or movie in another part of the city.

In Toronto, the best of nature and the city often intersect, and if you're willing to head into one of the city's ravines – some of which are strategically poised between various points A and B – you can easily take the road less travelled (it's the one that's more wooded). The wildest and deepest wilderness, the one closest to that Robert Frost moment, is found in Rouge Park, one of the world's largest natural-environment parks in an urban area. Rouge Park runs from the Oak Ridges Moraine in the north down to Lake Ontario along the far east side of Toronto, where Scarborough meets Pickering. The park ends at a nice beach with a good view of Pickering Nuclear Power Plant to the east, a fine backdrop for any picnic or urgent romantic moment. Up the Rouge River, in the northeast corner of the city, there's a series of hiking trails that starts just off Meadowvale Road, across from the Metro Toronto Zoo and is easily accessible by the 85 Sheppard East bus. The landscape here is closer to that of cottage country (and of Algonquin Park) than to Yonge and Bloor or even Trinity Bell-woods, even though it's all within the city limits.

The downside of wandering through this somewhat untamed chunk of big-country Toronto is the lack of essential urban walking services such as espresso machines. The closest coffee to these Rouge trails is a couple kilometres east on Sheppard. It's an

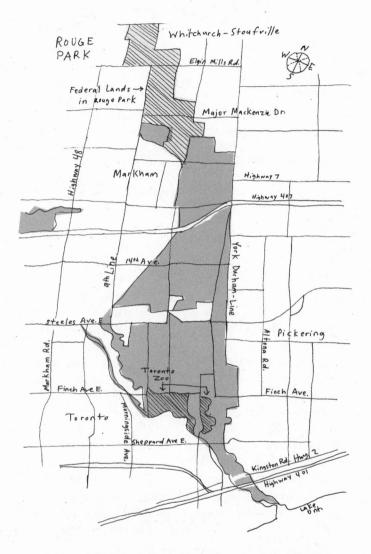

undercover Second Cup that hides in the lobby of a giant Home Depot, which seems appropriate in this landscape of bigness (big buildings, big spaces, big roads). Get off the bus at Grand Marshall Drive, just east of Morningside Avenue, for coffee and lumber supplies, and then start strolling east on Sheppard.

The walk from the Home Depot to the zoo is wide open, with lots of traffic lanes and high-voltage wires that pass by a few old homes on Sheppard that were there when the road was only two lanes, back when this was a seldom-travelled part of Scarborough. There's even a bike lane out here. The housing development on the north side of Sheppard was built in the New Urbanism style, and tries to mimic older, pre-car neighbourhood typologies. But like many of these developments, it's located far from the services that would make this place actually walkable. Still, the density here on the edge of Toronto is welcome. This corner of the city is the only one that touches rural Ontario; the rest of the 416 and 905 area code borders have been entirely consumed by sprawl. The Pickering Airport lands northeast of here have seen their development restricted since the early 1970s, when the federal government expropriated vast tracts of land for the proposed airport, which has yet to be built. The hydro corridor that cuts diagonally through Scarborough exits the city here, and from a few high places, you can look southwest and see the downtown skyscrapers.

The Vista trailhead is a short distance up Meadowvale from Sheppard, across from the zoo. Though the zoo is the best-known place for wild animals out here, there are some truly wild landscapes nearby. You can visit a number of these landscapes starting from Pearse House, a historical and natural interpretation centre housed in the 1869 Ontario farmhouse that was the homestead of James Pearse Jr., a stonemason who, along with his brothers, operated a sawmill nearby. The sign at the beginning of the Vista Trail lists a number of organized tours that start from the Pearse House, including an 'animal tracks- and scat-reading' winter walk that must be geared towards an audience of hard-core rural enthusiasts.

A few minutes down the Vista Trail, there's a bench that boasts one of the best views in the city, but not of the city. The bench doesn't face the CN Tower or any part of the Toronto skyline; rather, it faces across the hundred-metre-deep gorge created by Little Rouge Creek.

Sheer and dangerous cliffs drop down to the creek below, whose constant whitewater rush rumbles back up to the trail. From here, you can even see into the 905. The bench is dedicated to Rouge Park employee Patricia Joy Brooks with a little plaque that reads: 'Tragically taken August 2001, she fought and won so many battles, both personal and for the Rouge. She will remain forever young.' Finding her bench makes a solitary country walk less lonely.

Beyond the bench, the trail continues, following the gorge, and soon enters a forest of evergreens that's different than most of Toronto's deciduous forests, and that can be a bit of a shock in the winter months – so much green and thickness at a time when we're used to ravines stripped of foliage, revealing the usually hidden topography beneath. The trail gradually slopes downhill through the forest, and as I walked it, I passed other hikers, usually in couple or family form. The few solitary folks all had dogs, which I figure are mainly props, there to keep the walker from feeling like a pervert. There's something particularly suspicious about walking in a forest alone: people look at you warily. In the city, you can walk alone without guilt, but out here in the countryside even I started to wonder what I was up to. When I'd come across slower hikers, I'd make noise or cough before I overtook them to give them warning another human was nearby, a bit of social pretense that's hardly necessary when walking in the city.

The Vista Trail ends down at Twyn Rivers Drive, a curvy street that cuts through the park and connects the two parts of Sheppard Avenue. A short walk across a narrow pedestrian-unfriendly bridge to the Pickering side of the river brings you to the Orchard Trail, which heads back upstream. This trail is flat and low, and follows Little Rouge Creek quite closely, allowing for numerous side trips to the water's edge and good views up to the cliffs where Brooks' bench sits. The trail eventually leads to a long, straight road that's flanked by the Beare Road Landfill on the right and a barren mountain on the Pickering side. Turn left here and you'll arrive back at the Vista trailhead, the zoo and the TTC, which will carry you back to places much less wild. After a walk through the Rouge, gigantic Toronto seems, impossibly, even bigger. After all, it can contain all this too.

Kingston-Galloway and Guildwood Village

 neighbourhood jaunt   Connecting walks: None.

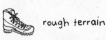 rough terrain

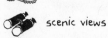 scenic views

Toronto has dozens of neighbourhoods with names many of us don't recognize. Those we do recognize, we know because they're celebrated or because they're notorious. The City of Toronto has designated thirteen 'priority' neighbourhoods, some of which have familiar names that fall into the latter category. Malvern or Jane and Finch, for example, are known for reasons residents there wish they weren't. So too is Kingston-Galloway, another one of those thirteen neighbourhoods, which is located in the almost-farthest reaches of East Scarborough.

Neighbourhoods are like people – bad reputations are easily acquired but hard to shake. But with neighbourhoods, there's the added injustice that that reputation can be spread by relatively few individuals. The crossroads of Kingston and Galloway roads would likely not have risen to notoriety had it not been for the Galloway Boys, the local gang that knew how to pick a memorable name and that gave the neighbourhood a bad reputation in the 2000s. The Galloway Boys' activities – which included the occasional murder – placed the area into Toronto's wider consciousness.

The curious thing about Kingston-Galloway, and a lot of neighbourhoods like it, is that when you're there, in middle of it, you'd never know it's a priority area. There are apartment towers, bungalows, townhouses, strip malls, used car lots, Starbucks, Tim Hortons and high schools – all things that resemble what a lot of Canada looks like. The landscapes of Canadian priority don't match the cinematic picture that's been painted of 'bad neighbourhoods,' so there's a sense of cognitive dissonance when you're there. The 1970s Bronx-on-fire is nowhere to be seen.

Just like in downtown Toronto, very different environments can exist close to each other, further undermining the cinematic (that is, American) image of blighted neighbourhoods that go on for miles. Walk south on Galloway a few blocks, across the GO and VIA tracks, and you encounter the big lawns and bigger trees of

The ruins of old Toronto reconstructed at the Guild Inn.

Guildwood Village, one of the wealthiest postal codes in the city. 'The other side of the tracks' is, as many clichés go, a reality.

At the south end of Galloway sits the Guild Inn, nestled in a tree-filled park high atop the Scarborough Bluffs, among eighty-eight acres of manicured grounds and woodland strewn with chunks of old Toronto buildings – the sculpture garden of lost Toronto. (Try visiting late at night during a full moon for the full ghostly experience.) The sculpture garden was started by Rosa and Spencer Clark, who collected bits of old Toronto buildings that were being torn down in the name of progress and set them up here. The main Guild Inn building, the Bickford residence, is an Arts and Crafts building that was constructed in 1914 and used by the Clarks as a Depression-era arts colony. It's currently abandoned and boarded up, deteriorating while the owner, the City of Toronto, figures out what to do with the historic building. In 2009, the low-rise 1960s 'Clamshell balcony' modernist tower was torn down, presumably at the behest of local residents who thought it didn't fit the historic character of the Guild (residents who themselves live in modernist split-levels and ranches). Perhaps it wasn't worth saving due to structural issues, but it was of a vintage that is out of fashion right now, just as Victorians were when Toronto's concrete towers went up in the 1950s and the gingerbread was seen as disposable.

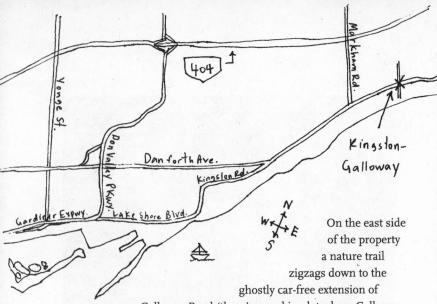

On the east side of the property a nature trail zigzags down to the ghostly car-free extension of Galloway Road (there's a parking lot where Galloway officially ends), leading down a steep ravine to the beach that stretches east and west for kilometres. Unless you think about what's on top of the bluffs, it's remarkable that a massive metro area of nearly five million people can just completely disappear.

This road was likely once open to cars, but today it's used only by pedestrians, cyclists and service vehicles that construct and maintain the elaborate breakwall along the bottom of the bluffs, which keeps the lake from eroding them further. Venture west along a human-made rock wall for a couple kilometres until you find a small beach and, just beyond it, a sculpture that looks a bit like a whale skeleton with metal ribs. Called the *Passage*, it marks geological time along the bluffs. Behind it, the very steep Doris McCarthy Trail (named after the Scarborough artist who lives nearby) climbs up the thick forest of Bellamy Ravine up to Bellamy and Kingston roads, where a TTC stop signals civilization.

East along the beach from the old Galloway Road, things become much more wild. The breakwall ends quickly and, after a stretch of rubble and rebar sticking out of the water, a narrow band of beach stretches for a few kilometres between the water and the bluff walls. A fifteen- or twenty-minute walk down the beach, there are some public-works ruins – a rare find in Toronto – that evoke the end of *Planet of the Apes*, when Charlton Heston finds the head of the Statue of Liberty on a beach under some sandy cliffs. People were here! What appear to be the concrete blocks are actually old early-Metro-era drainage culverts that were once part of the bluffs but now stand alone on the beach as a result of erosion. This beach continues

all the way to the mouth of Highland Creek, where there's a passage
up to a patch of back-country Scarborough (no TTC stops) and the
Highland Creek Wastewater Treatment Plant. Continue on by the
water and the beach leads to the end of Toronto at the Rouge River
outlet, which boasts prime views of the Pickering nuclear plant.

So close yet so far away, up on Galloway Road and back over the
tracks, sits the Boys and Girls Club of East Scarborough. On a June
day in 2009, I met Trichelle Primo there and she took me on a walk.
Primo has lived in Kingston-Galloway all of her nineteen years, and
she ran an after-school program out of the club. 'It's not as bad as
people make it seem,' she said. 'Everybody knows everybody.'

As we zigzagged around the neighbourhood, down a quiet postwar suburban street with the disproportionally mythical name of
Overture Street, through the Gabriel Dumont Co-op along Kingston
Road (home to one of the highest concentrations of First Nations
residents in Toronto) and near public housing buildings, she
greeted people and pointed out the obvious: the area is clean,
it's quiet and it's more like the rest of Toronto than we think.

The reasons this is a priority neighbourhood are somewhat
hidden at first glance, but as Boys and Girls Club Executive Director
Ron Rock explained, it's due to lack of services. 'Downtown, you
can walk a kilometre and you'll hit all kinds of services,' he said.
In East Scarborough, they are few and far between.'

Rock and I went up Galloway Road north of Kingston Road to
where it ends at Lawrence. He showed me around this part of the
neighbourhood, pointing out Toronto Community Housing buildings – often where the trouble with the Galloway Boys happened
before police broke up the gang in the late 2000s – and then the
East Scarborough Storefront nearby on Lawrence. Located in a
former police station, the Storefront is a collection of thirty-five
social agencies – 'a one-stop shop' – that share resources and offer
services. It provides a computer room, lessons on how to access the
internet and write resumés, space for community groups to meet,
courses on nutrition and even a community garden.

Sahar Vermezyari, coordinator of programs and services at the
Storefront, said they received 17,000 requests for services in 2008,
everything from 'how to find a lawyer to belly-dancing classes. We
want people to feel comfortable enough to ask for help.' Like Primo,

Fences and towers at Kingston and Galloway roads.

Rock also seemed to know everybody, engaging people along the way, asking a fellow at the Storefront how his job search was going. As the community catches up to the rest of Toronto service-wise, it's obvious there's already a strong network of people here who provide the solid human infrastructure that is as strong as the kind small towns are romanticized for having. *The King of Kensington* was set in downtown Toronto, Al Waxman's strut down the sidewalk in the opening credits evoking that traditional neighbourhood feel. If the CBC decided to reboot that sitcom today it could be set out here, because everything would be the same except for the topology: it's just wider and taller and there are lots more cars.

Wander the neighbourhood and you'll see physical traces of a small town. Before the crossroads-inspired name took over, Kingston-Galloway was known as West Hill, a name that lives on here and there on street signs and school buildings. West Hill was a busy stop on the road to Kingston, but it was eventually subsumed by Scarborough and, later, Toronto. On Lawrence, between community housing towers and townhouses, sits St. Margaret's church and park. Its adjacent cemetery is not fenced in, so the park blends into it. These are the kind of fuzzy boundaries we don't see as much in cities.

A Festival Market is held in the park each Thursday during the summer. Local vendors selling either produce or crafts and small items can rent a table for two to five dollars. I met with Sandra Hutley, one of the organizers, while wandering along. Hutley has lived in the area for thirty-five years and still calls it West Hill, a name, she said, that started to disappear when they lost their post office ten years ago. Like many long-time residents of Scarborough, she noted changes in the buildings that sprouted up in between the houses over the years. When you look at the area on Google Maps, you can see that Highland Creek wraps around West Hill, and it's easy to imagine that, when this was one of Scarborough's rural post office crossroads, it was isolated and very much its own place.

This market is important to the area, as there are few public places available for community gathering. In 2007, nearby Morningside Mall was torn down, replaced by an outdoor strip mall. It's similar what's been happening in Don Mills, where the former mall served as a neighbourhood hub, but the new outdoor shopping centre leaves little room for formal and informal community gatherings. We may have looked down our noses at mall culture, but for many places that developed rapidly when the car was king, they became town squares. Because they are privately owned, however, they can disappear in an instant, no matter how much they matter.

The lack of all-season public spaces in this neighbourhood makes a place like the Boys and Girls Club critically important. Primo had been going there since she was seven and said she felt like she grew up there. The club served over 16,000 kids in 2008, and in 2009 launched a campaign to raise $1.5 million to expand and open up the nearly windowless 1970s building, add new program rooms, arts, media and dance studios and expand the gym. The area's former councillor, David Soknacki, revealed his old-fashioned Red Tory self by donating his $30,000 councillor's severance to kick-start the campaign.

The club's motto, 'A good place to be,' will endure and become more apt with the expanded club. The feeling I got from the residents I met while hanging out in Kingston-Galloway is that it could be the whole neighbourhood's motto – something not even the Galloway Boys can take away. And, just like any downtown neighbourhood, it deserves a walk or two.

Scarborough City Centre and Bendale

 neighbourhood jaunt   Connecting walks: None.

dress to impress

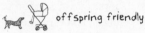 offspring friendly

You could forgive a visitor driving eastwards into Toronto on the 401 for thinking they've found downtown as they approach Scarborough City Centre. The cluster of skyscrapers surrounding the Scarborough Town Centre mall would be the envy of many mid-sized midwestern American cities. They shimmer on the horizon from kilometres away, and some are even lit up with phosphorescent colours at night. Should that visitor arrive and be told that this is Scarborough City Centre, you might also forgive him or her for being confused. Like North York City Centre and Mississauga City Centre, Scarborough City Centre has followed the 'if we call it a city centre the city centre will follow' model of city building.

The Scarborough Town Centre mall and the adjacent Scarborough Civic Centre both opened in 1973, and are separated by Albert Campbell Square, the Nathan Phillips Square of the then-city of Scarborough. Both squares are named after a former mayor and come complete with a skating rink. In 1985, the Scarborough Rapid Transit line continued the path of the Bloor-Danforth subway line to this area with a new not-really-a-subway, Ontario-built technology that was supposed to be the future of public transit. (Few cities bought it, Detroit being a notable exception.) When the RT train pulls into the station on its monorail-like track, it makes a strange electric hum that, paired with its late 1970s space shuttle styling, evoke low-budget science-fiction effects from that era and suggest that this is Spaceport Scarborough rather than a rail stop. This place often feels like a bit of the future we were promised by both science fiction and modern planning, one we never completely got.

The civic centre was used as Scarborough's city hall until amalgamation, and was designed by Moriyama & Teshima, the Toronto architects that designed both the Toronto Reference and the North York Central libraries. Though the civic centre came first, all three

People wait for H1N1 shots at the Scarborough Civic Centre in November 2009.

of these buildings have central atriums with zigzagging staircases. Keeping in the science-fiction theme, a sculpture by James Sutherland called *21 Points Equilibrium* is made up of reflective triangle shapes that begin outside and make their way up to the atrium ceiling. When Terry Fox ran through Toronto on his Marathon of Hope, he gave a speech by the pond full of goldfish (there are still fat ones swimming in there today) as onlookers crowded every level up to the ceiling. Seven years earlier, in 1973, Queen Elizabeth I stood in the same square to officially open the building. Inside the building, in a locked glass cabinet (as if waiting for eBay), there's a shrine to this event that includes the pen the Queen and her consort used to sign the opening documents. The faded pictures and dusty Union Jack are now memorials to Scarborough's former WASP-y demographic makeup, which has radically changed since this place was built.

The whole building is filled with these kinds of unintentional memorials to a city that no longer exists. Across from the former council chambers, there's a wall of plaques that commemorate various awards that were once given out, such as 'Poppy Appreciation,' and list presidents of this board or that. The tiles after 1998, the year of amalgamation, are blank, as if a silent apocalypse hit the city and everything stopped.

When the civic centre opened, it was the symbol of Scarborough's bright future. Inside there's still the architectural model of the 'site development concept,' which has a complicated keypad that used to light up various sections when you pressed the right numbers – more space-aged 1970s technology. It doesn't work anymore, as its electric power is unplugged, just as the building's political power was in 1998. Though the building is still busy and used for municipal offices, it once aspired to loftier civic ideas. A 1970 proposal letter from Raymond Moriyama summed up this spirit: 'We are very conscious of the contribution the new civic centre will make to Scarborough and our interest in the centre goes beyond the normal provision of Administrative Offices ... As a municipality, Scarborough has come of age. In just two decades it has been transformed from a rural agricultural area into one of the fastest growing municipalities on the continent ... It will be Scarborough's contribution toward making Metropolitan Toronto a World city.'

Somewhat sad to think we've been plagued by thoughts of our world-class status for over forty years. Scarborough was the bright future and it was big, so big that if we could fold it over the rest of Toronto, it would almost cover the entire city to the Mississauga border. Made up of a few dozen smaller communities – farm country post offices or tiny crossroads, in some cases – Scarborough was merely a township until it was incorporated as a borough in 1967. Though that farm heritage is just about gone (there are still a couple fields left in the far northeastern corner of the city, past the zoo), it isn't so far in the distant past that it doesn't live in Scarborough's collective memory.

In the summer of 2004, I was in an upper-floor room of a retirement residence on Sheppard Avenue in Agincourt, just north and west of the civic centre. I was there to see Bill Walton, a farmer born in 1919 on whose land the mall and civic centre were eventually built. There was a little metal Ford toy tractor by the window that looked out and over the sprawl to where his farmhouse once was, an area that's easy to find because of the condo skyscrapers. 'We raised grain and hay and we had pigs and quite a big orchard. The orchard was quite a thing at one time. It kind of petered out,' he told me. Farms in Scarborough often petered out like this, but this is no Depression-era story. Most farmers, including Walton, sold their properties. The Walton farm eventually became what the retail industry calls a 'super regional shopping centre.' Not unlike farmers on the edges of Toronto's sprawl today, mid-century farmers kept one eye on the crops and another on advancing development and land prices.

Back on Walton's former land, it's like a casino inside the mall: except for skylights that let in hints of the outdoors, this is an enclosed and self-contained universe. If you want to see Scarborough – not just the buildings or the highways, but the people – walk laps here, because it's Scarborough's downtown core. This mall was home to the very first Second Cup kiosk in 1975, and today it's where the Scarborough Walk of Fame is laid out (in the floor, by the food court). While the mall has been modernized inside, bits and pieces of 1973 modernism can be found around the periphery outside, like the concrete plain by the east Sears exit. While the main mall entrances have been updated, the department stores haven't been as quick, so they are artifacts from the era when they ruled the retail landscape. This big concrete patio is a place to pass through quickly, an annoying extra bit of distance from the doors of your car to those of the store. It's an important transitory space though: as loud and busy as it is inside the mall – casino-level loud sometimes – go outside and the open emptiness is abrupt and a bit of a shock. The patio just gets us ready for it.

Make your way east across the parking lot past McCowan Road and the open country, where the only sound is the hum of the highway. Though you're still surrounded by buildings, taking a walk here is not unlike walking through rural country: it's all big skies and wide vistas and the lingering feeling that walking isn't what you're supposed to be doing in a place like this.

Consilium Place is made up of the first cluster of high-rises that were constructed in the area, and they shoot out of the parking lot plains like the Rockies do when you're driving west through the Praries. They were built in the mid-1980s and wear that era's style boldly: J.R. Ewing could have had an office here. Despite being just a block away from the last stop on the Scarborough RT, the design of the area is very car-oriented, which makes it feel more like Dallas or Houston than Toronto. The steps leading to the front entrance are massive and wide and make you wonder what percentage of people going to this office walk up these grand steps instead of driving into the parking garage. Can you really know an office building if you don't walk through its front doors?

Further east, you'll see the newer condo buildings along Lee Centre Drive. These buildings hug the edge of the 401 and, while they're impressive from a distance – two of these towers appear to arc towards each other, as if about to hug and kiss – but they meet the sidewalk awkwardly. What could be urban isn't, and the busiest parts of the sidewalk aren't full of pedestrians but are where the constant car traffic enters each building (gated communities in a city that isn't supposed to have any). Peer through the lobby windows and you'll see that these modern buildings are decorated in a decidedly ticky-tacky style. Two of the indoor pools are done up in Roman temple style, complete with pillars and paintings of what looks like the Tuscan countryside. If you walk past the condos and south on Bellamy Road, you'll see real temples of a radically different style: many of the light industrial and commercial buildings here have been converted into evangelical churches which suggest this is, in fact, God's country. Just as ethnic neighbourhoods like the Danforth and Little Italy are branded with their own special street signs, Bellamy and Ellesmere could be called the Big-Box Jesus district.

It's lonely heading back east along Ellesmere on foot. The cars fly by but there are few people to bump into. Knowing how many there are in the mall is like being in a stadium parking lot on game day: crowded inside, quiet outside. Behind the civic centre, there's a stand of trees that were saved when the farmland was developed. The area to the south of this area is Bendale. If you want to see how Toronto works, how its past and its present co-exist, take a walk through Bendale, where the layers of our city are as visible as they are in Kensington Market or Corktown but in a different form.

The name 'Bendale' doesn't resonate with everyone who lives there – the word is scattered throughout the area, attached to schools or retirement homes, though the post office that bore its name is long gone. It's anachronistic and, like the neighbourhood itself, mostly overlooked by many of the people who live here.

Bendale's most striking feature is its sense of space. There's the city centre skyline to the north and the downtown bank head-quarters far to the west, the latter visible only on days with minimal smog. Instead of the CN Tower as a geographic landmark, Bendale has high-voltage power lines. They cut a diagonal swath through the neighbourhood, and through the rest of Scarborough, and never linger or come down to a human level; instead they're cold and reserved, headed straight for those towers downtown, feeding the empire all the electricity it can eat up. Standing in the middle of the hydro fields is like being in Montana, big-sky country again. You can even see the horizon, something that generally isn't in view anywhere within the built-up areas of the old City of Toronto.

Long before the power lines were put in, Bendale was one of the cradles of Scarborough civilization. Most of the activity took place along St. Andrews Road, a bucolic lane that curves around the small patches of forested ravine that run between McCowan and Brimley roads. (Walk south from the civic centre along either major street to find it, or take a circuitous adventure through the twisting residential streets between McCowan and Brimley.) When you're strolling down St. Andrews, the city might as well be a thousand kilometres away. On misty mornings, the road feels and smells like rural Nova Scotia. In the middle of this sits St. Andrew's Church, built in 1848. It still welcomes a Presbyterian congregation, some of whom are descendants of the Thomson family, the first European settlers in the area. You know they're important because the high school on Lawrence, David and Mary Thomson Collegiate Institute, was named after them.

The Thomson clan's homes are still on St. Andrews Road, and date back to the mid-1800s. Some bear historic plaques put up by the Scarborough Historical Society. The owners had great nicknames like 'Stonehouse Willie' and 'Springfield Jimmy,' names that referenced the geography and building materials of their houses.

The second wave of Bendale pioneers who filled up the new modern postwar homes were looking for the Canadian dream, the one we borrowed from America that involves backyards and driveways on winding cul-de-sacs. They came from downtown or from the streetcar suburbs around the Danforth or St. Clair and started families here. Their backgrounds were mostly English and Scottish, but some Greek and Italian folks were attracted to the area too.

One of the developments east of McCowan Road is known as the Ben Jungle because every street begins with the prefix Ben; there's Benlight, Benlark, Benfrisco, Ben Nevis, Ben Stanton, Benroyal and even Benhur and Benorama. It was on Benleigh, a quiet street lined with Pontiac Sunfires and Dodge Caravans, that seventeen-year-old Jeffrey Reodica was shot dead by police in May 2004 during a gang confrontation. The media often talks about the dangerous streets of Scarborough, and downtowners make jokes about 'Scarlem,' but this is the landscape where these incidents play out: typical Canadian suburbia that, more often than not, is as typically quiet.

As the European families grew up and out, in came the Filipinos, Chinese, Sri Lankans, Indians, Afghanis, Persians, West Indians and Somalis, and in the last couple decades, Bendale has gotten more and more interesting.The built environment suggests a *Leave It to Beaver* modernism designed with the car in mind. The plazas were built as rest stops on the way to real centres like Cedarbrae Mall or the Scarborough Town Centre. Yet so many of these new residents don't own cars and can't make it to these malls without a long journey. There are often long queues at windswept bus stops. Some of the plazas that are often criticized as bad urban planning have actually become centres for many people who lead what amounts to urban, or possibly even village-style, lives in a suburban landscape.

Today, these '50s- and '60s-era plazas better emulate the idea of Main Street than do downtown neighbourhoods like the Annex or Little Italy. There are no Starbucks, one-of-a-kind underwear stores or $100 haircuts here. If you look past the parking lots, these places are ungentrified, old-fashioned urban streets, places that people without cars, or without a lot of extra money, can get to. On McCowan, just south of Lawrence Avenue, there's a plaza with the neat old modish name, 'The Hub.' A Royal Bank and Shoppers Drug Mart serve as anchors close to the main intersection, but the rest of the development is all do-it-yourself stores. There are real barbershops – 'Tony's – $1 Senior Citizen discounts on Tuesdays, Wednesdays, Thursdays' – with faded glamour shots in the windows of guys with high-and-tight blow-dried hair. There's also the Paperback Exchange, McCowan Shoe Repair, the Asia Bakery and the New Suburban Restaurant, where you can get grilled cheese sandwiches, long, narrow, goldenish french fries and filtered coffee. (There are no espresso machines here.)

Over at the Hillside Plaza on Lawrence near Brimley Road, the corner Tim Hortons gives way to the Rasa Mini Mart. The mart's

Sri Lankan owner heads out to the airport every day at 4 a.m. to pick out fresh flowers for his customers to take to loved ones in Scarborough General Hospital. A couple of doors down, there's the First Class Bakery, which is also owned by Sri Lankans. It used to be run by Lithuanians. They make good croissants and really spicy vegetarian samosas. Above the bakery there's the Thunder School of Chess (the second floors of strip malls can be even more interesting than the first). Then there's Kathy S. P. Importers Fresh Fish Market, Emmy's In-Style Fashions ('Ladies, Mens, Diapers' reads the sign out front), the A1 Top Quality Florist, the huge Bombay Bazaar grocery store, Johnny Active Wear, the Liberty Restaurant & Bar and the Watch, Clock and Jewelry Repair Shop. Everything a real neighbourhood needs to sustain itself, including Comet Lanes, an eight-lane five-pin bowling alley out back.

These small businesses can survive and prosper in the shadow of the chains and malls because the rents out here are considerably cheaper than those downtown. In the mid-2000s, monthly rent of $12 or $13 per square foot was the average, compared to $23–$25 in places like the Annex or along Church and Yonge streets around Wellesley. In posher areas, it can get as high as $40. The affordable nature of these malls opens up room for innovation, low-budget eccentricity and services that cater to individuals rather than broadly defined demographics.

If you stand still, even for a short period, you notice that everybody seems to know each other here. People say hi or nod to each other the way you do when you run into someone you don't know that well but see every day. The stores are busy. Thomson Park is packed with multicoloured kids on summer days. The big mosque nearby on Lawrence (it was first housed in a former car dealership but now has an impressive new building) holds barbecues in the summer. It feels like a small town that's been invaded by the Torontonian mix we hear so much about but don't always see downtown. Out here, if you're on foot, you sometimes forget about the six lanes of constant traffic and bad planning and dowdy buildings. There are too marty ravines, people and strange store combinations to look at.

Dorset Park

 neighbourhood jaunt   Connecting walks: None.

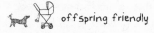 dress to impress

offspring friendly

When Highway 401 enters Scarborough at Victoria Park Avenue, its twelve to sixteen lanes move at high velocity in close quarters. Here, the Highway of Heroes is a city on wheels where the smallest mistake can be catastrophic. Out of the corners of their eyes – a glance any longer than a peripheral one is too long – drivers glimpse bits of Scarborough: the rooftops of houses, factories, townhouses, apartment towers, strip malls, big-box stores and more roads.

This is the landscape Torontonians who haven't set foot in the former borough in years (or ever) picture in their mind's eye when they hear 'Scarborough,' partly because of how pop culture and the news tend to portray this suburb. For folks passing through on their way to and from elsewhere, this backdoor view from the highway is simply 'Toronto.' It's big and not particularly pretty and, when you're travelling at 100 kilometres an hour or more, it begins to blur and repeat like an endless suburban movie set.

As eastbound cars pass Birchmount Road, passengers and particularly skillful drivers may take a longer look at the leafy area to the south. Large trees – including giant willows – catch the breeze on rolling grassy hills. Behind them there's a wide, balconied apartment tower, and more like it scattered farther on. There isn't any time on the freeway to wonder about this pocket of the city – it's gone before an impression of it can sink in – but this is the top of Dorset Park, a Scarborough neighbourhood of just over 24,000 people.

Though the City of Toronto designates it as such, the term 'neighbourhood' is not the most accurate descriptor for this large area that runs from the 401 south to just below Lawrence Avenue East. It is made up of a relatively narrow strip of residential land that's sandwiched between an industrial area to the west and the Scarborough RT line to the east. The southern part is largely made

up of single-family bungalows while the northern section above
Ellesmere, the one that's in view of the 401, features a mixture of
apartment towers and townhouses.

Standing in Glamorgan Park, by those aforementioned towers
and willows, the traffic on the 401 is white noise in the background, not terribly unpleasant, almost like the ocean surf (with
the occasional downshifting sputter from one of the big rigs – the
asphalt-sea version of foghorns). You can see the highway and its
blur of traffic in the gaps between the trees. From the park, the
highway looks as fleeting as the park looked from the highway.
The two places are close to one another, but they might as well
be a real ocean apart; they move at different speeds and there's
no communication between them. Here in the park, with that
white noise in the background, it's not immediately evident why
Dorset Park is another one of Toronto's thirteen 'priority neighbourhoods,' designated for focus because it doesn't boast the
social services other parts of the city do. The often-used but
seldom-interrogated nicknames 'Scarlem' and 'Scarberia'
seem ridiculous when you're actually here.

You can reach Glamorgan Park from Kennedy Road via
Antrim Crescent, which ends in a cul-de-sac by Glamorgan
Junior Public School. The school, its parking lot and the park
blend together, creating a large public space. Apart from the
trees, there are baseball diamonds, swings and other equipment,
a splash pad and washrooms: everything you'd expect from a typical Canadian park. The Canadianness of this park – the bucolic
semi-rural vibe that's often our shared image of this country, even
if it's false – seems almost cartoonish: witness the groundhogs
that peek out of the dens they've dug around the park. When I was
in the park in the summer of 2009, one of them had even created
an elaborate den and tunnel near a landscaping boulder at the
entrance of the school parking lot. Though it had built its home in
the path between the school to the park – hundreds of kids must
have passed by it every day – this groundhog seemed at home and
comfortable. Across Antrim, the grounds of the apartment tower
also help put the 'park' in Dorset Park.

I met up with three neighbourhood women and some of their
children near the groundhog boulder that summer. They were part
of a local group that had led a recent Jane's Walk, the community-

led walking tours that happen in the city every May. Abeer Ali, originally from Egypt, Feriba Mirza from Afganistan and Abeer Abukhaled from Saudi Arabia all call Dorset Park home and, within minutes, their love for their neighbourhood and the care they devote to it was clear.

'This is our hub,' said Ali, gesturing to the school and park. 'If you come late in the afternoon there will be five or ten families here.' Mirza continued, 'Here in the park, each picnic table will have a different family from a different place – Afghanistan, Saudi Arabia. Everybody shares sweets and our kids play with each other.'

Yodit Tsegaye, a community engagement worker with Action for Neighbourhood Change (ANC), a United Way–funded organization that operates in nine of the city's priority neighbourhoods, had also been along for the tour. 'The school has ESL classes and space for community meetings,' she said.'No services are provided in the area, so we use the schools as well as Toronto Community Housing buildings that provide us a little space.'

This is why one experiences some cognitive dissonance when standing by the park, wondering why this is a priority neighbourhood. The unseen things, those that are missing, are the problem. Downtown neighbourhoods, and those that are older and more compact, have services – community centres, libraries, public health facilities – that are usually just a short walk away from the homes of those who use them. Neighbourhoods like Dorset Park are so spread out that the same services are much farther away. Enter the fundamental design flaw in suburban planning that makes life difficult for the people who live here: areas such as this were built on the assumption that all residents have cars and will use them to get to the distant services, shopping malls and other activities. With the influx of new Canadians and less affluent residents, a pedestrian culture has been grafted onto an automobile landscape, and sometimes it's a hard fit.

We strolled along the side of the school to a place where the walking residents of Dorset Park collide with its poor design. A narrow sidewalk, fenced in with chain link on both sides, runs a few hundred metres between a condominium property and industrial land, then turns left for a similar length. It's an important passageway between the school and park and the residential area to the south. For those on foot, it cuts travelling time down considerably, but with only two entrances/exits and poor lighting, it can be an unpleasant and almost claustrophobic place.

'This is the most important problem,' explained Ali. 'During the winter and summer months there is no maintenance. Along here, this factory hasn't cut the grass for five years, so we don't know what might be hiding in there. When we walk through, it's one child at a time in a line because the fence is broken and it isn't safe for them.' They pointed out that the bottom of the chain-link fence was installed quickly and cheaply likely decades ago, and the sharp ends of the wire were now ready to catch the pant leg or skirt of pedestrians. Mirza said her six-year-old son got caught on the fence and fell face-first into the concrete, winding up with a bloody nose. 'In winter, we all hold on to each other to get through,' she continued. 'They do plough it, but at ten o'clock at night. What about at eight a.m. when everybody uses it?' Further down the pathway, the fence bends in where the condo parking lot plough pushed the snow, further encroaching on the public space.

We continued through the neighbourhood to a spot where the towers give way to townhouses. A makeshift path leads through a fence and over some curbs and bits of worn lawn to the parking lot of the plaza at Ellesmere and Kennedy. It's another curious bit of confounding design: the pedestrian thoroughfare to this plaza is well-used, yet it feels like a teenager's illicit back route. The plaza is an important to the neighbourhood, as it stocks the kinds of food residents want – halal meat, fresh bread – and houses services such as the ANC office. Set in contrast with the huge

In and around Dorset Park.

size of the half-empty parking lot, the poor pedestrian planning of this place is striking. In Dorset Park and so many areas of suburban Toronto like it, the population growth and demographic changes have outpaced the infrastructure, and the people-places are often accidental. They exist despite the lack of planning.

Like much of Scarborough, Dorset Park was nearly all rich agricultural land just a little over fifty years ago. Scarborough Township, as it was known, was dotted with small villages like Wexford, Bendale and West Hill. Doreen Brown has been a resident of the area since 1955, when Dorset Park was preparing to welcome the first wave of post-development residents. Brown has pictures of herself sitting on the foundation of her house as it was being constructed that year, only months after it was farmland. Of the days before and during the transition from rural to suburban, Brown said: 'Since the late 1800s, the areas of the present community of Dorset Park and the Kennedy Commons Plaza were all farmland. Eventually, around the turn of the century, several commercial merchants began to locate along Kennedy Road – especially between Sheppard and Lawrence avenues. Lansing Buildall, a lumber and building supply business operated by William Kitchen, was one of these merchants. His lumber yard was situated on the east side of Kennedy Road, just north of Ellesmere.'

Brown is a one-woman Dorset Park archive, and her house on Exford Drive is full of Scarborough artifacts. When I visited her

there, she showed me cardboard displays of the area's history that detail where the old can be found among the new, as well as the places that go back further than the Second World War. There's the original Rutherford Farm farmhouse at 34 Kecale Road (now the manse of St. Giles Anglican Church), which is today surrounded by standard suburbia. It requires a leap of imagination to see it alone in the fields as it once was. Brown then took me on a walk to Rutherford Farm and around her neighbourhood. You can't catch all the details on a quick pass through a place like this, details that, in fact, make it a place. Bits of history are scattered here and there – old homes, churches, graveyards – and even these 1950s bungalows are beginning to feel the weight of history. Entire families have moved in, grown up and moved out and, and the cycle has begun and even finished again in some cases. New becomes old (though not yet 'historic,' as that would imply a kind of universal admiration).

Brown is one of a rare breed of Dorset Park resident, an 'original' who still lives in the house that was built for her family. (They added a second storey at one point and now tenants live upstairs – an example of the kind of densification that happens downtown, too.) One of her cardboard displays details the wooden 'milk chutes' that each of these houses have, though they are no longer used for their intended purpose. The postwar and modern features on most of these homes makes these tiny doors for milk-bottle delivery seem anachronistic. Brown has documented what some of her neighbours have done to them: some use them to collect mail, others store yard tools in them and one tells stories of her son squeezing through the chute when he was locked out of the house as a boy.

Brown is active in organizing the local community, but laments the difficulty of getting people out to meetings. She's conscious of the new vs. old, high-rise vs. house divide among residents, and notices that many 'old-timers' aren't present at meetings. She tries to bridge those gaps when she can with events like 'get-to-know-your-neighbour night.' 'We don't want to think of this as North and South Dorset Park,' she said. Of all the new families moving in, including the women I met earlier (Brown had also participated in the Jane's Walk with them) she said, 'To me, it's like going back to when we moved in here. Everybody raising wee kids. It's just we were Anglo-Saxon and they are Middle Eastern.'

When Highway 401 was completed across the top of Toronto in the 1950s – it was then known as the Toronto Bypass, and later officially named the MacDonald-Cartier Freeway, though no one ever calls it that – it looked much like the standard four-lane high-ways that cross the Ontario countryside outside of major popula-tion areas. The 401, as well as the expansion of small country roads into arterials in the township, fed Scarborough's dramatic and quick growth. Though those groundhogs in Glamorgan Park seem out of place in an urban wilderness, fifty years is a blip in nature, so perhaps they're just waiting for us to move on again.

In what is now the Kennedy Commons shopping plaza, there's still a lumberyard at the site of Lansing Buildall. It's now a Rona, though William Kitchen lives on in the name of the street that bisects the parking lot. The commons is home to some large retail-ers, including a Chapters, a Metro grocery store and the AMC Theatre – there's nothing subtle about these places, as they can be readily seen from the highway – and though smaller than a true 'power centre,' it functions as an outdoor mall. Kennedy Commons is adjacent to Dorset Park, but it's big enough to attract people from other parts of Scarborough and the rest of city. So many Toronto strip malls are the cozy main street for their surrounding postwar neighbourhoods, designed to serve that purpose when the automobile made all the planning rules. The commons is too big to have such an intimate feel. It's more of a suburban-style 'high street.' The women I walked with from Dorset Park had reservations about shopping at the Metro – too expensive, not the right kinds of products – and did their shop-ping at the other nearby plaza. The size and scope of the commons take it out of the local scene.

Much of Kennedy Road itself functions in this way, somewhat independently of the Dorset Park community. The Kennedy Road

Business Improvement Area (BIA) organization, one of a handful of such organizations found in Scarborough – most are located within the old City of Toronto boundaries – describes the area as 'a popular local and regional shopping district ... [with] a wide range of large-format retail outlets, specialty shops, restaurants and entertainment uses. Enjoying both excellent vehicular and public transit access, Kennedy Road is truly a one-stop shopping destination with everything from tropical fish to house wares, car care to water sports, and off-track wagering to the latest movies.'

It's a strange description to read – a Wild West of unfettered retail – and just as strange a walk. The blocks are extremely long here, with few breaks for intersections. A walk down Kennedy is not unlike a walk in the country, where your path is rarely disturbed by traffic lights or obstacles. Such meditative strolls seem at odds with the suburban environment, but these streets are good for ambulatory thinking. There's lots to look at, too: there's an abundance of neon yellow and green lawn signs lining Kennedy that advertise various stores and products, and are perhaps a result of the numerous sign-making shops that do business along this road.

The BIA advertises proximity to public transit and, while this is strictly true – the Scarborough RT line runs parallel to the east side of Kennedy – both Ellesmere and Lawrence stations are an unpleasant walk away. Both roads are elevated over the transit tracks, so pedestrians must walk down relatively desolate service roads to get to the stations, which are tucked under bridges. The journey is particularly uncomfortable at night, when other foot traffic is light. In more dense parts of the city, a few blocks' walk to a subway station feels natural, and you do it without much thought. Out here, the same distance feels longer because there is less beauty, and fewer distractions and people.

The BIA has made improvements along Kennedy that include new light poles and fixtures, streetscaping and boulevard planters filled with lush and colourful flowers. Though they're meant more for car passengers more than pedestrians, such flourishes do have the effect of taming a huge street like Kennedy and making it less of a pavement desert. The BIA represents only the businesses along Kennedy and has no responsibility to Dorset Park itself, and it's telling that the priorities of urban beautification still revolve around automobile routes, while residents struggle for years for simple solutions to their pathway problems.

South of Ellesmere, you'll find the bungalows where long-time Dorset Park residents live next to the successive waves of residents who have made this place home. Black-clad European widows sit on their porches, across the street from houses flying Tamil flags. Walking around the quiet streets, it's clear that suburban neighbourhoods like these are to present-day Toronto what College Street, Dundas and Cabbagetown were to the city fifty or a hundred years ago: places that can absorb a varied population, where working-class Canadians and new Canadians – overlapping groups, for sure – can afford to buy homes and live out their version of the Canadian dream. It's a relatively inexpensive place in Toronto terms, but it's the 'blank-slate' nature of these areas (which unsympathetic folks might call 'sterile' or 'boring') that lets new forms of neighbourhood and urban culture flourish without the heavy, prescriptive history that some downtown neighbourhoods have. Out here, history is very much happening now, and there is no official guide to what comes next.

At first, Dorset Park seems not very different from the suburban Windsor neighbourhood I grew up in. It feels the same and, though I've never lived here, being in Dorset Park is like visiting a familiar haunt I haven't been to for a while. The landscape makes sense to me.

My old neighbourhood, though, was somewhat more exurban, with fields and forests nearby. Dorset Park is more urban, with curbs and strip malls. And while the suburb I grew up in has grown over the years, it's remained a quiet, suburban kind of place. Dorset Park and other neighbourhoods like it – some 'priority,' some not – have stayed largely the same in their landscape and infrastructure, but are really urban at heart, with all the mix and needs of any big city. Kids in exurbia can play in fields and forests, while the kids in Dorset Park – and there are a lot of them, many more than in downtown neighbourhoods – have less space for this activity, so places like recreation centres become critical.

The future for a place like this is bright because of its residents. Last year, Abeer Ali won a community-building award for her work in the neighbourhood. There's a picture of her accepting her plaque in the ANC office. 'I didn't sleep until I called my mom in Egypt,' she said. 'I scanned it in and emailed it to her.' The award is a small gesture but, according to Ali, 'what it also did was get a lot of other women to join in and help.' Here we see the beginnings of community activism that may one day evolve into a formidable organization like the high-rise-developer-crippling Annex Residents' Association downtown. If that happens, small things like that walkway won't take years to fix. The residents I met have just that kind of commitment to Dorset Park. 'Before this neighbourhood was a place people came and left,' says Ali. 'But now people try to stay.'

Thorncliffe, Flemingdon Park and Don Mills

pack a lunch

dress to impress

scenic views

Connecting walk: Danforth/
Crescent Town.

According to Graeme Stewart of ERA Architects, driving on the DVP between the 401 and Bloor is the most modern moment you can have in the city, perhaps even the country. As the road curves through the ravine, hundreds of high-rise apartments poke out above the forest, channelling one of those futuristic and utopian *Star Trek* cities. A number of these high-rises are located in the neighbourhood of Thorncliffe Park, just north of the Leaside Bridge, a span that's nearly as impressive but much less celebrated than the Prince Edward Viaduct a few kilometres south.

Standing on the bridge affords a beautiful view not just of the valley but of the DVP itself. The highway is a stunning piece of engineering as highways go, a two-way steel river that runs next to the slower Don River. Torontonians who don't want to drive to the country to engage in 'leaf peeping' can still see all the fall colours from this bridge, where the white mod high-rises of Thorncliffe Park contrast with the blazing colours below.

Thorncliffe is like a huge apartment island, and is surrounded by deep ravines on three sides. Light-industrial land separates it from Leaside, its upscale neighbour to the west. It's hard to imagine walking to Thorncliffe from anywhere, as it seems so cut off from the rest of the city, but when you walk up from the Danforth, it turns out that the valley is a bigger psychological barrier than it is a physical one. If you're at the northern end of the Leaside Bridge, stay left and you'll get to Leaside proper. But turn right at Overlea Boulevard and you'll find yourself where Thorncliffe begins. In the early 1880s, George Taylor named the house he built here 'Thorn Cliff.' Later, his daughter and husband turned it into Thorncliffe Farms, and then sold it to a Baltimore concern who built a racetrack that remained until 1952, when it was torn down so the area could be developed into apartment complexes. All that's left of the racetrack era are two short streets – referred to as 'places' – named Milepost and Grandstand.

Thorncliffe became, and still is, one of Toronto's largest rental districts, comprised of over thirty low- and high-rise buildings totalling nearly 6,000 units that are home to 13,000 residents. In her book *Leaside*, former Toronto councillor and mayoral candidate Jane Pitfield wrote that 'a unique piece of history ... all but disappeared' when East York Council renamed Thorncliffe 'East York Centre' in 1993.

Though the community is high above the valley, it is well-connected to the rest of the city. You can walk or bike to Thorncliffe from the Don Valley pathway where it passes through Seaton Park below. The route runs up a long and steep driveway that starts from the lower parking lot and leads up to Thorncliffe Park Drive. In the summer, you can watch people play cricket in the shadows of the tri-footed towers down in the valley, and observe the mountain bikers who regularly pop out of the forest after riding the single-track trails along the Don.

A walk through the neighbourhood after sunset is a Manhattan-like experience, a sea of sparking towers glowing from within. With so much glass, light is everywhere. You can hear the clinking of dishes and the laugh tracks of tv shows and you can smell food. But instead of stores and commercial activity, the space between buildings is covered in either pavement or grass and separated by fences. Still, there are people walking around everywhere, and the area doesn't have the dead-zone feel you might associate with tower-in-the-park design. Imagine if the fences were taken down and the areas between the buildings were animated somehow.

All the buildings in Thorncliffe surround the East York Town Centre, a mall that serves as the area's main street. Though many of Toronto's suburban tower communities were built for the car, Thorncliffe is remarkably walkable, as each building is no more than a few hundred metres from the mall. The town centre's interior has been renovated and is bright and new feeling. The only wonderful throwback is the huge combination five- and ten-pin bowling alley underneath the grocery store, complete with sunken bar and 1970s plastic booths.

Back outside, the twin slabs of the Leaside Towers located to the east of the mall stand out like giant monoliths from *2001: A Space Odyssey*, though instead of solid black they're glass and concrete. When they opened in 1970, they were Canada's tallest apartment buildings, and the penthouses could be rented for $750/month. For many newcomers who call this neighbourhood home, the idea called to mind by the word 'Canada' is not rural, pastoral or small-town, but an intensely modern place like this one.

This landscape continues across the Overlea Bridge to Don Mills Road and Flemingdon Park. Walking up Don Mills towards the Ontario Science Centre gives a sense of what a lot of Toronto outside the core is like: six to eight lanes of fast arterial traffic. For an alternate route, go back down that valley driveway to Seaton Park and walk up the ravine path towards Sunnybrook, but take the Science Centre exit (there are wayfinding signs all along) and come up past all the cascading concrete that was poured down the side of the ravine to form the science centre, a 1970s brutalist building designed by Toronto architect Raymond Moriyama. The science centre is a great example of how brutalism actually brings the inside outside and closer to nature better than other architectural styles. As you descend between the building segments inside, it's as if you're moving through the forest itself, but then you're deposited into another exhibit room en route to the bottom of the ravine. It's always curious to me why natural rocky environments are appreciated and held in wonder, but human-made ones are often the target of contempt.

The intersection of Eglinton and Don Mills is a ten-lane-wide no-man's-land tempered occasionally by intrepid squeegee kids and their requisite sad-looking dogs – reminders that you're still in the city. On the northwest corner of the intersection sits the former IBM headquarters (now home to motherboard-making

Celestica), which was built in the sinister, corporate-campus style of architecture popular in certain James Bond films and *Knight Rider* episodes. Some old-timers remember when IBM came here in 1951, at a time when Eglinton was little more than a dirt road. This was Toronto's modern postwar frontier, Canada's *Lebensraum* before sprawl smothered the dream.

Look south, back towards Thorncliffe, and then east, and you'll see one of Toronto's weirdest cityscapes: the Independent Order of Foresters skyscraper (home of the most oddly named insurance company ever), the Easter Seals office building (which is lit in a blaze of purple haze at night), a giant Mormon temple and a new subdivision overwhelmed by its towering neighbours.

Behind and south of all this is Flemingdon Park, Toronto's first planned apartment community, built between 1958 and the early 1970s on the farm of 1890s Mayor Robert John Fleming. It's a maze of townhouses and apartment buildings, with underground parking and courtyard playgrounds where, in 1965, *Ontario Homes and Living* said, 'Mothers can watch their children play from their windows.' Theoretically, it's exactly the jumble of homes, parks and passages I longed to grow up in while living the exurban life, but the 'Flemo Sux' graffiti, Belfast-like murals that say 'What's the point of getting drugs off the streets?' and many chain-link fences that block movement – there's a strip mall here, but all the fences make it hard to figure out how to get to it – suggest that utopia has not yet been reached, or, perhaps, has been lost. Flemingdon Park is worth a walk-through to find the niches that are rather cozy: small courtyards with trees, say, or the vast open space under the wires in the hydro corridor.

On a 2006 visit, we walked across Eglinton and climbed the terraced lawn of the then-abandoned and soon-to-be-demolished Bata Shoes headquarters that's set high above the DVP. The Bata building was another of Toronto's modern gems. Designed by architect John C. Parkin, it was like a pavilion straight out of Expo 67, though it had been built three years earlier. The Aga Khan has donated $200 million to build a centre for Toronto's expatriate Ismaili community here – expected to open in 2013 – with 75 percent of the site to become parkland. It's hard to argue with that, but being on that hill under the Bata building's concrete umbrellas afforded a fine view of Flemingdon Park and the Don Valley and CN Tower, all from the most modern of perches.

All the land to the north of here is Don Mills, Toronto's (and perhaps Canada's) most well-known suburb because it both invented and came to define what suburban living was in this country. While it's the geographic centre of Toronto, to walk Don Mills is to go back to the future, back to a modern vision of the future that's now over fifty years old.

The parkette on the northeast corner of Don Mills and Lawrence, in the centre of the community, is named after urban planner Macklin Hancock, a local hero. When he was just twenty-seven years old, Hancock took a leave from his graduate studies at Harvard to go to work for Toronto tycoon E. P. Taylor, the financier behind Canada's first planned suburb. Built between 1952 and 1965, Don Mills was, and is, a modern wonderland that garnered postwar headlines in local papers like 'The suburb that is to become Canada's most perfect city' and 'Toronto's bright satellite between the forks of the Don.'

E. P. Taylor lived a few kilometres east on Bayview at his Windfields estate – now home to the Canadian Film Centre – and began purchasing working farms in 1947. Taylor's plan was to build a new brewery – his holding company, Argus Corporation (later owned by Conrad Black), owned the O'Keefe Brewing Company – but in the end, a massive new community was planned. Hancock's plan, though brand new for Canada, was a modern take on the English Garden City model developed a half-century earlier, where residential, commercial, industrial and agricultural uses were balanced with greenbelts throughout.

Though it's relatively close to downtown, Don Mills is physically isolated, surrounded by ravines and railways. Turn onto any of the residential streets and you soon lose your sense of direction due to the twists and curves of the streets. Low-rise apartment buildings mix in with townhouses and single-family homes. Some of those homes have fantastic space-age designs, with massive panes of glass and roofs that slope to the ground.

This place is mother to most Canadian suburbs that followed. In 1977, John Sewell (who would become mayor two years later) said in a *Globe and Mail* article that already 'it is difficult to overestimate the influence of Don Mills on urban development in Canada. By the 1970s, the planning of every Canadian city was dominated by the suburban form espoused by Hancock.' Walking around the neighbourhood, you begin to notice subtle but important differences from many of the suburbs that came after. Over 200 different home designs were built in Don Mills, far more than are offered in contemporary suburban developments. You can still see the gentle roll of the Ontario countryside here. Homes and apartment parking garages are built into hillsides. For Sewell, developments that followed similar principles were 'the ghosts of Don Mills – but in a sad way.'

If you travel up to the fringe of GTA sprawl north of Major Mackenzie Drive, you'll find landscapes that look like images from clear-cut Brazilian rainforests, where the land is shaved down to an empty, muddy, uniform plain, waiting for streets and houses. In Don Mills, efforts were made to preserve and work around mature trees and, in some spots the narrow tentacles of ravines reach up between homes to the street.

The problem with suburbs is that they are neither city nor country; they try to do the impossible by being both. Don Mills might come as close as possible to attaining that balance. In the southeast quadrant, not far from the old Bata headquarters site, take a walk down to Moccasin Trail Park – it's tucked underneath Don Mills, by the DVP. An artificial pond was constructed here in the early 2000s to contain storm water, but it's already natural-looking and home to a rather extroverted beaver. If you follow the path nearby you'll come across a long cement tunnel that smells of pot and teenagers and that passes under the DVP into a clearing that leads to the Rainbow Tunnel (which northbound highway commuters can see from their cars). Through this looking-glass

Brand-new Don Mills and the now-demolished Curling Rink dome in 1960.

passageway you can see a quiet and hidden near-wilderness crossed by the paths along the Don that lead under what is likely Toronto's most impressive railway bridge. Look across the shallow river and you'll see the rusting ruins of the old Don Valley Ski Club.

Hancock's design incorporated nature and people from the very beginning. Karl Frank, a landscape architect who worked with Hancock and has lived in Don Mills since 1970, notes that many of the residential streets were narrower before Hancock's design, and that the natural watercourses were preserved. 'They wanted to avoid costly infrastructure,' recalled Frank in 2007. 'They tried to use as much of the topography as possible for drainage.' However, in the 1980s the soft shoulders and ditches were replaced with curbs and gutters for aesthetic reasons, and the natural absorption of runoff was curtailed. 'People just didn't like the ditches.'

Though it was built when the car was king, many residents of Don Mills, such as Jeanetta Vickers, who has lived here for forty-eight years, get along just fine without cars. 'It's very handy here. I don't drive, but I can walk everywhere,' she told me. 'There are a lot of seniors here who don't need a car.' Vickers said she raised her children in Don Mills, and now they and her grandchildren live there – 'once a Don Miller, always a Don Miller.' She describes a life that those marketing campaigns for developments north of Major Mackenzie try to conjure.

This utopian view of Don Mills is not shared by everyone, however. Author Lawrence Hill devoted a chapter in his book, *Black Berry, Sweet Juice: On Being Black and White in Canada,* to the neighbourhood. His parents moved from Washington, D.C., and settled in Don Mills in the early 1960s. 'It was a challenging terrain to navigate,' he told me. 'Nine out of ten days, it was a normal [suburban] life, hanging out at the rink, playing on teams. Then on the tenth day, somebody would spit in my face and call me a nigger. It happened enough to keep me off balance.'

For many ethnic minorities who were here during the WASP-dominated Toronto-the-Good era, this is a city-wide phenomenon. 'I may have faced similar things in other places,' says Hill. 'It's strange that my parents were fleeing one of the most highly charged racial places in the U.S., and they took us to Don Mills. They were looking for an escape hatch. Well, they found it. Then we had to find a way out.'

What Hill has in common with Don Mills fans like Vickers and Frank is concern that the 2009 redevelopment of the Don Mills Shopping Centre might destroy the sense of community. Originally a modernist gem, the outdoor plaza was converted into a covered mall in 1978 and became the de facto community centre. Don Mills lacks proper community gathering spots – even the bowling alley, movie theatres and curling club have closed – so the shopping mall became the town square.

Owner Cadillac Fairview has turned what was a lower-middle-class mall into an upmarket place called the Shops at Don Mills, hoping to attract consumers from outside the area. This gets to the heart of the problem of quasi-public spaces: what responsibility do the owners of such places have to their surrounding community? 'It gave the community its identity,' says Simone Gabbay, founder of the Don Mills Friends, an organization formed out of concern over the redevelopment that fears that the new centre will not really be geared to the community.

The Shops at Don Mills is an interesting and new exercise in planning for Toronto, the retail equivalent of New Urbanist ideas, like many upscale outdoor shopping areas built since 2000 in the United States. While there are still vast lots for parking – some will eventually be filled in with mid-rise condo buildings – the Shops recreates a series of traditional 'main streets,' though instead of being home to a variety of mom-and-pop stores, it's dominated by chains and large retailers. While there are still places for people to gather, they are generally all outdoors. That's why the folks who found a daytime home at the old enclosed mall are worried – this is wintry Canada, after all. Still, people were able to gather long before malls were invented. Maybe the sense of community Don Mills residents feel can endure just fine. For now, the Shops have a film-set quality to them: they seem like real streets, but slightly off. Things are too new, the street signs and bike stands look like Toronto's but just a little different. In the middle of it all there's a clock-tower sculpture called *Super Nova*, complete with 'exploding' bungalows flying in all directions, that was designed by Douglas Coupland. Like the sculpture, walking around the Shops is a bit of a dream, where reality is skewed just a bit, and that's probably a lot like how Don Mills itself felt when it was first built.

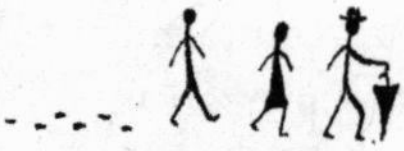

Eastish

The Danforth and Crescent Town

neighbourhood jaunt

dress to impress

offspring friendly

Connecting walks: Thorncliffe/ Flemingdon Park/Don Mills, Castle Frank/Brick Works.

Somewhere on the Prince Edward Viaduct, Bloor Street becomes the Danforth. There's no marker, but Torontonians shift from a western to an eastern state of mind while on this bridge. Michael Ondaatje used it as an inanimate character in his novel *In the Skin of a Lion*. 'The bridge goes up in a dream,' he wrote of its construction. 'It will link the east end with the centre of the city. It will carry traffic, water and electricity across the Don Valley. It will carry trains that have not even been invented yet.' One moment the pavement is soaring eastwards above the valley, the occasional train rumbling underneath, and the next it's part of a dense urban street. The change in topography is unmatched in Toronto. What's most remarkable is how flat and straight and perfect the road is throughout these changes, as if the road came first, and the Prince Edward Viaduct and the Earth rose up to meet it.

At 1 Danforth Avenue, you'll find the Adult Learning Centre, a mountaintop of modern institutional architecture completely surrounded by the on-ramp to the Don Valley Parkway. Various modish wings of the building lead back to community gardens and a secret pedestrian bridge over to Riverdale Park. Though it's somewhat neglected, this is one of Toronto's most unsung modern buildings, perhaps because of its island-like location. Between the school and the ultra-bright Pizza Pizza, there's a curious building that houses a Greek organization called the Thessalonikeans Society of Metro Toronto. The building's original purpose was somewhat more corporeal in nature: if you've ever wondered how Toronto built public washrooms in 1921, they did it like this, with this kind of style and elegance (today we build them – if we build them at all – with the hope that they work and little else).

At Broadview, two buildings, the CIBC building on the north side and the Playter Society building (where Guy Lombardo's orchestra played the third-floor hall regularly in the 1930s) on

The Prince Edward Viaduct leaps over the Don Valley.

the south side welcome visitors to the part of the Danforth they make tourist brochures about. It's one of the streets people use to define Toronto, bearing an iconic name with that definite article in front of it – *the* Danforth – as if it has an importance of place beyond that of being a major street. It's like a colonial territory or a realm of great consequence, echoing the way the British referred to *the* Sudan or *the* Levant back in the days of empire. It also appears in a line from a Barenaked Ladies song, where the fellas from Scarborough sing of going down to *the* Danforth. The use of 'the' could be a local Anglo-Saxon hangover – in the *Toronto Star*, writer Robert Thomas Allen described the character of the area up until the 1950s as overwhelmingly working class, 'a flat suburb of English, Irish and Scotch cops, TTC motormen and T. Eaton Company tie clerks.'

The Danforth has been the hardest stretch of 'destination' road in Toronto for me to cozy up to. It perpetually seems one lane too wide for walking and one too narrow for driving, and the trees are either stunted or non-existent; the summer sun is hot and unrelenting, the winter wind bitter and unbroken. At first glance, the retail strip between the Don River and Pape Avenue is dominated by too many Paul Frank underwear emporiums, fancy stationery shops and upscale knick-knack stores. It's boring, the kind of bland retail landscape people fear when the word 'gentrification' comes up. How many oddly shaped vases does one family need? It's also the best place in Toronto to be run over by a yummy mummy pushing a ridiculously oversized SUV stroller, though a number of other neighbourhoods (Bloor West Village, Leslieville, the Junction) also jockey for that position.

Just west of Broadview, at Number 121, there's a tiny passageway that leads north/south to A & V Aluminum, an infill development *avant la lettre*, and a bit of very old-fashioned mixed-use heritage. Across the street and a bit east of here, at Playter Boulevard – the Playters were an original Loyalist family – the 'All Canadian' Mister Transmission was replaced in the late 2000s by a Shoppers Drug Mart building that, while it does meet the sidewalk, is a glorified big-box structure, only one storey tall in a place where there should be three or four floors above the retail. Though Mister Transmission is gone, it and A & V represent what Toronto once was: a provincial working-class city. Businesses like this were, and sometimes still are, located on our main drags, not tucked away in a hidden district. It's details like these, some of which you don't see at first, that make the Danforth worth getting to know.

In the 1950s, waves of Italian immigrants settled in those working-class houses surrounding the Danforth, replacing the tie clerks. The Greeks who followed eventually turned the area into what the local BIA calls the largest Greektown in North America. At its height in the 1970s, there were between thirty and forty thousand Greeks living in the area. But like so many other inner-city ethnic enclaves, the first- and second-generation Greeks started to move out to suburbs like Scarborough and North York in the late '70s, selling their homes to 'white painters' who moved in and fixed them up, shifting the prices and demographic in a decidedly upwardly-mobile direction. The ethnic strip remains, as they have in other neighbourhoods, anchored by the restaurants and Alexander the Great Park at Logan.

The Carrot Common is a good example of this transition. Opened in 1984, it won a City of Toronto urban design award soon

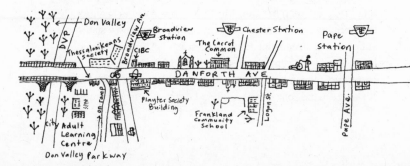

after. Inside the Big Carrot – a worker-owned co-op, and the guilt-free version of the corporate Whole Foods – phrases like 'wellness' and 'well-being' are printed on nearly everything, and customers shop with their bike helmets on. An employee once told me, on condition of strict anonymity, that when she started working there, 'it felt like Sesame Street, everybody cheerfully saying hello to me by name.'

A bit further east, around Jones Avenue, the Danforth returns to its working-class roots. Gone are the high-end coffee chains and mid-scale restaurants; instead, a nearly continuous line of independent stores, bars and low-rise architecture styles stretches to Victoria Park. This is where the east side's great unsung view starts: to the south, Lake Ontario has a looming presence, a rare thing in most of Toronto's urban areas, where the lake might as well not exist.

Around Greenwood you hit a dead zone. A persistent anomaly, the zone stretches for two long blocks of empty lots, abandoned buildings and big LCBO and Beer Store parking lots that suck the life from the street. (The two latter buildings are representative of the booze retailers' consistent corporate philosophy of being as un-urban as possible.) The Roxy, an old boarded-up movie house, was for sale the last time I visited, its former grandeur not altogether obscured by neglect and plywood. Somebody had rearranged the letters on the sign above the door to say, 'For a scare convert to drugs etc 3 large enemas 4 afternoon delight,' a message containing enough of the original intent to seem like a legitimate entertainment option. A mixed-use Carrot Common–style development was to fill in this empty area in 2010 but, as with many new Toronto developments, there was a public debate over how high the towers should be during the planning stage.

Madeleine Callaghan, who lives near the Greenwood intersection with her husband and two kids, remarked that when they

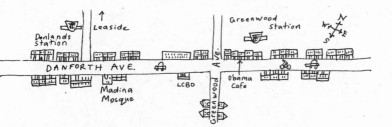

moved here in 1997, they 'were the second young family on the street. Slowly, it became all young families. Everybody said the intersection was just about to turn for the better, but it didn't.' It's remarkable how some retail strips can remain unchanged even as the surrounding neighbourhood becomes more desirable.

The Danforth mix picks up again past Greenwood. This post-Greektown stretch of relatively low rents is important – tech or cultural industries would call this an incubator for small businesses and arts organizations – and looks a lot like a museum of small-time capitalism. It also boasts a fine collection of irony-free bars that provide space for everybody to feel comfortable. For instance, you could stop in at Noah's Ark, further along at Dawes Road, an old roadhouse established in 1905. Go on a Thursday night and the locals will force somebody in your group to do karaoke, and then when you're leaving they'll ask you to come back and visit anytime. Good cities need places like this.

At Main Street, on top of the Hakim Optical building, a pair of huge red eyeglasses watches over the street omnisciently, like the billboard eyes of Doctor T. J. Eckleburg do in *The Great Gatsby*. Main Square, opposite the eyeglasses, is a dense community of high-rise towers whose utopian 1970s plaza has been neglected and is now host to underutilized retail and unkempt concrete planters. Even the pool area has been filled in. So many people come and go through the square (the Main Street GO train station is just south of here) that it should be a great Toronto space, yet, for everyone except the local residents who use it despite its state, it's a missed opportunity.

Just past Main hulks a large Canadian Tire store, one of the biggest crimes against Toronto's urbanity. Though it seems like a crown corporation, the way Tim Hortons does, and so should have our best interests at heart, this company enjoys plunking down big-box stores where a more detailed touch is needed (though the

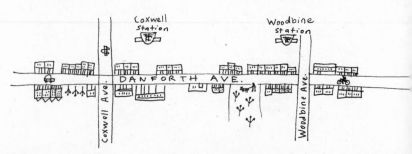

LCBO is certainly no model of urban design sensibilities, either). Like the Shoppers back at Playter Boulevard, the Canadian Tire meets the sidewalk, but gives the pedestrian a lot of nothing, just a blank wall and one entrance. These cookie-cutter one-size-fits-all shops may be easy for the company, but they're bad for the city.

Past Warden Avenue, the Danforth becomes just Danforth Road. Looking back into the city, you can see the slope down towards the Don and enjoy a perfectly straight view all the way into the heart of midtown. Though it's a mall with a big parking lot, the Shoppers World Danforth at Victoria Park is an interesting hybrid of a strip mall and what must be the city's shortest mall – there are just a handful of stores in its truncated arcade. This was once a Ford factory, but when Shoppers World built in 1962 it was replaced by what was the second Eaton's store outside of a downtown area.

The old City of Toronto, East York and Scarborough all meet at the corner of Danforth and Victoria Park avenues – not exactly a 'four corners' kind of place, but three will do. Walk north on Victoria Park a few blocks and you'll find Crescent Town, a self-contained mod spaceship of a community that rises high above the ravine of Taylor Creek Park, a landmark last bit of East York concrete before the former borough gives way to Scarborough. Crescent Town is attached to Victoria Park subway station by a long covered walkway, and it's the first thing you see out the north side of the train when it exits the tunnel.

Much of Crescent Town's public space is raised up on pillars, hovering above mud and parking lots, allowing for grassy parkland and passageways. Yvonne Bambrick, now a registered downtowner

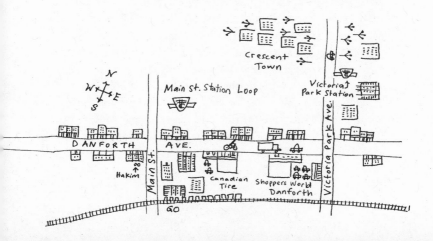

The Crescent School in 1933, on the spot where Crescent Town stands today.

and the executive director of the Toronto Cyclists' Union, spent her first eighteen years happily positioned with her parents in a condo on the twenty-ninth floor of a building in Crescent Town. 'It was as hip as lofts are today, but with a lot of young families,' said Bambrick. 'There were lots of three-bedroom units.' Places like Crescent Town demonstrate that when units are built big enough for families, kids can live happy vertical lives, too.

Bambrick would walk her dog in the Taylor-Massey Creek ravine and take swimming lessons in the pool at the attached Crescent Town Club. A few years before she arrived, a young Kiefer Sutherland was one of the development's first residents, and a student at Crescent Town elementary school.

This area was once named Dentonia Farm. The farm was owned by the famed Massey clan in 1897 and named after Denton, Susan Massey's maiden name. It was here that the Masseys raised the cows that provided the milk for their City Dairy Company, which was located on the northeast side of Spadina Crescent, in a building that's now owned by the University of Toronto. In 1933, Susan donated her mansion and forty acres of Dentonia Farm to the Crescent School (for Fancy and Exclusive Boys). In 1969, the private school moved to its current location on Bayview near the

Bridle Path, and this land was redeveloped as Crescent Town. The name Dentonia lives in the moniker of the adjacent city-owned golf course.

Crescent Town is still a vibrant place, with people populating the open spaces, even on cold nights. Crescent Town restaurant, snug in the centre of the neighbourhood, still has laminated place-mats that list cocktail suggestions from the swinging era when this place was built.

Parts of Crescent Town could use some sprucing up, and some of the broken and burnt-out lights should be replaced. Bambrick pointed out that, in recent years, some of the concrete 'hiding' places in the main courtyard by Victoria Park station have been removed, making it less dodgy for late-night walkers. Still, the pedestrian-oriented mix of modern concrete utopian space next to forested ravine – a very Torontonian kind of place – is largely intact.

Downtown East Side Zigzag

  pack a lunch

 dress to impress

offspring friendly

Connecting walks: Yonge, Harbourfront, Nathan Phillips Square/PATH, YMCA, Dundas, Castle Frank/Brick Works, Gerrard.

Standing down where the Esplanade meets Yonge Street, it feels like the bulk of the city is towering above you, more so than anywhere else in the city. The east side of the city core has a special view of downtown – from the west the buildings gradually build up to the core, whereas on the east it's an abrupt rise, like an electric mountain range next to low-lying plains. The effect is dramatic, and ever so big-city, a valuable feeling in a city like Toronto, which is eternally preoccupied with how it measures up. Parking lots here have been converted into new condos and what was once a back-alley kind of place is now dense and filled with people.

A few steps east of Yonge, between the Esplanade and the railway corridor, there's a large condo building that's remarkable because it's Toronto's larger, yet unsung, flatiron building. Our famous flatiron, the Gooderham building, is just a block away, on the corner just east of Yonge where Front and Wellington streets meet. It gets all the tourists snapping photographs, while this one looms unheralded, almost invisible despite its size, looking like the prow of an unreal ship slowly passing in front of the skyline. Behind it is the Hotel Novotel, a postmodern creation that references a European vision of what a hotel should look like.

Across from the unsung Flatiron on the Esplande, you'll find yourself at the back door of what was once the O'Keefe Centre, later the Hummingbird Centre and, more recently, the Sony Centre for the Performing Arts. This building hosted legendary Russian dancer Mikhail Baryshnikov after he defected from the Soviet Union in June of 1974 and was spirited away first to journalist John Fraser's apartment and then to the Caledon Hills just outside of the city before he finally found his way into the arms of Leonard Bernstein, Jackie O. and the rest of New York's arts society. This door is the tiny passage to that notable life. That Cold War drama was able to play out down here because Victorian-era

Torontonians decided to extend the city south of Front Street, where the original shoreline of Lake Ontario was located.

A little further east from here, you'll find the beginnings of Church Street. There are two Church streets in Toronto – the one below Gerrard Street and the one above. People talk about the northern section of the street more, since it's where out-of-towners go during Pride Week, the part locals are perpetually worried is becoming less gay, or straighter. People have been worried about the state of the Village for at least a decade now, and every time a bar or gay-owned shop closes, the fretting begins anew. Neighbourhoods like Church Street are delicate, as community interests and the free market have to be synchronously directed in order to produce a beloved neighbourhood.

Far from these queer concerns, Church Street has a rather unglamorous beginning in a parking garage. Though it's unsung (perhaps we should brand this area of Toronto the 'Unsung District'), the view from down here in the St. Lawrence Market neighbourhood shows Toronto's urbanity at its zenith, as a bowl of buildings – some old, some new – rises in each direction. It feels safe and solid: we are protected by buildings here. The steep slope up to Front Street is the result of fill that softened a twenty-foot cliff to the original beach below, where the Town of York's first substantial wharf was built.

Though the lake view from Front is gone, the Gooderham building is still photographed hundreds of times a day. This part of Toronto is the city's most Parisian quarter in terms of scale, but it also feels like a 1980 period piece. Maybe it's the font of the St. Lawrence Centre for the Arts logo, or Derek Michael Besant's 'peeling facade' mural on the back of the flatiron building, but Front Street evokes the last days of Toronto's 1970s 'City That Works' era. Meanwhile, the odd little cabana-like Pizza Pizza building on the northwest corner, which replaced a fine old bank, is from the 1980s 'City That's Broken' era.

North of here, Church Street quiets down, and it remains in this calmer state for quite a number of blocks. Just below King Street at Colborne Street sits one of the few parking lots in the city that may actually be all right, as it affords a view from tiny Leader Lane – once the brokerage centre of Toronto – of the side of the King Edward Hotel up to the still-mothballed penthouse

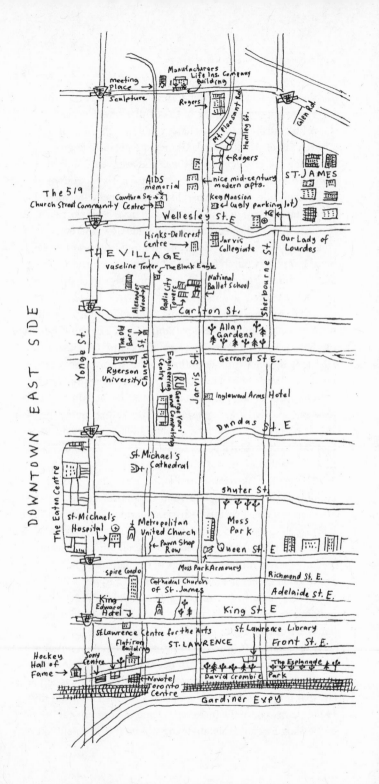

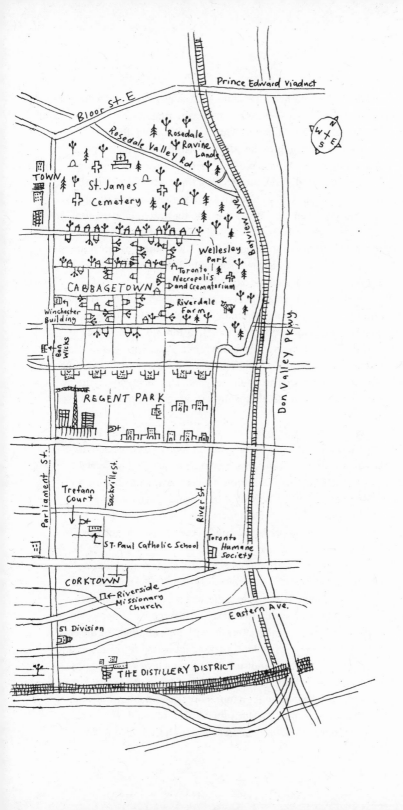

ballroom. It's another bored-out urban canyon view and a glimpse of a sheer part of that electrical mountain range.

At King Street, St. James Anglican Cathedral – the first of three churches that give the street its name – was, for a time, the centre of social life in old York, and the source of all things Toronto the Good (it remains so for a few). A few blocks north, the Metropolitan United Church at Queen remains a hub of community meetings – it was home to the anti-amalgamation rallies of former mayor John Sewell's Citizens For Local Democracy group in the 1990s, and its front lawn is now home to the chess hustlers who relocated from outside the Yonge and Gould Sam the Record Man in 2003.

A block north, St. Michael's Cathedral is the Catholic counterpoint to St. James' Anglican redoubt. These three churches form a kind of religious triumvirate that, like Toronto itself, seems to effortlessly contain a variety of divergent viewpoints. In the middle of this, the Spire condo building rises above all their steeples, the triumph of civic secularism in a city that still seems to dig the church, but whose steeple shadows no longer dominate the streets and the culture.

Opposite the Metropolitan United Church stretches Toronto's pawnshop row. It looks like a 1960s or '70s film scene shot in an ungentrified city (*The French Connection*, or even *Midnight Cowboy*). McTamney's is Toronto's oldest pawnshop, buying and selling here since 1860. Most of the pawn industry is on the up and up, this block is where underground and hidden desperation manifests itself, as emotional bonds between people and objects are broken for quick cash.

Ryerson University and its giant 'RU' signage dominates Church at Dundas. As many campuses do, Ryerson makes the street less interesting here, because instead of individual storefront variety there's a mono-block. The George Vari Engineering and Computing Centre is a recent block-long addition on the east side of the street – it filled in a parking lot between Church and the magnificent Merchandise Building, which was once a Simpsons, and then a Sears warehouse, and is now a residential loft conversion. The building is a four-storey glass fishbowl of student life that was designed by Moriyama & Teshima Architects, of Toronto Reference Library and Scarborough Civic Centre fame.

North of Gerrard, Church becomes busy and diverse again. This stretch used to be residential all the way up to Bloor, but over time the big houses were either torn down or converted into stores and bars. The venerable Barn, which was carved out of a rambling Victorian house, was closed for a few years after the owner's murder (his lover was accused but later acquitted), but it's open again, and functions as the kind of gay bar every good city has: it's a big, slightly dirty social trawler where anybody from any scene can hang out now and then. It, like those pawnshops, seems to be from another era and sensibility, and like so many enterprises of this nature, it could close again at any time.

As Toronto's gay scene moved from Yonge to Church in the 1980s, that old sensibility of queer bars behind darkened windows evolved into a much more conspicuous street presence. This was always a gay area, from the early 1800s, in the legendary days of possibly gay magistrate Alexander Wood (that's his statue with the conspicuously bulging crotch at Alexander and Church), to the '50s and '60s, when the City Park Co-Op and Village Green apartment complexes were built (the latter includes a round building endearingly nicknamed 'Vaseline Tower'), residential structures where a single man or (less frequently) woman could live alone and in relative privacy.

Church-Wellesley's kind of urbanism is ideal. Church along here has one of the liveliest streetscapes in Toronto (it filled in for Pittsburgh in all five seasons of *Queer as Folk*), with enough bars to keep people around until late at night but enough of everything else to keep it populated and functional by day. With a few grocery stores, a butcher, restaurants and other services, it's a completely self-contained neighbourhood – it's not a surprise that lots of not-so-gay folks want to move into this kind of *Sesame Street* urban landscape.

In you look at the changes in the neighbourhood through the Diversity-our-Strength–motto lens, it's all good, but for those worried about the demise of Church, it's useful to think of how other ethnic strips have evolved. The Greeks don't live en masse on the Danforth anymore, nor do the Italians along St. Clair, but the ethnic strips there remain, and people visit because the areas still feel Italian or Greek. Bars may come and go, but Church is anchored by visible institutions and places like the

519 Community Centre, the AIDS Memorial and Cawthra Park, the AIDS Committee of Toronto and that Alexander Wood statue. Even the CBC's *Battle of the Blades* figure skating show that put life back into Maple Leaf Gardens in 2009 after a decade of neglect was good for the community because it was the gayest event the place had witnessed since Liberace performed there in the 1950s. While Church Street isn't cool with the hipster queer kids (all it takes is a few promoters to change that), and the need to stick together in one area for security is much less powerful now, the Village is still critical, if only for this moment: imagine a gay kid coming from a less tolerant place like Timmins, Jamaica or Afghanistan, arriving at Church and Wellesley and, for the first time, seeing this vibrant, celebratory strip. No offence to those three places, but this is why cities are salvation: you can see, immediately, that you belong here, just as you are.

As Church moves north, its overtly gay vibe fades into the institutional feel of Bloor Street East. Here you'll find the typical Toronto mix of old Victorian houses that have been converted into bars, restaurants or businesses next door to taller, modern build-ings, proof the two styles can coexist close to each other without offence. On the northeast corner of Church and Bloor, a large stainless steel sculpture by Kosso Eloul called *Meeting Place* is the kind of public art kids like because they can run up and touch it and, in this case, look at themselves in it. Further east, on the north side of Bloor, the Manufacturers Life Insurance Company building has the finest putting-green-style lawn in Toronto, which is kept safe behind a tall wrought-iron fence.

A little farther on, there's a relatively rare-for-Toronto T-inter-section where Jarvis, one of Toronto's most contentious streets (for a brief period of time) meets Bloor. On February 20, 2009, at 8:02 a.m., city councillor Denzil Minnan-Wong sent a message on Twit-ter that said, 'Used the middle lane on Jarvis St to get to work. Fast and efficient!' When questioned about it later, he said, 'It was a great way to get to work. Imagine driving to work and not having to wait in gridlock! It was fantastic!'

The exclamation-mark-mad muckraking councillor was inten-tionally wading into the contentious debate about the future of Jarvis. At the same time, he betrayed the strange panic that causes drivers to think that anything that threatens the dominance of the automobile in urban design is somehow a declaration of war on the car. Jarvis, once the most beautiful street in Toronto, has been reverse-gentrified and turned into a fat arterial traffic pipe between North Toronto and downtown. The City's 2009 Jarvis Street Streetscape Improvement Plan, championed by long-time local councillor Kyle Rae, aimed to return the street to some of its pedestrian-friendly glory.

The shrill tone of the histrionics employed by, for lack of a better term, the car lobby, might have led residents to believe the city wanted to close Jarvis and hand it over to ambulatory south-of-Bloor Bolsheviks. It's the kind of rhetoric that ages quickly and makes the past look more backwards than it was. As early as 2000, Councillor Rae told Christopher Hume of the *Toronto Star* that 'What [the plan was] trying to do is bring back something the city lost many years ago ... a dignified and safe street with a park and a boulevard.' The plan, which was approved in February 2010, included wider sidewalks, more trees and possibly a bike lane, but the main item fanning Rosedale's anti-improvement rhetorical flames was the removal of Jarvis's unique middle lane, which reversed direction depending on the rush-hour flow.

What the Minnan-Wongs and four-wheeled-folk of Toronto hadn't noticed was that a 'residential urbanization' had taken place along the strip in the preceding decades, a change that was easy to miss while speeding by in a car. Walk Jarvis and you quickly notice the incredible residential density, and how much of its past grandeur still remains.

Today, Jarvis still begins in grandeur of a kind, along Bloor's Insurance Company Row. The Manulife building is now the most impressive building here representing the industry. (The Rogers headquarters on the corner used to give it a run for its money when it was the Confederation Life, a company that went under in 1994, long before insurance company failure was bailout fashionable.) Here, Mt. Pleasant Road, opened in the early 1950s, and once referred to as the city's first expressway, funnels all that Rosedale and North Toronto traffic onto Jarvis, traffic that was the reason behind the widening of the street in the 1960s.

Artist Michael Snow's best-known pieces of public art in Toronto are *The Audience* (the grotesque figures shouting and hanging off the building formerly known as SkyDome) and

Flightstop (the famed flying geese in the Eaton Centre). But hidden behind the Rogers corporate campus at Mt. Pleasant and Bloor is *Red, Orange and Green*, the giant stainless steel tree sculpture Snow built for Confederation Life in 1992 that includes cutouts of his equally famous 'walking woman' figure from the 1960s. The sculpture was originally placed in a very public spot, where Mt. Pleasant splits off from Jarvis, but you can now find the sculpture on the Huntley Street side of the Rogers campus, near where the Christian talk show *100 Huntley Street*'s studios once were. Snow once told me that the building owners 'without discussion or permission moved the sculpture to the backyard. This was a big deal: the street needed to be closed for big cranes. The title of the sculpture refers both to traffic lights and the seasonal colour changes of tree leaves. It was explicitly designed for that corner – in the work there are references to nearby shapes. It was made to be seen driving by, as well as more contemplatively from the side-walks.' On another occasion he joked that when Rogers bought the SkyDome he was afraid that they would move *The Audience* as well.

South on Jarvis, and opposite the Rogers headquarters, there's a block of wonderful mid-century modern apartment buildings made from angular yellow brick and glass that look as sharp as Glenn Gould's *Goldberg Variations* of the same era. One of the buildings is appropriately named 'Massey House,' as the Massey family lived just down the street in the Keg Mansion, what is now one of the most unique chain-restaurant locations in the city. To understand the Jarvis story, stand across from the Keg at the corner of Cawthra Square (which leads back to the AIDS memorial on Church). From there, you'll see two massive Richardsonian Romanesque mansions (they look like smaller versions of Old City Hall), high-rise and low-rise apartment buildings and then, south of Wellesley, Jarvis Collegiate Institute, the public high school where so many Torontonians of note went and where so many Canadians of future note currently study. These good things are slightly diminished by one of Toronto's ugliest parking lots, which sits in front of the Keg Mansion like a blunt piece of public art representing the crimes against Jarvis.

Nearby, the details that make Jarvis great abound. At Wellesley, on the northeast corner, Plaza 100 – a narrow, wide and high concrete building complete with rooftop swimming pool – is surrounded by mod parkettes defined by Expo 67–era avant-garde sculptural shapes. Sit on one of the benches and the potential Jarvis has to return to its former, welcoming state is obvious.

Until I walked Jarvis to write this – that is, until I paid close attention to the street – I hadn't noticed the Hincks-Dellcrest Centre just south of Wellesley at number 440. The Hincks-Dellcrest is a children's mental-health facility that's housed in a brutalist masterpiece tucked away behind some trees. A few steps down, at 432–438, the Jarvis Court apartments have gorgeous prewar De Stijl tile and window designs. (So many details only reveal themselves when you're on foot.) Across the street, round apartment towers rise behind a Second Empire mansion that could have been the inspiration for the house in Hitchcock's *Psycho*. At this point, Jarvis begins to seem like it should be a cherished architectural museum rather than Toronto's shortcut.

The most recently celebrated jewel in Jarvis's heretofore secret crown of gems is the Canada's National Ballet School, a perfect collision of new and old, with glass and steel surrounding old mansions and the former CBC headquarters, itself once the Havergal College school for girls. The condo towers that rise behind – appropriately named Radio City – are the latest additions to this dense residential neighbourhood.

South of Carlton, Jarvis begins to look more fortified. The Inglewood Arms rents rooms daily and weekly, the Allan Gardens park has an underwhelming street presence, and the traditional downtown sex-worker 'stroll' lives here – guys in cars really do drive by slowly in the evening looking at the sidewalk like they're extras in *Taxi Driver*. Meanwhile, the fenced-in Moss Park Armoury is a bad urban neighbour, taking up space and giving nothing back.

In 2007, Toronto gave Lombard Street – a short street between Victoria and Jarvis streets south of Richmond – the honorary title of Gilda Radner Way. Radner, the comedy legend of *Saturday Night Live* fame who died of ovarian cancer in 1989, performed at 110 Lombard, an 1886 fire hall that was home to the Toronto location of the Second City comedy troupe from 1974 to 1997. This location was also the launch pad for Canadian comedians Mike Myers, John Candy and Eugene Levy. Today, the building houses Gilda's Club, where cancer patients and their families can gather.

Back on Jarvis, the fine and urbane St. James Park flanks
the west side of the street as it moves back into the St. Lawrence
neighbourhood, where there's no questioning the street's vibrancy.
Here, Jarvis no longer has its magic centre lane, and traffic is
forced to squeeze into two lanes – and farther south into one –
during non-rush-hour times when street parking is allowed. All
that fuss over a street that wasn't really a highway after all? The
tamed highway passes agreeably by St. Lawrence Hall, built in
1850, and down to Front Street.

Across the street from the beloved south building of St.
Lawrence Market, which houses the best selection of fresh fish,
vegetable and meat in the city, its northern counterpart, the square
brown brick building at Jarvis and Front streets, sits like a dowdy
and stern aunt frowning at happy Toronto. Built in 1968 to replace
an earlier market building, the structure has a few elements of
modern style inside, but not enough to make it beloved in any
way. That was slated to change when, in 2009, the city announced
a design competition to rebuild it to a more pleasant standard.
(There has been a market in this location for over 200 years, and
at one point a canopy connected the south building and an earlier
version of the northern one.) Though its home is not the most
attractive, the Sunday antique market held here each week is
the best-curated garage sale in the city.

Jarvis slopes along the side of the market, another hint of
the long-buried beach that was once adjacent to the building.
The Esplanade, which runs behind the building, may be one of
Toronto's most beautifully and grandly named streets, but when
you're here, its narrow width and relatively short length do not
live up to that fine name. The street is a fraction of the wide waterfront promenade it once was. By the mid-1800s, the railway had
pushed its way across the front of the city, laying tracks along the
Esplanade. Landfill eventually extended the waterfront away from
the Esplanade, leaving the city with what we have today: a cute
urban street with a very big name. East of here, the Esplanade
runs alongside the David Crombie Park, named after the 'tiny
perfect mayor' of 1970s Toronto who presided over the construction of what has become a not-so-tiny perfect neighbourhood. One
of Toronto's largest-ever urban projects – a peek at archival photos
shows much of the St. Lawrence neighbourhood was just parking

lots by the 1970s – the area combines rental housing with condominiums, co-ops and even a school and community centre built
into some of the mid-rise buildings. It's a kind of urbanity we
don't see much of in Toronto.

The park and the Esplanade are a natural corridor leading
east to the Distillery District. As the West Don Lands are built up,
the isolated, island feel of the Distillery – an isolation that's not as
strongly felt if you approach the area from the west – will diminish
and the city will grow up around it. Walk through Parliament
Square Park at the end of the Esplanade, past the subtle plaque
that explains that this was the site of Ontario's (then Upper
Canada's) first Parliament building, which was burnt to the
ground by American attackers during the War of 1812. Then travel
across Parliament Street to the corner of Mill Street, where you'll
find the Toronto condo that is most likely to poke you in the eye.
The Pure Spirit condo and loft tower includes a glass flatiron-style
podium that comes to a perfect and dramatic point at Parliament
and Mill streets. Historical-architecture purists may not like where
it's located, but glass towers adjacent to the preserved Victorian
industrial buildings of the distillery occupy a space in the growing
tradition of a unique Toronto look, a look that should be celebrated

Watch you don't get poked in the eye by the Pure Spirit building.

(when it's done right) for preserving historic buildings and making them part of the evolving and living city. The building replaced an ugly parking lot, and it opens up a new grand entrance into the Distillery District that finally properly connects the site with the St. Lawrence neighbourhood.

Apart from a few places like the Distillery complex, the 51 Division police station and other old warehouse buildings, Parliament Street's lower half is not particularly pretty. Some of the older parts of the street are rundown, while newer bits are often clunky and ugly. There have been tragedies here, too. On the northwest corner of Queen and Parliament, keep your eyes to the sidewalk and try to find the granite plaque that bears the names of the ten residents of the Rupert rooming house who died in a December 1989 fire. After the tragedy, concerned tenants, landlords, community workers and housing advocates formed a group called the Rupert Coalition, which fights for increased safety inspections of rooming houses and the development of more safe and affordable housing units.

Parliament's desolate feeling ends north of here at Dundas, with the Regent Park revitalization project's new glass and brick buildings. Finally, after decades of hiding from the sidewalk, the Regent Park public housing complex, for the last half of the twentieth century one of Toronto's greatest blights, now has a real street presence. As people and stores move in (all former residents were given the option to move back in), and the rest of the project is continued by further razing the older parts and replacing them with mixed-income housing (and a return of the old street grid), the Parliament streetscape will change dramatically, and the revitalization will also shift the psychological boundaries of this neighbourhood and that of Cabbagetown, its neighbour to the north.

North of Gerrard, Parliament seems to achieve the perfect balance between gentrification and the urban hodgepodge that makes cities exciting. We struggle to find an equilibrium for these forces in many neighbourhoods across Toronto, but Parliament can handle places like the somewhat fancy bar above the Tim Hortons in the Winchester building and the crummy Coffee Time across the street, and the million-dollar homes east of Parliament that are a stone's throw from the hardscrabble St. James Town high-rises on the west side at Wellesley. Hardware stores, antique stores, pubs like the House of Parliament, the Halifax Fish Market and the venerable Ben Wicks coexist just fine with a beastly Esso Station, the No Frills supermarket and some rather sketchy bars towards Gerrard, where a guy once told me he would break my bike if I didn't give him some change. (I didn't, and he was bluffing.) In the summer, the lovely old lady who used to work nights at the Coffee Time said things like 'Hi, dear' as she sat outside, watching high-heeled patrons of the fancy bar smoke.

It's remarkable that these places exist and don't seem to be under pressure to move. Old-timers argue that the real Cabbagetown was south of Gerrard and was destroyed when Regent Park was created. But the idea of a neighbourhood is what's important; the borders that define a place often shift. David, the bartender and manager at the Ben Wicks pub, once told me that while many people walk down Parliament, few go past the Shoppers Drug Mart a quarter of a block south of Carlton. He says people think there's nothing happening beyond it. (The Ben Wicks is located on the wrong side of this equation.) Psychological divides are hard to overcome; sometimes it takes a new skyscraper to do it.

Old Cabbagetown was an Orange bastion of mostly working-class Irish Protestants, a Little Belfast devoted to crown and empire. Cabbagetown was political currency, as the Toronto writer Morley Callaghan explained in a newspaper article in 1987: 'If you were from Cabbagetown, it meant you really belonged to Toronto. It was the working man's area, where there was a neighbourhood feeling, where people were sort of proud to be living, and they produced politician after politician. To be a member of the Orange Lodge and born in Cabbagetown had all kinds of splendid possibilities. A man like Tommy Church could become mayor six times, always proudly announcing that he was a Cabbagetown boy.' I don't recall 1990s-era Toronto mayor Barbara Hall ever mentioning she lived in Cabbagetown. She does, and has for nearly forty years now.

The most visible workers in Cabbagetown now are tasked with the eternal upkeep of those old homes (the sound of hammering will never cease), many of which still have genuine McCausland stained-glass windows (a very special thing, Cabbagetowners will tell you). At Halloween, a candied version of noblesse oblige plays out as the neighbourhood welcomes a flood of children from neighbouring (and far less affluent) St. James Town. One home

The white tower cluster of St. James Town.

spent $175 on candy and was out by 7:30 p.m. None of this will
solve class divides, but the mix that plays out between the very
different in Parliament neighbourhoods is Toronto at its best.

From many vantage points in Cabbagetown, you can see the
towers of St. James Town peeking out from between Victorian
gables. Wellesley is the divide, with high-rises to the north and
low-rises to the south. From a distance – especially from the east,
across the Don Valley – St. James Town looks like one of those
stylized cityscape illustrations where a cozy cluster of skyscrapers
quickly gives way to a low-rise suburban or rural landscape. It
looks as if it's a solid mass, but up close, from any direction, St.
James Town is porous: there is no right or wrong way to get in,
no main or backdoor entrance.

On a number of occasions, people who should know better –
smart newspaper columnists or even friendly city-minded folks –
have suggested that walking through St. James Town is something
that just should not be done, as if they'd be embarking on some
kind of wild urban adventure through the set of a 1970s Charles
Bronson film. That isn't the case. There are around 17,000 people
living in this cluster of towers. It's the area with the highest residential density in Canada, and there are always people around,
whether it's noon or midnight.

To grasp how it's put together, St. James Town is best explored
without a plan. Subway stops make for good official entrances to

neighbourhoods, and the Glen Road exit of the Sherbourne subway station at the top of the neighbourhood should be St. James Town's grand entrance. Instead of being welcomed to the neighbourhood, people exiting the subways were for years met by the oft-lamented demolition-by-neglect Victorian houses that lined Glen and were often used as film sets because abandoned buildings are so rare in Toronto. (As of this writing, there are finally plans in the work to renovate them.) Boarded-up homes continue around the corner, down Howard Street to Sherbourne itself – one of these houses even collapsed in on itself in the early 2000s and is now an empty lot.

Though many, if not most, of St. James Town's residents are pedestrians and transit users, there's no crosswalk at Howard Street to stop the steady flow of cars on Sherbourne. Across from where this crosswalk should be, there is a row of Second Empire buildings, some of the few remnants of the original neighbourhood that was cleared out in the 1960s to make way for the swinging-'60s vision of bachelor apartments that were the first incarnation of St. James Town. Today, only a handful of buildings – like the World Laundry on Parliament at Wellesley – remain from this era. The buildings along Howard appear as though they were prepared to be demolished when the march of towers suddenly exhausted itself.

Ghosts of those razed streets can also be found all around the neighbourhood. Though cars can't make it through it, Ontario Street still cuts a straight line down the middle of St. James Town and, with a little work, could become a fantastic linear neighbourhood plaza. Walk down off Rose Avenue or Bleecker Street, which still connects Wellesley and Howard. Between Bleecker and Sherbourne, there's a raised space that connects the three apartment towers along here in much the same way public spaces are connected in Toronto's Crescent Town and London, England's Barbican Estate. While people and cars pass constantly underneath – the entrance to the neighbourhood and the connection to the No Frills grocery store are busy areas – the parkland floating above is derelict, a modern ruin. Two eroding staircases lead from either street up to this platform of broken tiles and concrete-framed lawns. As of this writing, the soothsaying white-and-block-letter development sign down on the street, which announces an upcoming remake of the retail podium of these towers, is likely also the reason it's been left to rot. For now, though, it's possible to be alone in the middle of 17,000 people, with a near-bird's-eye view of St. James Town and the city to the east, including the stunning and un-Toronto-looking Our Lady of Lourdes Church on Sherbourne.

Inside St. James Town there are more block letters, this time used more elegantly in the names of the Winnipeg, the Halifax, the Montreal, the Calgary, the Edmonton and the Vancouver. Never let them say Toronto doesn't think about the rest of Canada – we do, and we proclaim our connection to other cities via the most appropriate form: the skyscraper. The northernmost tower, the Toronto, has a mature pine forest (as do many institutional and residential buildings from this era) in its rather large front yard along Howard Street, along with half-round planters and interesting angular pathways through the trees with benches for resting. However, what might be a well-used space is often empty because of the fences that surround it, which leave nowhere to go once inside.

While St. James Town is porous at its edges, wandering around inside can be a challenge because there are even more fences separating the various tower properties, making natural and desired routes on foot often impossible. More than once, I've walked a logical route through the buildings only to be blocked in by chain link or a cheap knock-off of a wrought-iron fence. Some of those fences have been turned into inadvertent and somewhat beautiful sculptures by people who have locked their bikes – many dozens of them, all in varying states of disrepair – there.

In the middle of St. James Town, along that ghost of Ontario Street, there are often impromptu markets selling fruit and vegetables, while closer to Wellesley, by the Food Basics grocery store, a flea market runs when the weather is good. One vendor who sells rugs along the Wellesley sidewalk can be seen, at the prescribed time, kneeling in the direction of Mecca on those rugs. All this hints at the tremendous capacity that is locked up in the surrounding towers. The people in them know how to make and do things and, given the chance, could likely create a flourishing local economy.

It wouldn't take much to make this area nice: remove the fences, make sure landlords keep their properties in shape (and ploughed in the winter, which is often a problem), get some lighting that doesn't burn the retina and keep it clean. The city life is already here, it just needs some respect. Nicer spaces will bring more people out. Add in some infrastructure that would support the markets that already exist and we have the potential for a new Toronto attraction.

At the southeast corner of St. James Town, a neglected parkette with a modish concrete sculpture marks the transition back into the deep Victorian jungle of Cabbagetown. Follow Wellesley east to Sackville Street, which bisects the neighbourhood as well as the entire east side of town. Sackville begins at a chain-link dead end and it's downhill from there, as all of Cabbagetown's northern edge is pressed up against St. James Cemetery, one of the city's finest burial places. The first block of Sackville is a little stub of road that extends north of Wellesley for a hundred metres or so. To the south, the street is a consistent line of Victorian pleasantness made so by pioneering gentrifiers – so-called 'white painters' – in the early 1970s.

Sackville does run noticeably downhill. On a bike you can coast all the way to Gerrard if you're liberal in your interpretation of what a stop sign means. On foot, the grade results in effortless walking. It feels strange to say this, but one of the nicest things about Sackville, and Cabbagetown in general, are the fences. These aren't the six-foot-high suburban fences I grew up with, but proper low wrought-iron fences with squeaky gates that close with a bang and rattle. They mark the divide between public and private in the gentlest way, inviting and allowing the exchange of pleasantries between residents and those passing by. When you see it happen on warm spring days, you realize this is as it should be everywhere.

From spring until late summer, the southern entrance to Cabbagetown, at Sackville and Gerrard, is a fertile gauntlet created by rival corner stores that display an explosion of portable foliage for Cabbagefolk to pick up in their red wagons. To the south is Regent Park, marking perhaps the most abrupt and dramatic social and economic shift in Toronto. Though I don't claim any knowledge of what happens inside the Regent Park buildings, nothing out of the ordinary ever happens when I pass through the area, though based on urban folklore one might be forgiven for expecting a Detroit-like no-go zone. Pass through a few times and Gerrard stops being a mental barrier at the south of Cabbagetown.

There are usually kids shuffling about with a ball of some kind, teenagers voguing like they're listening to a 1970s Springsteen song and people taking groceries out of 1989 Honda Accords – all the same stuff that happens in the rest of the city. Regent Park is more like the rest of Toronto than it is different.

Though the area was completely redeveloped in 1948, and the southern part of Cabbagetown – what Hugh Garner called 'the largest Anglo-Saxon slum in North America' in his novel *Cabbagetown* – was razed, you can still follow Sackville Street and see traces of the ghost of the Sackville that once was as you head south. Midway through Regent Park, by where Oak Street was once lined with homes (made famous by the 1953 NFB film *Farewell to Oak Street*), the four quadrants of Regent Park spread out in each direction. Each was slated in 2010 to be revitalized in turn, a second major razing of the area that leads one to wonder about the permanence of what we build. At Dundas Street you'll find St. Cyril and Methody, a Macedonian-Bulgarian church where you can see and listen to West Indian wedding receptions taking place under fluorescent tube lighting if you're passing through on a Saturday night.

Just south of Dundas, the former Sackville roadway is filled in with grass and blocked by a large iron fence, but pedestrians can easily pass here because the sidewalks are still exactly where they would be if the street was intact. Farther south, by the Regent Park Community Centre, it's harder to follow Sackville's ghost, as a wading pool, some elaborate concrete ramps and a neglected, paved-over tree pit have been installed there over time. This is technically called 'Sackville Green,' so the name lives on, and includes a sign stating this is an alcohol-free zone, complete with a crossed out picture of a martini garnished with an olive on a toothpick.

Towards Shuter Street, Sackville regains its form and passes though Trefann Court, an area whose planned redevelopment in the 1960s was halted by a historic community effort to keep the small neighbourhood intact (led in part by John Sewell, who would become mayor in the late 1970s). In what is now the yard of St. Paul Catholic School on Queen at Sackville, lies the burial ground of hundreds of Irish refugees who came to Toronto in 1847 after fleeing the Great Hunger. Today, they're beneath a paved playground with an asphalt baseball diamond nobody would ever want

to slide into home on. Here, Sackville faces its greatest hurdle –
the twin elevated roadways of Richmond and Adelaide. Directly
in front is the green, impenetrable berm the roadway is built on.
However, head east and find a secret passageway that feels illicit
but allows pedestrians to pass through to King Street via a parking
lot under the highway.

The lot skirts the side of the Riverside Missionary Church, best
known for its 'Prepare to meet thy God' sign, which drivers up on
Richmond pass on their way into the city. Just east on King is the
Sackville Playground. From the park, there's no sign of Richmond
Street. This park was created in the 1960s when Richmond and
Adelaide became super-arterial roads; existing streets and build-
ings were removed, leaving this new space.

There is a crosswalk on King here that leads to that last
existing bit of Sackville, which extends one block down to Eastern
Avenue, where it finally comes to an end. Remarkably, and with
the exception of the traffic light at Gerrard, the pedestrian has
the right of way, through either stop signs or push-button cross-
walks, the entire length of Sackville from the cemetery to Eastern
Avenue. Even though it's been chopped up, blocked and rerouted,
Sackville Street still lives on foot.

The area south of Queen is called Corktown, and below it is
the Distillery District, which we encountered from the other side
on Parliament earlier in this essay. I once spent an afternoon
following Dennis Keliher around Corktown circa 1890. Keliher
was the sole character in *A People's History Distilled*, a wonderful
historical mobile play in which he led an audience on a walking
tour of the Distillery District, where he worked, and out into
Corktown, where he lived.

When the play ventured outside the preserved Distillery
confines, this most-necessary Toronto mythologizing got exciting.
At Mill and Cherry streets, we encountered the unrelenting wooden
wall that surrounds the West Don Lands development. The wall
went up seemingly overnight in the mid-2000s, and everything
inside it began to be removed to make way for a new community.
Keliher mentioned living here, a nod to the fact that this area was
residential over 100 years ago. Once, in the early 2000s, I tagged
along to a late-night warehouse party in this area. I can't remember if it was any good or who threw it, but the building it was in is

now gone, and with it most of my memories of that night. When this development is complete, people will again return to live here.

The West Don Lands regeneration has been twenty years in the making, but not begun in earnest until the mid 2000s. In the late '80s, the 'St. Lawrence Square' scheme – later renamed Ataratiri – was a City of Toronto proposal for a massive mixed-use and affordable housing development that saw more than $300 million spent on a project that didn't happen. Planning fetishists can visit the St. Lawrence library branch and look through report after report on Ataratiri: 'Social Structure Analysis'; 'Noise and Vibration Study'; 'Soil Analysis'; 'Flood Protection Options.' Reading them is like listening to George and Martha talk about their non-existent son in *Who's Afraid of Virginia Woolf?* When the economy and local housing market collapsed in the early 1990s, the project was unable to get private investors on board, and in 1992, Bob Rae's provincial government cancelled Ataratiri. Now, with the current, seemingly neverending Toronto real-estate boom, Waterfront Toronto's (the arm's-length city agency overseeing waterfront development) new plan for the area is well underway.

Before the fence went up here, Bayview Avenue and Front Street met in a derelict, post-urban kind of place where one could imagine the bad guys dumping bodies unnoticed in the darkness. Around parts of Corktown there remains an element of fleeting dereliction that is rare in Toronto, like the unkempt urban prairie that grows between Richmond and Adelaide not far from the Sackville playground.

One time, I revisited the area alone and wandered the streets, going up alleys, finding original Corktown cottages and sneaking under the flying Eastern Avenue roadway where film crews store New York City cabs. Getting lost and a little dizzy, I repeatedly forgot I was in Toronto until I'd turn a corner and Toronto's skyline, so sheer when viewed from the east, came into view. There's lots of Corktown left, but you have to find it among all the concrete of elevated expressways.

At River and Queen streets, on the edge of Corktown, you'll find the Toronto Humane Society building, which bears a dedication to pianist and benefactor Glenn Gould. It reads, in part, 'The Toronto Humane Society gratefully acknowledges the generous legacy left to thousands of abused, lonely and abandoned animals ... a musical and humane legacy to the world.' Surrounding it are heartbreaking 'Pawprints on our heart,' memorials to Toronto pets that include 'Gigi Mak – Beloved member of our family,' 'In memory of Benny Bergman – A gentle soul' and 'Porky Alfino – Our funny little man. We'll miss you.'

Further on Queen, after it merges with King Street, wipe the THS-induced tears from your eyes as you hit Corktown and the end of the downtown east side, which ends at the Don River. When commuters cross the Don, the bridge they travel on is part of a 1990 artwork called *Time: And a Clock* by Eldon Garnet. It includes the stainless steel words 'This river I step in is not the river I stand in' and a clock. Across the river, in South Riverdale, at Queen and Broadview, more phrases alluding to time are embedded into the sidewalk, the words 'Time is money, money is time' perhaps contributing to some east-side anxiety. At a third site, by Jimmy Simpson Park near Logan Avenue, Garnet installed four steel pennants each emblazoned with the one of the following words: *coursing, disappearing, trembling, returning*. The pennants announce that the Don River is near. This work, which begins at the river that serves as the city's physical divide and which creates an even more significant psychological one in many Torontonians, helps drag the two sides of the river, and the city, together. Looking back, the skyscraper cluster doesn't seem so far away, but there is much to find in between.

Castle Frank and the Brick Works

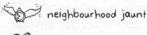 neighbourhood jaunt

 dress to impress

few services

Connecting walks: Danforth/
Crescent Town, Downtown
East Side.

If you don't have a sense of the local history, Castle Frank subway station might seem like a misnomer. There is no castle in sight when you exit, though some of the Rosedale manses to the north might think they're castles. It's a swell station, though, with a little dome and a lot of horizontal glass: a classically modern mid-1960s TTC structure from the transit commission's Kennedy-esque era of station-building. South across Bloor, Castle Frank Crescent sits on the edge of the Don Valley, and is home to the Rosedale Heights School for the Arts, a Toronto version of the art school from the movie *Fame*, and formerly Castle Frank High, a trade school. This whole area is the end of a ridge that's surrounded by buried creeks and ravines, though modern development obscures some of it. The obvious and celebrated Prince Edward Viaduct leaps across the valley, but west on Bloor the bridge over Rosedale Valley Road is nearly as impressive. It's a massive yet often-overlooked piece of infrastructure; from below, the bridge and the nearby subway tube appear triumphant.

Rosedale Valley Road down below is a beautiful, not-so-secret downtown escape route for motorists. People moving more slowly can catch a glimpse of the remains of the old Castle Frank carriage drive carved into the slopes of the ravine if they look closely, especially when the trees are bare. The name 'Castle Frank' was always used tongue-in-cheek, first for the summer home of Upper Canada's first lieutenant governor, John Graves Simcoe – it was more a wooden country lodge than a castle, so they went for an over-the-top name, demonstrating that a sense of humour was possible even in the hard days of early Toronto – which he named after his son Francis. The lodge was located south of where the TTC station is now, but it burnt down in 1829. Whatever archaeological traces still exist are likely buried in the garden of one of the homes on Castle Frank Crescent. Down in the valley, the carriage drive the Simcoes used to get from York to their lodge can be seen at the back of St. James Cemetery, sloping east towards Bayview, where it once turned north and went up the other side to the erstwhile castle.

To get a sense of this obscured ridge, take a walk around the high school – a modern mid-century gem itself – where it hugs the top of the ravine. At its easternmost point, there's a unique view into the underside of the Bloor viaduct, where the subway trains rumble by, popping out of their underground tunnel and finding themselves suddenly high above the ground. Here, too, there's a long wooden staircase leading down to Bayview Avenue. It's worth the climb down to feel just how big the bridge's arches and concrete anchors are. (They built 'em big back in 1917.) In front of the school, there's a small plaque that tells the story of Castle Frank, though it's often obscured by art students smoking cigarettes.

Rosedale proper starts north of Bloor and of the station. Walk directly up Castle Frank Road until you come to a pedestrian passageway on the right. It leads into Craigleigh Gardens, a fine and nearly secret urban park that was once the grounds of a large estate. It was bequeathed to the City, and today the fancy dogs of the Canadian aristocracy do their business here. Along the northern edge, find the dirt paths that lead down the ravine wall to 'Milkman's Lane,' a gravel path that continues into the valley. Stay right at the fork at the bottom (left leads up to Mount Pleasant Road and, eventually, to the Yonge and

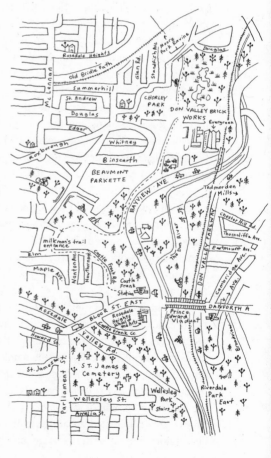

St. Clair neighbourhood) and pass by the Bayview/DVP off-ramp. You'll surprise motorists not expecting to see a pedestrian at eye level as they round the curve.

If you ever find yourself in a class-war shouting match with a Rosedale resident, call their neighbourhood a swamp – you wouldn't exactly be lying. Below the mansions perched on the edge of the Don Valley is the Binscarth Swamp, a hardwood wetland that expands in the spring, sometimes overtaking the trail that leads to the Brick Works. These wetlands were restored in the early 2000s, and seem far away from Castle Frank station, even though at this point they're only about a fifteen- or twenty-minute walk away.

A little further on, the Don Valley Brick Works will appear through the trees on the right, no more than a twenty-minute walk northeast of Castle Frank station (that is, if you're not slowed by the many distractions along the way). For nearly a century, the Brick Works drove a wide and deep industrial wedge into Rosedale. That sounds dirty and violent, and perhaps it was, but this place built the city. Between 1889 and 1984, the site produced the bricks that built Old City Hall, Casa Loma, Convocation Hall, Queen's Park and countless homes throughout the city. Extending beneath Rosedale mansions, the quarry is one of the few places in the city where we can see our geological history – there have even been fossils of an extinct species of scary-sounding 'giant beaver' found here. A woman who lived above the quarry on Douglas Crescent told me that, before the industrial site was closed, she and her neighbours would have to adjust the pictures in their homes and count the plaster cracks whenever the workers dynamited at the site. Since 1987, millions of dollars have been poured into the Brick Works to restore some of the buildings and create a sprawling wetland in the old quarry complete with an elegant, zigzag boardwalk.

The old corrugated metal buildings here sat vacant for nearly two decades. Urban infiltrators found ways inside them and their pictures are plentiful on the internet, as are stories of the guy who made the site his home. Evergreen, a non-profit environmental organization, has been slowly converting the site into a $55-million 'international showcase for urban sustainability and green design,' – a nature-ish version of the Distillery District. Through this plan, they've not only created the aforementioned wetlands, but they're also restoring many of the heritage buildings on the site. Past

Restoration and wetlands at the Don Valley Brick Works.

proposals weren't as kind or public-space minded: in the 1980s, a developer called Torvalley planned to build 750 houses on the slopes of the quarry, and commercial buildings at the bottom. Rosedalians and an ad hoc group called the Friends of the Valley stopped all that. Located in the former borough of East York, the development would have meant a huge increase in the municipality's tax base, which was relatively small compared to its wealthier neighbours.

Those residents were unsung urban heroes who set the stage for a series of events to unfold, events that created the unique industrial-urban-wilderness mash-up we have today. The Brick Works can be visited anytime, but they're especially fun to visit at night. When the drive-in crowds have gone and the summer farmers' market has packed up in late afternoon, the site becomes a dreamy place that you might have all to yourself. Late one hot July evening, a friend and I sat on the boardwalk and had a long talk – long talks take on greater importance and come easier in surroundings like this – our feet dangling above the lily pads and frogs, with a view of the St. James Town electric mountain range rising above the trees. In the background, traffic on the DVP hummed at a steady rate. Later, we climbed the circular path to the Governor's Road Lookout, high above the Brick Works site, from which you can see a panoramic view of the entire valley. As this giant project is completed and Torontonians add the Brick Works to the everyday parts of the city, this point will be a busy and beloved place. As it should be.

Gerrard Street

pack a lunch

dress to impress

offspring friendly

Connecting walk: Downtown East Side.

At the time of Confederation, Toronto was a tight grid of small streets that hugged the lakefront. The Toronto Gaol, or Don Jail, was a severe sight on a hill across the valley. Today, Gerrard Street still crosses the Don River just east of what's now Cabbagetown. The Don is the great psychological divide between downtown and everything east, and at Gerrard it's a straight and shallow ditch of a river. The open space of the valley – which is narrow here too – as seen from the Gerrard Street Bridge can still evoke what it may have been like to leave the core in the city's early days and travel east on a dirt road, the Don Jail looming on the other side of the river.

Despite its ominous look and the stories of the Victorian atrocities (and more recent ones) that have taken place here, the Don Jail was constructed as a reform jail, where prisoners could work in the fields outside. Stand in front of it, under the dead eyes of the Father Time carving set into the doorway arch, and it's easy to imagine the last moments of the convicted before they were brought inside.

Some of Toronto's worst and most notorious villains have spent time here. The bank-robbing Boyd Gang – described as 'the most desperate criminals ever locked in the Don Jail' by a newspaper of the time – escaped from from the jail while awaiting trial for the murder of a police officer in 1952. (It was their second escape from the Don, where the gang members had met in the first place.) Their escape sparked an eight-day manhunt that entranced local news organizations. Two members of the gang were later hanged back-to-back at the jail. And in 1962, the last execution in a Canadian jail took place here, and involved another double hanging, this one of murderers Ronald Turpin and Arthur Lucas. Even former Maple Leafs president Harold Ballard spent time in the Don Jail after he was convicted of fraud and theft in the early 1970s.

The Don Jail: a building that would intimidate even the most hardened criminal.

For some time the future of the old jail was uncertain, as it was a difficult building to find a new use for, and its position high on the hill was marred by an unfortunate parking lot used by corrections workers at the still-functioning 'modern' Don Jail attached to the east end of the original building. (The term 'modern' is used here only to date the building to the mid-1900s, as current overcrowding conditions are often described with Dickensian adjectives.) As of 2006, the old jail building is part of a new expansion of Bridgepoint Hospital. Michael McClelland of ERA Architects, the firm that has been restoring the building for Bridgepoint, has called it 'one of the most intact British-style prisons left in North America.'

The Don Jail was built between 1857 and 1864 by architect William Thomas, an English transplant responsible for many early Victorian buildings in Toronto. The jail's design was progressive in that it allowed a considerable amount of light into the central atrium and came equipped with a ventilation system that was better than those in most homes at the time. Rent *Cocktail* if you want to see it pretending to be Tom Cruise's 'Jailhouse Bar.'

By 1977, the conditions in the old part of the jail were so bad that there were calls to raze the building. Ontario's correctional services minister at the time called the conditions in the building a 'monument to human degradation and misery,' but then-alderman and soon-to-be-mayor John Sewell, one of those responsible for saving it, rebuked him, saying, 'On that basis, the first thing that should come down is the Legislature Building. More terrible things have happened there than anywhere else.'

Across the street from the jail, in the corner of a parking lot, there is a ceremonial Chinese gate that was erected by the local BIA in 2009 after years of fundraising. The gate marks the entrance to Toronto's East Chinatown, which, while not exactly forgotten, has been struggling for years. With the Spadina Chinatown downtown and the suburban Agincourt Chinatown (or 'Asiancourt,' as it is sometimes called) and Markham Chinatown (home of the Pacific Mall) to compete with, Gerrard's Chinatown is marked by empty storefronts sandwiched between not-particularly-fancy Chinese restaurants, internet cafés and a few grocery stores. The area feels a little like Queen West West (the now hip, once not-hip stretch of Queen west of Bathurst Street) did at the turn of the most recent century, when the streetscape was that of an old recession-battered Toronto. (Though nobody likes empty storefronts, trying to decipher what they once housed is a fun kind of amateur archeology.) Gerrard may be destined to face the same gentrifying forces that are shaping Queen East a few blocks south and the Danforth a similar distance north. For now, though, the surrounding neighbourhood's high property values are certainly at odds with Gerrard's down-market character.

To get a sense of Riverdale, hang a left up Howland Road, which runs north of Gerrard a block east of Broadview Avenue, just as Chinatown

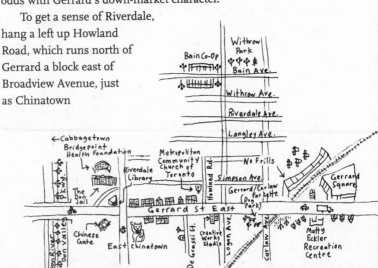

begins to fade out. One block up at Simpson Avenue, you'll see the Metropolitian Community Church of Toronto or, as it's better known, the Gay Church. It's here that Canada's first same-sex marriage was performed in 2001. It was a benchmark of Toronto's tolerance and progressive nature, but note that the church's long-time reverend Brent Hawkes performed the ceremony wearing a bullet-proof vest.

Follow Simpson one block east and Logan Avenue five blocks north and find, in the heart of deepest, darkest Riverdale, Canada's first social housing project: the Bain Co-op. Built between 1913 and the mid-1920s by a group of Toronto philanthropists who called themselves the Toronto Housing Authority, the Bain was influenced by the egalitarian Garden City urban-planning movement that started in England in the late nineteenth century. The idea was to have a balance between residences and green space.

The Bain has 260 apartments that range from one- to four-bedroom units and a population of approximately 400, but you would never know it. The first time I stumbled upon the Bain, I was completely surrounded by it before I realized I was in something different, a place a little more planned out and dense than the rest of Riverdale. The Bain is just below a mild escarpment that runs through Riverdale and can turn an alley or quiet street into a San Franciscan slope for a block. The differences in elevation and density of houses and trees gives it a Swiss Family Robinson feel.

Underneath a canopy of massive London plane trees with bark that looks like desert camouflage, the Bain's grassy courtyards seem too big for such a tightly built community, but they fit in with ease. They give way to footpaths that lead through a jungle of secret tiny patios. Children's toys are left out all night, porches are stuffed with bric-a-brac and laundry hangs between buildings on those old-fashioned pulley lines.

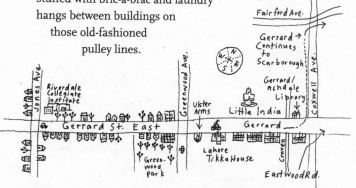

The cozy Bain Co-op loves to compost.

On warm summer nights, you can overhear conversations, televised baseball games and other, less recognizable sounds of domesticity. Few places are so public and intimate at once.

The community here seems to mirror the close-knit architecture. The Bain has had a softball team since the early 1990s, holds craft shows and street festivals and even has its own closed-circuit TV station. And those egalitarian Garden City ideals are expressed in the affordable rents: in the late 2000s rates ranged from under $800 for a one-bedroom to a stunningly low $1,286 for a four-bedroom. There are also subsidies available for co-op members who are in short-term financial difficulty.

This is social housing with none of the woes postwar developments like Regent Park, Moss Park and Don Mount Court have suffered. Eric Arthur, the late Toronto architect and professor, and the author of the seminal 1964 work *Toronto: No Mean City*, would take his students on walks through the Bain. In the late 1960s, he was already saying it had much to teach about how to make low-income housing livable and built to a high standard. Today's condominium developers could learn something from this place, too: maybe if they'd build more three- or four-bedroom units, families who can't afford houses of their own could still live downtown like they do at the Bain.

Back out on Gerrard, Riverdale's coziness gives way to Gerrard's continued rough urban state. Not rough as in dangerous, but in the sense that there are no Starbucks outlets. De Grassi Street is here, a road that competes with Yonge for the status of most famous in Canada due to the various TV shows that were named after the fictitious Degrassi Junior High and Degrassi High schools. (The series of series actually began with the mostly forgotten *The Kids of Degrassi Street*, which was filmed using local children as actors in a park on the street a block south of Dundas, just a five-minute walk from here.) For those of us who grew up outside of Toronto, the shows based on De Grassi were a portal into what our teen lives might have been like had we lived in the city: more walking and attached houses, both radical things when seen from suburban Canada.

Just around the corner, there's a storefront that used to be painted with slogans like 'drunk drivers are lousy lovers' and 'Welcome to Metro, 156 languages spoken, including French,' a rare example of curmudgeon-graffiti. In the 1970s and early 1980s, the shop was called Handy Andy's Tailors, and the proprietor would regularly change the signs in the window to attack then Prime Minister Pierre Trudeau, to proclaim that abortion was murder and to tease Quebec for its language laws. The signs continued to change long after the owner closed the store itself, until the messages were finally frozen in time. That 1990s axe continued to grind away well into the new millennium, enabled by the cheap rents in the area. There's little pressure to sell or lease when there are so many other empty storefronts, so an informal landmark like this can exist for a long time and then suddenly simply disappear, as this one did in the late 2000s when a new owner renovated it for future retail uses. These days, it's mentioned only in passing now and then when a memory is sparked. 'Hey, wasn't this where … ?' Once something physical disappears in the city, our memory of it no longer has a place to root, and it becomes fleeting, sometimes even forgotten.

The fact that Gerrard can still support this kind of weirdness makes it more interesting than some more celebrated, gentrified parts of the city. The street is made up of a mix of residential and commercial buildings, and the line between the two is often blurred: storefront windows look into makeshift living rooms lit by harsh fluorescent tubes, while some front porches lead into computer and electronics stores.

There's a little forgotten-in-plain-view park at Carlaw Avenue that backs onto the railway tracks that transport thousands of GO train commuters each day. One year, a local woman named Shannon took it upon herself to dig up the lawn in one corner and plant a vegetable garden, complete with compost bins, little brick walkways and water barrels.

Beyond the Carlaw underpass lies Gerrard Square, one of Toronto's less successful urban mall experiments. (It's nicknamed 'Gerrard Scare' by those unsympathetic to its presence.) The mall underwent a complete renovation in the late 2000s. Before the renovation, a fictionalized version of it was used as the community hub in a short-lived CBC soap called *Riverdale*, an unsuccessful Canadian version of *Coronation Street*. (Though it's unsung in many ways, Gerrard seems to have found its way into Canadian television mythology.) With the renovation, the Square lost its traditional anchors (Sears, BiWay) and then found new ones (Staples, Home Depot), and it's now a stucco fortress with a somewhat antiseptic interior. It's much less interesting now than it would have been if it were populated by the hodgepodge of tenants that make so many past-their-prime, second- and third-tier malls interesting by allowing for informal community hubs to develop (low-rent malls don't want to kick anybody out). It's worth a wander, though, as the change in environment from Gerrard is dramatic. I've found myself in that Home Depot on more than one occasion, somewhat panicked and surrounded by burly contractors, trying to find the one item that will make some problem go away. It makes railing against big-box stores more difficult (though, as you will have seen elsewhere in this book, not impossible), because they have what people need, even if it's hard to find. This particular Home Depot is about as urban as they get, and comes with a parking garage rather than acres of parking lot.

There's a McDonald's at Gerrard Square too, right next door to the old one that was torn down. In addition to moving 100 feet, the new McDonald's went upscale, with a Starbucks-like interior and comfortable chairs – it's perhaps the most gentrified place along much of Gerrard. Casting no judgment on the food served inside, I still dislike the place. The destruction of a perfectly serviceable building is a waste of energy and resources, and this redesign also wasted an opportunity to take back more of the parking lot and establish a retail streetscape along this busy stretch of Gerrard. (In fact, the old McDonald's met the street with windows looking out from Playland onto the sidewalk.) For now, a parking lot endures, but such places can be easily filled in.

Gerrard continues east, becoming mainly residential for a number of blocks until Greenwood, where it becomes a retail strip again. A block further east is the Ulster Arms, a dive tavern that's the last old Orange Toronto bastion before the street gives way to the much less dour India Bazaar, 'the largest marketing place of South Asian goods and services in North America,' according to the area's marketing copy. The informal beginning of India Bazaar is dominated by the ever-expanding Lahore Tikka House. The restaurant always had a chaotic campsite look to it, but the two-storey restaurant they're building there will dominate the street and make the restaurant one of the first South Asian establishments to build its own new structure. (As of this writing, though, the building seems to be under perpetual construction.) The India Bazaar strip was first established in the early 1970s, when the Eastwood Theatre started showing Bollywood films. Institutions such as theatres and places of worship establish beachheads in many ethnic strips, and the community follows. And like many strips, those communities eventually move on, a newer, more mixed and, well, Torontonian, population moves in, but the ethnic shopping remains. In the summer, some of the stores expand onto the narrow sidewalk, where they sell cane juice (a year's worth of sugar intake in one cup!) and roasted corn. It probably violates a number of city bylaws but, like Chinatown, this appropriation of the sidewalk for public-private uses is a break from the usual orderly way of doing things in Toronto. Like the East Chinatown we passed through just a few blocks back, this South Asian area now competes with newer suburban clusters that are cropping up in places like Brampton.

Before you catch the Gerrard streetcar north on Coxwell, take a walk south down a curious street called Craven. An oddity of planning, the west side of Craven is dominated by a long fence behind which you can see the backyards of homes on the adjacent street. On the east side, a string of homes – some tiny, some tall, some just plain weird – continues down to Queen Street. Like a lot of places along Gerrard, this street functions differently than the rest of Toronto. Gerrard continues east after a jog up Coxwell, becoming mostly residential again, and later even industrial, and eventually ends quietly in Scarborough, a few kilometres after it loses its streetcar tracks at Main Street.

The Beach

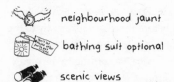 neighbourhood jaunt

bathing suit optional

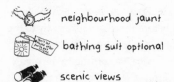 scenic views

Connecting walks: Dundas, Downtown East Side.

As the 501 Queen streetcar heads east past Coxwell, it enters an inter-
zone between neighbourhoods. Here Leslieville fades and the Beach
appears. Though hard-liners will always point out where the historic
or official boundaries of a neighbourhood are, people have some
fuzzy latitude when it comes to identifying with the neighbourhood
they like. In 2000, when I was moving to Toronto, my future room-
mate and I drove down Queen East, thinking it would be the same as
Queen West. It wasn't – the east side was quieter then, and wasn't yet
on the rest of the city's radar. But in the decade that followed, the east
has started to look more western. Restaurants, galleries and the usual
shops that mark a neighbourhood with rising property values are
plentiful. The end of this line – the Beach – has always been solidly
middle class.

The inter-zone between Coxwell and Woodbine now includes a multiplex theatre and an off-track betting facility, as well as parkland that leads down to Lake Ontario, ensuring a physical divide between the neighbourhoods. The gambling room is a vestige of the Greenwood Racetrack that was once on Woodbine, at the foot of Lake Ontario, one of many horse tracks around Toronto that have disappeared. In the 1990s, there was a debate over what to do with this vast tract of land, as many wanted more parkland and others wanted it developed. The compromise reached saw some land dedicated to a park and, on the rest, five streets of dense housing built in the New Urbanist style. While the buildings here are single-family homes, they keep their garages in back-facing laneways, and there are no parking pads or driveways out front. When the complex was built, many criticized it for being sterile or banal, but if you look at archival pictures of celebrated Toronto neighbourhoods like the Annex or Little Italy, you'll find that they looked the same when they were built: new, awkward and treeless. Give this place twenty or thirty years – landscape architects talk in terms of decades rather than years – and it will start to blend in with the surrounding neighbourhoods. The mid-rise condos that were built on Queen Street itself will, with the patina of age and a more diverse mixture of tenants, look more like the retail strips of older neighbourhood too.

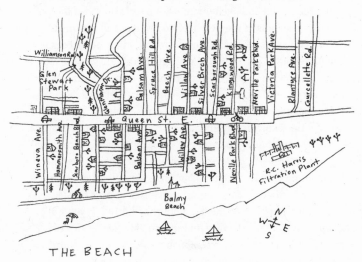

THE BEACH

The Beach starts beyond Woodbine. In the mid-1980s, Beach residents declared they didn't want to be another Yorkville and fought the high-rise condos and chains that were trying to move into the neighbourhood. Starbucks eventually moved in, but the neighbourhood's look and feel has largely been preserved. The Beach has always struck me as a shade of what a small Ontario cottage town may have felt like in the 1920s. It might be the handful of white picket fences just east of Woodbine or the way the residential streets abruptly end at the actual beaches that line the lakeshore. Wander around for a bit and, without any thought or effort, you're suddenly on the sand listening to waves, which is just the way summer holidays are supposed to work. Even the wooden boardwalk itself blends smoothly with the grass next to it.

And though you'll hear Torontonians use both terms, the Beach residents also definitively declared that the area is, in fact, 'The Beach' and not 'The Beaches.' In the 1980s, the City installed fourteen street signs that said 'The Beaches,' and eventually removed them due to controversy. In 2006, the Beach BIA (then called the Beaches BIA) held a poll, and 58 percent of those who voted went for 'The Beach.' Both sides claimed their version was historically correct, but the new name is better because it turns this chunk of Toronto into an inhabitable notion: most people only visit the beach, but residents of the Beach get to live there all the time.

The centre of the Beach is Kew Gardens, where an elaborate castle-like children's play area is 'dedicated to all the smiling faces you see around here.' It's reminiscent of the 'innocent amusements' that Joseph Williams advertised in 1879, when Kew Gardens opened on Queen Victoria's sixtieth birthday. Williams had spent thirteen years turning a portion of his land into the park, which was named after his favourite place in England. According to his advertisements, people could dance and 'obtain all temperate drinks, but no spirituous liquors,' which seems about right for uptight old Toronto. Today, you can get spirits without hassle, though lattes appear to be the neighbourhood drink. If you walk and sip, watch out for moms with huge SUV strollers – they're everywhere. They should use reasonably sized Victorian prams in better keeping with the spirit of the neighbourhood.

The Beach was always a place of amusement for the rest of Toronto. Until 1925, the area between Leuty and McLean was home to the Scarboro Beach Amusement Park, and another park was located at the end of Queen near Victoria Park Boulevard, where the R. C. Harris Filtration Park currently resides. Both parks are now gone, but adventure can still be had where the Glen Stewart Ravine gently touches Queen Street. The ravine begins as a civilized dip meandering north from Queen between fine residential streets until, after a few blocks, it goes deep, surrounded by steep walls and covered in a thick forest. You can lose your sense of direction in here: you think you're moving due north, but you veer east and west at times, following the course of an ancient stream. On occasion, you can hear the sound of trickling water. My friends and I walked here in the pitch black of night once, barely able to follow the path, which was lit only by the shafts of light from houses sitting high above at the ravine's edge and by the glow of our mobile phone screens. The path eventually leads to a steep staircase that deposits hikers in from vast wilderness onto Kingston Road, the Beach's upper main drag, where civilization comes in the form of flower shops and cute pubs.

Back down on Queen, the end is near. At Neville Park Boulevard – an odd dead-end street that fills up a ravine of its own – is the terminus of the 501 streetcar, a small loop where water trickles onto the tracks, an effort the TTC makes in some locations to muffle the steel-on-steel squealing of turning streetcars. Next door is the place in Toronto most likely to have people saying, 'They don't build 'em like they used to': the R. C. Harris Filtration Plant, which overlooks Lake Ontario. Dubbed the 'Palace of Purification' by Michael Ondaatje in his novel *In the Skin of a Lion*, the plant has undergone extensive renovations and the art deco buildings are as beautiful as they were when they were built.

Sadly, we don't get to see 'em like we used to, either. Since 9/11, interior tours have been cancelled, so many of us will never know just how magnificent this public work really is. The exterior is best visited at night. Follow the service road and staircases around the buildings and down to the beach. Standing here, with the waves crashing and the vastness of Lake Ontario roiling south, it's easy to feel like Jay Gatsby looking out over Long Island Sound on the grounds of his estate, but instead of a personal prewar empire at our backs, we collectively share in the Palace of Purification.

The Port Lands and Leslie Spit

 pack a lunch

 dress to impress

 scenic views

Connecting walk: Downtown East Side.

Toronto can be a chameleon, looking and feeling dramatically differently depending where your feet are planted. It's why this town, like Los Angeles, can play so many other places in films. The lack of a distinct look – a problem for some – frees up the city to be many things, even fantasylands. Toronto seems like a page out of a graphic novel when viewed from the Port Lands: a stylized city where the cluster of downtown skyscrapers is immediately adjacent to a wide-open landscape of freeway on-ramps, swampy scrubland and industrial wasteland. Think Gotham City, where the darkness at the edge of town is not so far away from the bright lights of the city centre. With the addition of a glass-point tower at the Gooderham Distillery on the north side of the Gardiner, this view is even sharper today than it was in the early 2000s.

There are two kinds of escapes in Toronto: the natural ones in the city's celebrated ravines and valleys and the industrial ones, which are quieter now than in the productive past. At the corner of Cherry Street and Lake Shore – one of just a handful of entrances to this massive tract of semi-industrial, semi-abandoned Port Lands – the Gardiner Expressway, some cement silos and a draw-bridge over the Keating Channel provide an appropriate backdrop to a part of the city that was invented by us in an earlier era and is being reinvented now.

The Keating Channel is the mouth of the Don River – or what became of it. The disused drawbridge here has an operator station that sits on a diagonal pedestal – a bit of near-abandoned modernist whimsy that's in contrast with the older industrial heritage of the area. There are still railway tracks running alongside the roadways in places. Vestiges of the days before the trucking industry made individual spur lines obsolete, the tracks are like capillaries that no longer carry blood to cells.

The Don River itself originally meandered down its valley like a minor Mississippi and emptied gently into the marshy delta of

Ashbridge's Bay where silt was deposited and there was a gentle and wildlife-filled transition from river to lake. Beginning around 1912, the bay was gradually filled in with material excavated from the foundations of the new buildings that were going up in the rest of the city. Natural curves became right angles and the zone between land and lake became formal and abrupt. Like a lot of Toronto's waterfront, from Sunnyside to Scarborough, the ground we walk on today is often transplanted from somewhere else, just like the city's population.

Today, the Don makes an abrupt right turn after it passes unceremoniously beneath the Lake Shore–Gardiner highway stack. From the intersection of Cherry Street and Lake Shore, wander immediately west along Villiers Street, which runs parallel to the channel (there's even a bar here called the Keating Channel – remarkably, there are a few oases in the Port Lands where you can get a drink), and at the Don Roadway find a path through the brush to the end of the Don River. The tall, concrete piles of the Gardiner rise right out of the water and, after major summer rainstorms, debris, some of which has likely travelled kilometres downstream, crashes into the steel bank.

The Don Roadway ends further south at oversized and lonely Commissioners Street. In the middle of the street, there are high-voltage towers and, adjacent to them, the giant new Pinewood film studios sit amid vacant industrial buildings. Things here are airport-scaled, and the size and space tell a silent story of unrealized industrial potential. On late evening walks here, we've come across film sets that use the roadway as a kind of drag strip where *Mad Max*–style chases play out. It's a surprise this isn't a popular spot for illicit drag races and street racing, – the suburban arterials seem to have cornered the market on that kind of activity. A little further east, a right on Bouchette Street leads to Basin Street, which dead-ends at its namesake, the giant turning basin for the port. This unsung body of water is massive and affords back-door views of the mothballed Hearn Generating Station and the new Portlands Energy Centre, which opened after its builders won a battle with nearby residents opposed to its construction. It's easy to feel sympathy for the residents – nobody wants to live near a power plant – but herein lies the rub of places like Toronto's Port: does it continue to fulfill our industrial needs or does it completely clean up and become part of the shiny new post-industrial city?

Backtrack to Cherry Street and you'll near the 'port' part of the Port Lands. Lake freighters are often docked at the piers here. It's always a surprise to find a working ship here because, though this is our port, we seldom think of ourselves as a port city, partly because we never really succeeded at being one. After the St. Lawrence Seaway opened in the 1950s, the Toronto Harbour Commission (precursor to the Toronto Port Authority) developed this area to welcome an expected shipping boom. The big ocean-going container ships continued to stop in Halifax and Montreal, however, and, like in many ports in Europe and North America, much of the work here had dried up by the 1970s and '80s.

Since the Port Lands are so near both the water and down-town, there have been many plans to do something with the area over the decades. In 1975, a $75-million plan to turn this into an industrial park with jobs for 10,000 people was floated, then sunk. Fast-forward a few decades and the redevelopment of port areas into living and working (and decidedly not industrial) places was the trend in Toronto as well as in other cities, led perhaps most famously by the U.K.'s London Docklands, where developments like Canary Wharf created entirely new communities.

In the 1990s, Toronto tried to spur on devel-opment here with a bid for the 2008 Olympic Games – this is similar land to the kind of urban industrial area that will host the London 2012 Olympic Games. When Beijing was awarded the 2008 games, the area languished again, though small developments have found success here and there. In 2009, the city was awarded the 2015 Pan Am Games, for which the city plans to build a 2,100-unit village with 8,500 beds; sports facilities, such as a fifty-metre pool and a 400-metre track; and retail space, restaurants, a medical centre and entertainment centres. When the games are done, this will all presumably be converted to community and residential uses.

Leslie Street Spit

As I write this, prior to the construction that will precede the games, the Port Lands remain a mysterious and mixed-up land-scape, especially at night. An outlet of the T & T Supermarket chain opened here in 2007, a brightly lit island that, on one visit,

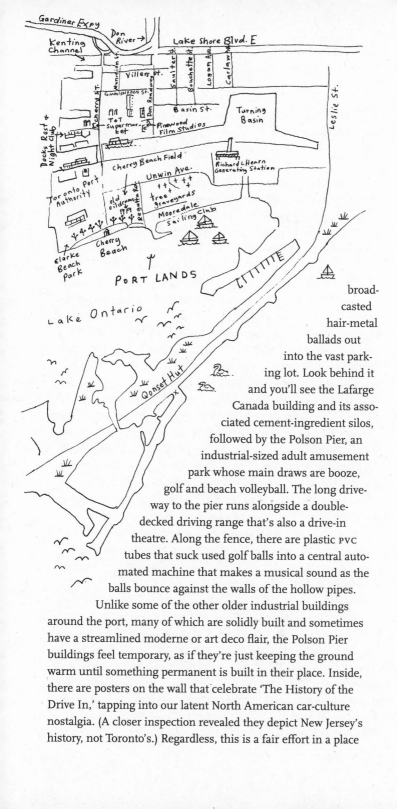

broad-
casted
hair-metal
ballads out
into the vast park-
ing lot. Look behind it
and you'll see the Lafarge
Canada building and its associated cement-ingredient silos,
followed by the Polson Pier, an
industrial-sized adult amusement
park whose main draws are booze,
golf and beach volleyball. The long driveway to the pier runs alongside a double-
decked driving range that's also a drive-in
theatre. Along the fence, there are plastic PVC
tubes that suck used golf balls into a central auto-
mated machine that makes a musical sound as the
balls bounce against the walls of the hollow pipes.

Unlike some of the other older industrial buildings
around the port, many of which are solidly built and sometimes
have a streamlined moderne or art deco flair, the Polson Pier
buildings feel temporary, as if they're just keeping the ground
warm until something permanent is built in their place. Inside,
there are posters on the wall that celebrate 'The History of the
Drive In,' tapping into our latent North American car-culture
nostalgia. (A closer inspection revealed they depict New Jersey's
history, not Toronto's.) Regardless, this is a fair effort in a place

where common history is often subordinate to common recreation. The history of this location is harder to celebrate, as it's about work – and dirty work at that – rather than *American Graffiti*–style nostalgic memories. The few locations of old and heavy infrastructure may be where such feelings can be successfully channelled, like the next drawbridge farther down Cherry that spans the turning basin channel. To stand under the massive cement counterbalances (they're as big as some of the trucks that cross the bridge) that hang off the north end of the superstructure is to wonder about your own mortality, and about how such weight could simply hang there in mid-air for so many decades.

Walk south of the bridge and Cherry Beach comes into view. It's a good view, too. With the white beach house at the end of the road, followed by the lake and the thin and rocky shore of the Leslie Street Spit in the background, it feels very much like you're approaching a Muskoka lodge. For a brief time, the ferry to Rochester, New York, docked nearby, giving this 'end of Toronto' place a bit of international verve, though the now-closed shed-like ferry terminal just looks shed-like, unromantic and, like the Polson Pier buildings, quick and temporary. The facilities at Cherry Beach were greatly improved by the city in the 2000s, but there's still much wild territory to explore to the east and west of the beach house. To the west, paths lead through a thicket of trees growing out of the sandy soil to the Eastern Gap, where Ward's Island was once attached to the mainland until an 1858 storm broke the passage open. For a time, a group called Promise held weekly Sunday afternoon dance parties here, but they've since moved to the eastern side of Cherry Beach after coming to something of a truce with the police, who would routinely unplug the generators and shut the party down.

After dark, cars pull in and out of this parking lot late into the night. Few people get out, and the windows steam. Today's secret sex is benign compared to Cherry Beach's past reputation – one that's less *Happy Days* and more *Sopranos*. In the early 1980s, Toronto band Pukka Orchestra wrote 'Cherry Beach Express,' a song that will likely never play at the Policeman's Ball, with lyrics like: '52 Division, handcuffed to a chair / I'm trying to line up, to fall down the stairs / I tell you I am innocent, I try to explain ... That's why you're riding on the Cherry Beach Express / Your ribs are broken and your face is in a mess / And we strongly suggest you confess, I confess.'

Unwin Avenue leads east parallel to the shore, straight towards the abandoned smokestack of the old Hearn Generating Station – opened in 1951 but mothballed in 1983 – which dominates the horizon. It's an impressive piece of industrial heritage and architecture, one that has lured many clandestine urban explorers (one of whom died when he fell through a hole in the floor). Buildings like this are almost 'too big to tear down' – but what to do with them? Some have suggested it should get the Tate Modern treatment and become a second site for the Art Gallery of Ontario, but that kind of money is hard to come by in Canada. For now, it's an impressive backdrop for the still-rough Port Lands.

The staged car collision scene in David Cronenberg's *Crash* was filmed along Unwin (look for the recognizable railway tracks adjacent to the road), and you'll also find the City of Toronto's 'tree graveyard' here, where old stumps go to compost. A number of small, long-established sailing clubs like Water Rat line the shore. These clubs are a poor man's version of the Royal Canadian Yacht Club, providing cheap access ($150 a year) to the lake for people who can't afford to moor or tow a boat but want to get out on the water in their kayak or tiny catamaran.

The Day-Glo artificial turf of the new soccer fields that are also along Unwin replaced a yard of massive, rusting oil drums. Friends and I explored here once, squeezing our bodies through narrow passages and into huge metal rooms where our voices reverberated. I watched from the ground as the crazy-brave among us climbed the rickety staircase that snaked around the side of the largest drum to what I was told was a magnificent view of the skyline. Rusty and full of broken glass, it was the kind of ruin rare in Toronto, a city that, though it's almost in the Midwest, and though it suffered its share of industrial exodus after the Free Trade Agreement was signed in the late 1980s, tends not to let its abandoned areas stay abandoned for too long.

The Port Lands remain the kind of dirty land big cities around the world are often ashamed of, like the long swampy strip of refineries, rusted industry and container ports people pass through in New Jersey as they head into or out of New York City. Though often maligned, places like New Jersey are the engines

cormorant

that keep the shiny and clean parts of the city running. They're also the places where industries we might not like to look at – and where a lot of working people – can find a home. As we figure out exactly what to do with our Port Lands, we need to decide if we really want to erase all of its roughness. As fuel prices increase, will we return to moving ourselves and our stuff by water again? Will we need more power plants to make our creative-class microprocessors function? Maybe most importantly, do we want to preserve space for places within the city limits where people can make physical things?

As Unwin passes the Hearn plant and crosses a small bridge, the industrial wilds begin to give way to natural ones. A road to the right passes through a prairie-like grassland to the 'Outer Harbour Marina,' home to larger crafts than places like Water Rat can welcome. The Marina sits at the head of the Leslie Street Spit, a wild piece of artificial land that sticks out of the eastern Port Lands five kilometres into Lake Ontario. There is a small trail that leads off the marina road to the Spit Road (really an extension of Leslie Street) but the main entrance to the Spit can be found farther down Unwin, where it meets the end of Leslie Street proper. It's an odd main entrance to such a vast park: during weekdays it's closed, and there are signs warning not to pass as this park is continually expanded by trucks full of debris rumbling up the Spit Road. The road seems like a country highway, complete with yellow line down the middle. Despite the signs, after the workers leave the Spit in the later afternoon, a small invasion of runners, cyclists and walkers take over the area. The big gate remains shut even when the Spit is open to the public, lending a feeling of trespass, which may not be such a bad thing.

I've been out on the Spit in a variety of circumstances. I often come alone, on a bike ride, as there are no stop signs or traffic lights to interrupt my momentum. It's remote yet urban enough for some strange sights, like the fire I saw burning out of control in a pile of rubble one evening that looked like movie-set fires from *Full Metal Jacket*, or the man I saw once who squatted suddenly in the middle of the road, pulled down his pants to take a crap and then quickly hiked up his pants and walked away, waving at unseen spectres in the air.

Another night, in deep February, a group of us rented snow-shoes from Mountain Equipment Co-op and started a trek out on the Spit in –18°C temperatures. The wind was blowing in from the east and Lake Ontario had a mighty roil that night. The spray from the crashing waves covered everything with a few inches of ice as if an apocalyptic winter storm were ravaging the city. In the super-cold, the city makes a humming sound in the distance – perhaps from cars or rooftop HVAC units singing in unison – but it's as if it's vibrating, trying to keep warm. We didn't make it to the end, as the shoes we rented were for wet snow and the crystal and grain-like snow had us sinking with every step. That night, we didn't pass anyone else. For a brief time, surrounded by a metropolitian area of 4.5 million people, we had a few kilometres to ourselves.

On a less Siberian night during the summer, three of us rode bikes together in the darkness, encountering a handful of other cyclists and walkers at first, then nothing but the open dark road. For a while we rode a few hundred metres from each other, only our blinking lights marking our locations. I rode with no hands, enjoying the slightly out-of-control feeling of a nighttime bike ride and putting all trust in my memories of where the road was the smoothest. Perhaps not smart, but as close to flying as possible.

About halfway out along the Spit, we started to hear an ear-piercing Hitchcockian sound: thousands of cawing buzzards. Soon it was all we could hear and we abandoned our bikes and walked down wooded footpaths toward the noise, which was now accompanied by an overwhelming fishy stink worthy of the Digby, Nova Scotia, scallop fleet, though here the Bay of Fundy was replaced by a Toronto skyline obscured by the silhouettes of circling birds. The vegetation became stunted and the trees leafless, both victims of a fowl strain of herbicide. We only had our LED bike lights with us, which were more useful for avoiding bird corpses than finding our way. Then, like the final interior scene in *The Birds*, a hidden flock suddenly spoke up in unison, the birds revealing themselves all around us. We retreated quickly, only then noticing that in the darkness

we had missed signs warning us this was an environmentally
sensitive area.

This wilderness was unplanned, but it was man-made, as were
the rest of the Port Lands. The Toronto Harbour Commission
began building the Spit in the 1950s to serve as a breakwater for
expanded port activity. Though the steamers didn't come, Toronto
kept growing, and all the rubble and waste of our city-building
were dumped here. As it grew, the Spit was colonized by cotton-
wood and poplar forests that include some 400 plant species.
By day, it's obvious that those terrible buzzards we encountered
at night are just cormorants, gulls and some 300 other species
of birds, migratory and resident. When the Toronto and Region
Conservation Authority (TRCA) took over management of the
Spit twenty years ago, they turned it into a nature preserve.

In 1976, a plan was floated to build a $26-million aquatic park
with marinas, an amphitheatre and even a waterskiing centre.
Soon after, the 'Friends of the Leslie Spit' was formed, and they
lobbied the City to keep the space public and turn it into the
nature preserve it has become, one that changes and grows with
every new truckload of debris. It was named Tommy Thompson
Park, after the former Toronto Parks and Recreation commissioner
responsible for those great 'Please walk on the grass' signs.

The Spit ends at Vicki Keith Point, where Keith began and
ended some of her marathon swims across the lake. It's a jagged
place littered with twisted metal and chunks of Toronto's buildings
and sidewalks – the kind of place you could hurt yourself, the kind
adventurous kids find so magical.

It's also an unlikely place to find an iconic piece of architecture. Yet this rough landscape is the perfect context for just such a
thing: a rusting Quonset hut abandoned halfway out on the peninsula. The same waves that cover everything with a frozen crust in
the winter also mercilessly spray this building in the summer. The
building takes its name from Quonset Point, Rhode Island, where
the first such hut was commissioned almost seventy years ago.

On one visit to the hut I came across a feral tabby cat that was
guarding the entrance with a series of long meows that coincided
with the sound of a loose board banging in the wind – a scene
straight out of a low-budget horror film. Inside, a red bench from
an old van awaited any visitor who got past the guard cat.

At about 3.7 metres in length, this Quonset is smaller than most. You can see the faded words 'Testing Building,' above the front door. The hut once housed the Port Authority's gauge for measuring lake levels and was later used for storage when the Port Authority moved its equipment to the foot of York Street. According to Ralph Toninger, supervisor of environmental projects with the TRCA, the move was made after 'staff complained they were afraid to go inside because of all the raccoons and things' living there. The bulldozer often parked by the hut is a testament to the continued growth of the Spit, and one of the reasons why it is open to the public only on weekends and holidays.

The expanding part of the Spit where trucks spend weekdays dumping construction material is just east of the Quonset. You can climb over raw chunks of buildings and sidewalks, sometimes finding clues as to where in Toronto they came from. If you didn't know better, it would be easy to think this is some bombed-out version of Toronto after a terrible war.

It was the threat of war that prompted the Quonset hut's design. In July 1940, the U.S. Navy's Bureau of Yards and Docks issued contract NOY-4175 to two firms, the main one being the George A. Fuller Co., to build a 'shore-based aviation facility' at Quonset Point.

The Fuller design team, headed by architect Otto Brandenberger, looked to the earlier Nissen Hut as inspiration for easy-to-erect, portable buildings for Quonset Point. Constructed with corrugated steel in a semi-circle shape, Nissen Huts were first used during the First World War. Keeping the shape and shell, Brandenberger's Quonset design added insulation and versatility. There were forty-one variants, including dispensary and surgical huts, laboratories, laundry facilities, hospital wards, barbershops, morgues and tailor shops.

When they were first designed, Quonsets typically cost between $800 and $1,100 to produce. After the bombing of Pearl Harbor in 1941, demand for the huts rose to 150 a day. Eventually, Stran-Steel, the company that supplied the corrugated metal, was awarded the contract. By war's end, more than 150,000 huts had been produced; their shape was as familiar as a Jeep, and as symbolic of military agility. After the war, the Quonset hut became part of the North American landscape when the U.S. military sold off surplus huts for $1,000 each. Stran-Steel also began manufacturing huts for commercial and residential uses.

A 1944 article in *Architectural Forum* titled 'Hutments to Housing,' heralded an extension of the Quonset into postwar life, listing a number of civilian uses and noting that 'such a structure could be erected by the owner himself, with the help of his neighbours, particularly if they had military experience setting up huts.' Stran-Steel's marketing campaigns read like a page out of the mid-century, cocktail-cool modernity handbook: 'Quonsets: American answer to American needs.' 'Dress it up, or use it straight.' 'Look around you, America, at the clean flowing lines of a building that's changing your world.' Quonset huts became houses, supermarkets, garages, greenhouses, paint stores, small factories, and even theatres and dance halls. They were outfitted with brick façades and hoisted up to serve as a second floor. In some small towns, the most happening nightspot was a Quonset hut.

Though a Stran-Steel logo can't be found on the Leslie Street Spit hut today, it appears to be an original. It has played a role in films over the years, including *Bulletproof Monk* and *Canadian Bacon*. It was even converted into an east-coast fishing shanty, complete with lobster traps, for the 2006 Michael Douglas film *The Sentinel*.

'We had a request to blow it up shortly after the filming of *The Sentinel*,' says the TRCA's Toninger. 'At the time we said no, but unfortunately some kids set fire to it, and now we can't find anybody who wants to blow it up.' While incendiary punks may be no match for a building that was designed to withstand war, 'progress' is another matter. Toninger says the hut will one day be bulldozed – and thus it will itself become part of the Spit as the city eats itself and rebuilds.

Back out at the entrance to the Spit, it's a short walk up Leslie to Lake Shore Boulevard, past an array of satellite dishes and community gardens. To the east, another stack rises on the horizon, this one part of the Ashbridges Bay Wastewater Treatment Plant, perhaps as impressive an industrial operation as the Hearn plant but, being a sewage plant, somewhere farther down the list of infrastructure we like to celebrate. The connection to the city along Leslie is as strange as the Cherry Street one, but instead of a comic-book landscape, it feels like you've been transported to a

The toughest and loneliest Quonset hut in Toronto.

suburban arterial on the periphery of the city, or somewhere along the 401 or QEW. Twinned Tim Hortons and Wendy's restaurants sit across from a Burger King, and both structures are located in big supermarket parking lots across from a Canadian Tire. This landscape comes into view slowly, like a mirage, causing some cognitive dissonance: we're getting closer to the city but it looks like we're farther away from it than ever.

Perhaps after so much post-industrial and natural wilderness, the re-entrance to the city needs to be slow, tempered by these big-box comfort stations, just as divers require decompression after scuba diving to avoid getting the bends. Pass through this inter-zone territory and soon, just a few more blocks up Leslie, you'll find Queen Street and the cozy streetcar city we expect to find in Toronto.

Acknowledgements

Early and substantially shorter versions of the essays in this book have appeared in three places. Many started out in *EYE WEEKLY*, first as general city pieces, then as a column (which was first called 'Stroll' and, later, 'Psychogeography'). Special thanks to Edward Keenan for editing those two columns all along (as well as this book) and to Bert Archer, who first asked me to contribute to *EYE WEEKLY* back in 2004 and let me write about the city the way I wanted to write about it.

Parts of this book also appeared in the *Toronto Star*'s 'Insight' section (previously called 'Ideas'). Editor Alfred Holden is tireless in his pursuit of ideas, and often a brief email encounter or conversation about something random will become the basis for a new article. His own writing in *Taddle Creek* magazine was an early inspiration as well.

My colleagues at *Spacing* magazine have been the finest people I could have hoped to work with over the past seven years. They have tolerated my pieces – some of which are included in this volume – coming in just as the presses started to roll. *Spacing* editors Matt Blackett, Dale Duncan, Dylan Reid and Todd Harrison all contributed to this book in various ways.

Also under the *Spacing* umbrella, thanks to Anna Bowness and Jessica Duffin Wolfe, who not only helped with various pieces in this book, but have been crucial to developing the identity of this Toronto *flâneur* character all along. They've helped me by drawing connections between the Toronto of today and the Victorian literature that helped inform how we think about and appreciate cities. That all the people above (and below) are also friends makes work not seem so work-like.

Thanks to the *Toronto Star* and its image bank GetStock (getstockphotos.ca), and to that paper's past and present staff photographers for the use of many of the photos that appear in these pages. The complete list of photographers appears on page 303 – I extend personal gratitude to each one.

Though I fell in love with Toronto long before I moved here, the people I've met here – the human infrastructure of my city – have made life in Toronto exceed all expectation. This book is a collaborative effort, and the brains of many folks around the city have been picked over the past ten years, as various people contributed thoughts and direction to this exploration of Toronto, or simply came along for the walk. My parents, Charles and Pat, and my sister, Danielle, eventually came around to the idea that walking around Toronto is, in fact, almost a real job, and provided support from afar. Closer to home, thanks goes out to the following people:

To John Bentley Mays, who generously agreed to write the fore-word for this book, for Toronto chats. His own exploration of Toronto, *Emerald City: Toronto Visited*, was the first book I read about this city when I arrived and, though it was not designed explicitly as a guide book, I used it as such, reading a chapter and then exploring that part of the city on foot.

To Toronto's former Poet Laureate, Pier Giorgio Di Cicco, who led me to think about Toronto, and cities, in broader ways. Historian Stephen Otto also provided many phone calls, emails and chats filled with advice, encouragement and background I'd not have found else-where. And to the unsung Toronto Public Library librarians who keep the wonderful and valuable local files full.

To the folks at Coach House – Christina Palassio, Evan Munday, Alana Wilcox, Kira Dreimanis and Stan Bevington – for publishing the things they do and making this book possible. To *EYE WEEKLY* for their support of my writing over the years and for their enthusi-asm for co-publishing this book. And to Marlena Zuber, for coming on that second walk and thinking it would be a good idea to make psychogeographic paintings and maps, many of which are scattered throughout this book.

To Todd Irvine, Liz Clayton, Yarika Rose and Christofer Williamson for being around for in-between, unofficial walks, explo-rations and chats. To Windsor folks like Christine Arkell and Nancy Yim for keeping the home in hometown. To Michele Kasprzak for thoughts on these city matters and ongoing, deeper explorations of place, space and technology. To Melissa Taylor for illustrating my *flâneur* column in *Spacing* and for early encouragement to write down my thoughts on the city in a presentable way.

To Ana Serrano at the Canadian Film Centre's media lab for providing us a space to invent *[murmur]* in 2002, and to Gabe Sawhney and James Roussell for co-founding it with me, giving me an excuse to scratch the city a little deeper for stories. And now, to Robin Elliot for carrying the project on to new places. To young

Sebastian, who has become a fine four-footed furry *flâneur*
companion who leads me around the city with a psychogeographic
method of his own. And to Michael Cobb, for much love and
ridiculous and critical amounts of support.

The passage on page 10 is taken from Walter Benjamin's *The
Arcades Project* (Cambridge: Harvard University Press, 1999). Page
11 quotes Rebecca Solnit's *Wanderlust: A History of Walking* (New
York: Penguin, 2000). Page 14 includes an excerpt from Pier Giorgio Di Cicco's December 7, 2004 speech at the Mayor's Round-
table on Art and Culture. Lyrics from Morrissey's 'Everyday is Like
Sunday,' which appeared on his album *Viva Hate* (UK: hmv, 1988),
appear on page 42. The passage on page 57 is taken from Amy
Lavender Harris's essay 'Toronto's Tower of Babel' in *The State of
the Arts: Living with Culture in Toronto* (Toronto: Coach House
Books, 2006). John Bentley Mays' *Emerald City: Toronto Visited* is
quoted on page 66 (Toronto: Viking, 1994). The description of the
Ontario Legislature on page 73 is from Charles Dickens' *American
Notes for General Circulation* (London: Chapman & Hall, 1842). A
line from F. Scott Fitzerald's *The Great Gatsby* (New York: Scrib-
ner, 1925) appears on page 148. A passage from Alfred Holden's
essay 'Dupont at Zenith' appears on page 148 (Toronto: *Taddle
Creek Magazine*, 1998). A passage from Walter Benjamin's *Moscow
Diary* (Cambridge: Harvard University Press, 1986) is used on
pages 152–153. An essay by Veronica Madonna published in
*Concrete Toronto: A Guidebook to Concrete Architecture from the
Fifties to the Seventies* (Toronto: Coach House Books, 2007) appears
on pages 179–180. Lines from Robert Frost's 'Stopping by Woods
on a Snowy Evening,' originally published in New Hampshire,
appear on page 202 (New York: Henry Holt and Co., 1923).
Michael Ondaatje's description of the Prince Edward Viaduct from
In the Skin of a Lion (Toronto: McClelland and Stewart, 1987)
appears on page 240, and his description of the R. C. Harris Filtration Plant from the same book is on page 285. Jane Pitfield's
description of Thorncliffe Park in her book *Leaside* (Toronto:
Dundurn, 2008) is quoted on page 231. Hugh Garner's description of Cabbagetown, from his novel of the same name (Whitby:
Ryerson Press, 1968) appears on page 266. A verse from Pukka
Orchestra's 'Cherry Beach Express' (Toronto: Solid Gold Records,
1984) is quoted on pages 290–291.

Photo and Illustration Credits

All maps and illustrations by **Marlena Zuber**. Marlena makes maps, illustrates books and magazines and is a member of the glam-pop indie band Tomboyfriend. She also helps run the non-profit art program Creative Works Studio. In 2008, Marlena partnered with writer Stacey May Fowles to produce the illustrated novel *Fear of Fighting*. View her work on the web at www.marlenazuber.com.

Index

Typeset in Scala and Scala Sans
Printed and bound at the Coach House on bpNichol Lane, 2010

Edited by Edward Keenan
Copyedited and designed by Christina Palassio
Proofread by Alana Wilcox

Coach House Books
80 bpNichol Lane
Toronto ON M5S 3J4

416 979 2217
800 367 6360

mail@chbooks.com
www.chbooks.com